BRYN THOMAS was born in Zimbabwe, where he grew up on a farm. His wanderlust began early with camping holidays by the Indian Ocean in Mozambique and journeys to game parks in other parts of Africa.

Since graduating from Durham University with a degree in anthropology, travel on four continents has included a Saharan journey in a home-built kit-car, a solo 2500 km Andean cycling trip and 40,000km of rail travel in Asia. In 1989 his first guide, the *Trans-Siberian Handbook*, was shortlisted for the Thomas Cook Guidebook of the Year Awards. He has travelled widely on the Indian subcontinent and is co-author of Lonely Planet's *India* and *Britain* guides.

He first trekked in Nepal in 1983 and has since visited the Annapurna region seven times.

Trekking in the Annapurna Region
First edition: 1993
This third edition: 1999

Publisher
Trailblazer Publications
The Old Manse, Tower Rd, Hindhead, Surrey, GU26 6SU, UK
Fax (+44) 01428-607571
Email: info@trailblazer-guides.com
www.trailblazer-guides.com

British Library Cataloguing in Publication Data
A catalogue record for this book is available from the British Library

ISBN 1-873756-27-5

© **Bryn Thomas**
Text, maps and photographs (unless otherwise credited)

© **Jamie McGuinness**
Cover photograph

Editor: Patricia Major
Cartography and index: Jane Thomas

Every effort has been made by the author and publisher to ensure that the
information contained herein is as accurate and up to date as possible. However,
they are unable to accept responsibility for any inconvenience, loss or injury sus-
tained by anyone as a result of the advice and information given in this guide.

Printed on chlorine-free paper from farmed forests by
Technographic Design & Print (☎ 01206-303323) Colchester, Essex, UK

TREKKING
IN THE
ANNAPURNA
REGION

B R Y N   T H O M A S

WITH ADDITIONAL MATERIAL AND RESEARCH
BY CHARLIE LORAM AND JAMIE McGUINNESS

TRAILBLAZER PUBLICATIONS

For Jane

Acknowledgements

From Bryn: It takes more than one person to compile a comprehensive and accurate guidebook. I am greatly indebted to the numerous people who have helped me with the research and execution of this project through its three editions. First, I'd like to thank my sister for the long hours spent drawing and updating the route maps (without which this guide would not be what it is), for compiling the index and helping with the production. I'd also like to thank Patricia Thomas for her thorough editing of the text and much more, and Anna Jacomb-Hood for holding the fort while I was in Nepal. Thanks to Charlie Loram for updating the Annapurna Circuit sections, the side routes to Gorkha and Begnas Tal, and to Jamie McGuinness who updated the Annapurna Sanctuary section, assisted with last minute corrections to the Annapurna circuit and researched the expedition-style treks and the peak climbs. Thanks to Juddha Bahadur Gurung of ACAP for providing the information on the Sikles Trek, and to Tara Gurung, also of ACAP for many useful suggestions.

I'm grateful to the many readers who have written in with suggestions and advice, in particular: Angela Millard & Martin Bray, Robert Badner, Jane Bensberg and Gail Tilford, Jolyon Webb, Ron King, Phil, Nicholas Le Ray, Jolanta & Monika Glabek and Claire Di Cola, Theo Kiewiet, Lawrence Daly, Michel van Dam, Markus & Magrit Eyger, Leslie Kodish, Brett Medson, Judy Mort & Tim Walker, Anthony Lyons, Paul Hindle. Thanks to Henry Stedman (who helped with the last update) for the photo opposite p96, Tara Winterton for the language section and for continuing contributions to the text; and Rosemary Higgs for explaining Bagh Chal. I'd also like to thank Chris Beall, Lisa Choegyal, Bhakti Hirachan, Lilli Eriksen and Torben From, Simon Cohen, Heather Oxley, Vijaya Shakya, Cassie Cleeve and Peter Knowles for help and suggestions.

From Charlie: For advice, companionship and help on the trail many thanks are owed to: Nancy van Hees (Holland) and Anouschka Bakkenist (Holland) who kept an eye out on the low route between Tal and Karte; Peter Viklund (Sweden) for providing information on the low route from Pisang to Manang; and Russel Benton (UK) for his work on the Tatopani to Ghorepani section. Thanks to Gary Koppelman (USA) and Ken Hadzima (USA) for a diet of raw noodles which provided more realism to our Herzog-esque exploits up a snowy Khangsar Khola and also for providing new information on the side-trip to Dzong and the east-bank trail via Thini and Dumpha. For information, suggestions and the best DB on the whole Circuit I'd like to thank the HRA team at Manang: Dr Jim Duff, Dr Torrey Goodman, Rejane Belanger, Govinda and Indira.

From Jamie: While trekking the friendliness of the local villagers, the hospitality and wholesome food in the lodges and the curious mix of trekkers never ceases to amaze me. Many villagers, lodge owners, cooks, indomitable porters, guides and trekkers answered questions, offered advice and comments on a diverse range of topics, never questioning why. Thank you everyone. For providing more specialised information I would like to thank: Mrs Gurung of Tiptop Lodge, Dovan (surely the best lodge of the region), Radha Gurung of the comfy Cozy Lodge, MBC, Narendra Lama, Rajesh Gupta, Ms Tara Gurung and Tej Rimal, all of ACAP. The information on Bandipur was kindly provided by Ralph and Pam Rosenburg.

Many trekkers and climbers have accompanied me on some rather wild trips, considerably enriching the experiences, and in some cases enabling them to happen. Thanks especially to the hardcore: Gyalgen, Pasang and Nima, sherpas par excellence from Traksindo, Ah, Malia, Ulrica, Michael and Fred for surviving around Dhaulagiri, Reid 'pill-popping' Tiley, Andy 'bag o'shite' Emms, Richard Minson, Torrey 'Ventolin' Goodman and Suzanne for the most memorable mountaineering failures.

And thanks to Mr Tek Dangi of the newly-formed Nepal Tourism Board and the helpful staff at the Department of Immigration for endless visa renewals.

A request

The author and publisher have tried to ensure that this guide is as accurate and up to date as possible. However things change quickly in this part of the world. Prices rise, new lodges are built and trails are rerouted. If you notice any changes or omissions that should be included in the next edition of this book, please write to Bryn Thomas at Trailblazer Publications (address on p2). A free copy of the next edition will be sent to persons making a significant contribution.

Updated information will shortly be available on the Internet at **www.trailblazer-guides.com**

Front cover: Trekking near Ngawal, Manang Valley (photo: © Jamie McGuinness)

CONTENTS

INTRODUCTION

The history of trekking in Nepal is surprisingly short. Until 1948 the borders of this mysterious Himalayan kingdom remained firmly closed to outsiders and the race to climb Mt Everest, which had begun in the 1920s, was conducted from Tibet. As the first mountaineers entered the country reports of their exploits were widely publicised. The first peak over 8000m or 26,000ft to be climbed was Annapurna, by Frenchman Maurice Herzog in 1950. Everest was conquered by Edmund Hillary and Tenzing Norgay with a British team in 1953.

The ensuing blaze of publicity focussed world attention on Nepal and in 1955 Thomas Cook organised the first guided tour to Kathmandu. The tourists were welcomed and entertained by Boris Lissanevitch, the legendary White Russian who ran the only Western-style hotel in the country. They were met by King Mahendra who is reported to have watched in disbelief as the tourists haggled amongst each other to buy up all the curios they were shown. The King immediately recognised a source of foreign exchange of rich potential and the experiment in tourism was declared a success. An industry was born that is now the country's top foreign currency earner.

While Boris Lissanevitch is often credited with being the father of tourism in Nepal, the man who initiated the sport of trekking is Colonel Jimmy Roberts. He led a small party of American tourists on a short trek in 1964, with porters, tents and all the paraphernalia of a mountaineering expedition. This set the style for guided treks and is essentially how they are organised today. The word 'trek' is derived from the 'Vortrekkers', the Dutch pioneers who travelled across South Africa in their ox-carts.

The trekking routes themselves are nothing new, having existed as a network of paths ever since there have been people in the mountains. Some, such as the trail up the Kali Gandaki, are old trade routes leading to Tibet. For as long as there have been traders driving their pack animals along these routes there have been *bhattis*, tea houses where they could get a meal and spend the night. Discovered by budget travellers in the 1960s, tea-house trekking is now the most popular way to trek in Nepal.

Had Robert Louis Stevenson lived today and had the opportunity to go trekking his 'To travel hopefully is a better thing than to arrive' might well have emerged as that favourite misquotation, 'It is better to travel than to arrive'. Trekking is most emphatically not about arriving; the interest and enjoyment is along the way. Trekking is about walking at whatever speed suits you, slow or fast, for as many or as few hours per day as give you time to enjoy the scenery and to experience something of the culture; here an ancient, Tibetan culture. There could surely be no better place to do this than among the highest mountains and deepest valleys in the world, with some of its most friendly and welcoming people.

PART 1: PLANNING YOUR TREK

With a group or on your own?

To travel properly you have to ignore external inconveniences and surrender yourself entirely to the experience. You must blend into your surroundings and accept what comes. In this way you become part of the land and that is where the reward comes.
Dame Freya Stark

The modern trekking holiday has evolved from the Himalayan mountaineering expeditions of the first half of this century. It is hardly surprising, therefore, that the two basic types of treks to choose from today reflect the styles of these early expeditions.

Most expeditions were grandiose affairs involving enormous quantities of equipment and armies of porters to carry it. The packing-list for Maurice Herzog's 1950 Annapurna Expedition ran to 50,000 items. There were, however, a few mountaineers (Eric Shipton, for example) who preferred to travel light picking up basic supplies as they went and partly living off the land, like the local traders who travelled along the many trade routes to Tibet.

Today's trekkers have the choice of joining an organised trek with accommodation in tents and everything carried by a team of porters or travelling independently, staying in *bhattis* (tea houses or lodges) along the main routes; they carry their own packs or employ a local porter.

TEA-HOUSE TREKKING

Carrying your own pack and eating and sleeping in village tea houses is the cheapest way to trek. On a very tight budget it would be possible to get by on as little as £3.50/US$6 a day. A daily budget of £6/US$10 would be better and £10/US$16 would be difficult to spend.

Since the route up the Kali Gandaki has been an important trade route for centuries, the network of lodges is well developed in the Annapurna region but things have been changing fast on the bhatti scene recently. When the first few hippies stumbled into the lodges in Tatopani in the late 1960s, they could expect nothing more than *daal bhat* (rice and lentils) and a place by the fire to unroll their sleeping bags. There are still some basic places like these to be found but most resourceful lodge-owners have adapted their premises and services to the needs (or whims?) of the modern Western traveller. Sometimes lavatories are still just a hole in the ground but there has been some advance in sewage disposal and some lodges have even installed flushing Western-style sit-down loos. In many places hot showers and varied menus are available. There are now some lodges that are more like small hotels than traditional tea houses.

The pros and cons

Apart from being cheap, the advantages of tea-house trekking are that it is easy to arrange (just get a trekking permit and hit the trail), and that it allows you to stop where you want and to make changes to your itinerary as you wish. Since you're using local services, more of the money you spend stays in the local economy. Staying with Nepali families gives you more of an insight into the country and its people than you might get on an organised trek, sleeping in tents. The main drawback to tea-house trekking is that it is confined to the main routes and at the height of the season on the main trails the lodges can be quite crowded.

Guides and porters

A **guide** is really not necessary since most routes are easy to follow and local people are helpful over giving directions. A guide can, however, greatly increase cultural appreciation and interaction with local people by explaining things and acting as interpreter. On the main trails, however, most of the lodge owners speak English.

More independent trekkers are beginning to employ a **porter**, which is an excellent idea. For £3-7/US$5-12 a day, it's best to employ someone locally (see p92 for how to go about it). Apart from the advantage of taking a load off your back, the money you spend directly benefits the local economy. Another option is the **porter-guide**, who speaks good English and will carry a light pack but charges a little more than a porter. He (or she: see below) will also be able to teach you some Nepali.

Nepalis are unable to understand why Westerners who earn in a year what few Nepalis could earn in a lifetime seem to prefer to carry their packs themselves. You should not feel in any way guilty about employing a porter or porter-guide – quite the reverse, in fact.

❏ **Single women trekkers**

If you're a single woman contemplating a trek but concerned at travelling alone there are several ways to find a trekking partner. In Kathmandu you can leave a message on billboards at the Kathmandu Guest House and at the Pumpernickel Bakery. On the main trails in the trekking season, however, it's very easy to find people to walk with.

For something more organised, **Three Sisters Adventure Trekking** (☎/🖷 +977-61-24066, email: lllsisters@cnet.wlink.com.np – lower case LLL) PO Box 284, Lakeside, Khahare Pokhara 6, is the first trekking agency in Nepal to cater exclusively for women trekkers. It's run from their budget lodge, Chhetri Sisters Guest House, in Pokhara. Apart from providing a useful service to trekkers, the project has the potential to help women in Nepal, too: 'Our dream to empower the women of Nepal is a long hard path to undertake but the potential jewels at the end are so great it must be travelled' (The Three Sisters).

GUIDED TREKKING GROUPS

The early Himalayan mountaineers would recognise and, no doubt, approve of the style of the modern guided trekking groups. Accommodation is usually in tents and food prepared in the camps, so large numbers of porters are required to transport everything.

Although levels of service vary from agency to agency, if you book a trekking holiday through an agency in your country you can usually expect a representative from the company to be always on hand from the moment you arrive at the airport.

Where to book – at home or in Nepal?

The alternatives are booking through a trekking agency in your country (addresses listed below) or, on arrival, with a Kathmandu- or Pokhara-based agency. Trying to make arrangements with a Nepalese agency from abroad by phone or fax can be difficult, although many places now have email addresses.

Booking a trek once you've arrived in Nepal is a cheaper option than signing up abroad. You will, however, need to allow at least three days to make arrangements.

If you're pressed for time, it's better to book with a travel agent at home or go tea-house trekking.

The pros and cons

Most people sign up for a guided trek because it is easy to arrange. Some, however, may be doing so because they don't realise that arranging a tea-house trek themselves is really very easy. Others join guided treks because of the higher levels of comfort and food that are offered (except with the cheapest agencies).

Although most guided treks in the Annapurna region follow the standard tea-house trekking routes some adventurous agencies offer itineraries off the beaten track, a few of which include high altitude routes and even a little mountaineering. If you're interested in climbing one of the trekking peaks (see p235) in the Annapurna region, probably the best way to do it is to join a guided trek operated by an adventure travel company. Perhaps the biggest advantage of joining a guided trek is to get away from the standard routes: easy to do since you're camping.

The main drawbacks to the guided trek are that it is more expensive than tea-house trekking; that by staying in tents rather than lodges you have less contact with village Nepalis; and, of course, you are stuck with a fixed itinerary.

In theory, trekking with an agency should be more environmentally friendly than tea-house trekking since groups are required to use kerosene rather than precious firewood. In practice, if kerosene is used at all it will only be for the group members, not for the porters (except in Annapurna Sanctuary). If kerosene is provided for them, they may save it to sell after the trek.

TREKKING AGENCIES

Outside Nepal there are many specialist agencies offering guided treks in the Annapurna region. Treks range from a few days to several weeks and may include sightseeing in the Kathmandu Valley, river-rafting trips, and visits to Chitwan National Park. Most agencies have a representative company in Nepal.

Trekking agencies in the UK

Most prices include return airfares from London and all accommodation in Nepal, usually in tents. A few operators have started offering guided treks with accommodation in tea houses. Prices are £1100-£1500 for a three-week trip. It is, however, just as easy (and cheaper) to arrange these yourself in Nepal.

Prices for fully-guided treks with accommodation in tents are £1500-£1900 for 24 days including the Annapurna Circuit and around £1700 for 21 days with the Annapurna Sanctuary. Several operators now feature treks to Mustang for about £2900 for 24 days. Note that the number of days spent trekking is about five to seven fewer than the total tour length.

Adventure trekking agencies offer some interesting routes that may include some mountaineering. Some, for example, combine the Annapurna Circuit with a climb of the trekking peak, Chulu East (6200m/ 20,305ft) – 30 days for about £2200.

● **Bufo Ventures** (☎/🖻 01539-445445) 3 Elim Grove, Windermere, Cumbria LA23 2JN, organises tailor-made treks for groups or individuals.
● **Classic Nepal** (☎ 01773-873497, 🖻 01773-590243, email: classic-nepal@himalaya.co.uk) 33 Metro Ave, Newton, Alfreton, Derbyshire, DE55 5UF, feature a good mix of standard routes and adventure treks including Mustang. Trekking peaks include Chulu East and Pisang Peak.
● **Encounter Overland** (☎ 0171-370 6845, 🖻 0171-244 9737, email: adventure@encounter.co.uk, www.encounter.co.uk) 267 Old Brompton Rd, London SW5 9JA, offers guided treks in the region.
● **Exodus Expeditions** (☎ 0181-675 5550 🖻 0181-673 0779, email: sales@exodustravels.co.uk, www.exodustravels.co.uk) 9 Weir Rd, London SW12 0LT, have a wide range of guided treks with accommodation in tents or tea houses.
● **ExplorAsia/Abercrombie & Kent** (☎ 0171-973 0482, 🖻 0171-730 9376) Sloane Square House, Holbein Place, Sloane Square, London SW1W 8NS offer a large selection of standard and adventure routes.
● **Explore Worldwide** (☎ 01252-760000. 🖻 01252-760001, email: info@explore.co.uk, www.explore.co.uk) 1 Frederick St, Aldershot, Hants GU11 1LQ, offers a number of treks.
● **Foreign Window** (☎ 01568-709042, in Nepal: ☎ 061-23523, 🖻 61-21523, email oskar@anand.mos.com.np) runs the luxurious Laxmi Lodge (see p138), used by Abercrombie & Kent and Cox & Kings and Naturetrek. Foreign Window can also arrange up-market tailor-made treks in the area.

● **Footprint Adventures** (☎ 01522-690852, ▤ 01522-501392, email: sales@footventure.co.uk, www.footventure.co.uk) 5 Malham Drive, Lincoln LN6 0XD, offer several guided treks in the area.

● **Guerba Expeditions** (☎ 01373-858956, ▤ 01373-858351) Wessex House, 40 Station Rd, Westbury, Wilts BA13 3JN, leads small group treks off the beaten track in the Annapurna region.

● **Himalayan Kingdoms** (☎ 0117-923 7163, ▤ 0117-974 4993, email: 101460.2022@compuserve.com, www.himalayankingdoms.com) 20 The Mall, Clifton, Bristol BS8 4DR, have several treks in the region, including Mustang. Their expeditions section (☎ 0114-276 3322, email: expedit ions@hkexpeds.demon.co.uk) organises more ambitious trekking and mountaineering holidays.

● **KE Adventure Travel** (☎ 017687-73966, ▤ 017687-74693, email: kead venture@enterprise.net, www.keadventure.com) 32 Lake Rd, Keswick, Cumbria CA12 5DQ) offers several guided treks including the Mustang trek.

● **Mountain Travel & Sobek** (☎ 01494-448901) 67 Verney Ave, High Wycombe, Bucks, HP12 3ND (see: Trekking agencies in the USA).

● **Naturetrek** (☎ 01962-733051, ▤ 01962-736426, email: sales@nature trek.co.uk, www.naturetrek.co.uk) Chautara, Bighton, Nr Alresford, Hampshire SO24 9RB offer bird-watching tours in the area, covering the Kali Gandaki, Marsyandi or Mustang.

● **OTT Expeditions** (☎ 0114-258 8508, ▤ 0114-255-1603, email: andy@ottexpd.demon.co.uk, www.ottexpeditions.co.uk) South West Centre, Suite 5b, Troutbeck Rd, Sheffield S7 2QA, is a mountaineering and adventure trekking company.

● **Roama Travel** (☎ 01258-860298, ▤ 01258-861382) Shroton, Blandford Forum, Dorset DT11 8QW specialise in individual treks.

● **Sherpa Expeditions** (☎ 0181-577 2717, ▤ 0181-572 9788, email: she rpa.sales@dial.pipex.com, www.sherpa-walking-holidays.co.uk) 131a Heston Rd, Hounslow, Middx TW5 0RD, have over 20 years experience in Nepal and a wide range of guided treks.

● **Terra Firma** (☎ 0181-943 3065, email: terrafir@globalnet.co.uk) offer several treks in the Annapurna region.

❑ **On the trail with a trekking group**

A typical day on the trail with a guided trekking agency begins with a cup of tea in bed ('bed tea'), followed by a bowl of hot water for washing. After a good breakfast (usually including porridge or muesli, and eggs), the day's trek begins.

Group members carry only a small day-pack containing camera, documents, water-bottle and jumper. The pace is usually leisurely, allowing kitchen staff to race ahead to prepare another meal at the designated lunch spot.

A couple of hour's walking follows and the group arrives at the next camp well before sun-down. This allows time for relaxing and taking in the spectacular scenery, writing up diaries or, for those with excess energy to work off, games of volley-ball or frisbee. After a large dinner most people are in bed by about nine.

● **Tribes Travel** (☎ 01728, 🖹 01728-685973), 7 The Business Centre, Earl Soham, Woodbridge, Suffolk IP13 7SA offer a short cultural trek including Ghandruk and Chandrakot.

● **World Expeditions** (☎ 0800-0744135, 0181-870 2600, 🖹 0181-870 2615) 4 Northfields Prospect, Putney Bridge Rd, London SW18 1PE feature a range of standard treks.plus a 25-day trek around Dhaulagiri.

● **Other UK operators** offering tours in the Annapurna region include **Bales Worldwide** (☎ 01306-885923, 🖹 01306-740048) Bales House, Junction Rd, Dorking, Surrey RH4 3HL; and **Ramblers Holidays** (☎ 01707-331133, 🖹 01707-333276, email: ramhols@dial.pipex.com) Box 43, Welwyn Garden City, Herts AL8 6PQ.

Trekking agencies in Continental Europe

● **Austria   Okistra** (☎ 0222-347526) Turkenstrasse 4, A-1090 Wien. **Supertramp Reisen** (☎ 01222-5335136) Helferstorfer St 4, A-1010 Wien.

● **Belgium   Anders Reisen** (☎ 013-33 40 40) Refugiestraat 15, 3290 Diest. **Connections** (☎ 02-512 50 60) Kolenmarkt 13, rue Marche au Charbon, 1000 Bruxelles, with branches in Antwerpen (☎ 03-225 31 61), Gent (☎ 091-23 90 20) and Liège (☎ 041-22 04 44). **Joker Tourisme** (☎ 02-648 78 78) Boondaalsesteenweg 6, Chaussée de Boondaal 6, 1050 Bruxelles. **Divantoura** (☎ 03-233 19 16) St Jacobsmarkt 5, 2000 Antwerpen. **Roadrunner** (☎ 03-281 16 50) Belgielei 209, 2018 Antwerpen. **Divantoura** (☎ 09-223 00 69) Bagattenstraat 176, B-9000 Gent.

● **Denmark   Inter-Travel** (☎ 33-15 00 77) Frederiksholms Kanal 2, DK-1220 Kobenhavn K. **Marco Polo Tours** (☎ 33-13 03 07) Borgergade 16, 1300 Kobenhavn K. **Topas Globetrotters** (☎ 86-89 36 22) Skaersbrovej 11, 8680 Ry.

● **Germany   DAV Summit Club** (☎ 089-64 24 00) Am Perlacher Forst 186, 81545 München. **Explorer** (☎ 0211-379 064) Huttenstrasse 17, 4000 Dusseldorf 1. **SHR Reisen** (☎ 0761-210 078) Kaiser Joseph Strasse 263, D-7800 Freiburg.

● **Iceland   Icelandic Student Travel** (☎ 01-615656) V/Hringbraut, IS-101 Reykjavik.

● **Ireland   Maxwells Travel** (☎ 01-677 9479) D'Olier Chambers, 1 Hawkins St, Dublin 2. **Silk Road Travel** (☎ 01-677 1029) 64 South William St, Dublin 2.

● **Italy   CTS** (☎ 06-46791) V. Genova 15, 00184 Roma.

● **Netherlands   Nepal Reizen Snow Leopard** (☎ 070-388 28 67) Calandplein 3, 2521 AB Den Haag. **Himalaya Trekking** (☎ 0521-551 301) Ten Have 13, 7983 KD Wapse. **Nederlandse Klim en Bergsport Vereniging** (☎ 030-233 40 80) Oudkerkhof 13, 3512 GH Utrecht. **SNP** (☎ 024-360 52 22) Groesbeekseweg 181, 6523 NR Nijmegen. **Adventure World** (☎ 023-5382 954) Haarlem. **NBBS** (☎ 071-22 1414) Schipholweg 101, PO Box 360, 2300 AJ Leiden. There are also branches in Groningen (☎ 050-126 333), Amsterdam (☎ 020-20 5071), Utrecht (☎ 030-314 520) and

Rotterdam (☎ 010-414 9822). **De Wandelwaaier** (☎ 020-622 6990) Herengracht 329, 1016AW Amsterdam. **Terra Travel** (☎ 020-275129) Singel 190H, 1016AA Amsterdam. **Royal Hansa Tours** (☎ 050-127799) Stoeldraaierstraat 11, 9712 BT Groningen.
● **Norway Worldwide Adventures** (☎ 22-564200) Oslo. **Terra Nova Travel** (☎ 47-2 42 14 10) Dronningens Gate 26, N-0154, Oslo 1. **Eventyrreiser A/S Adventure Travel** (☎ 22-11 31 81) Hegdehaugsvn 10, 0167 Oslo.
● **Spain Banoa (Bilbao)** (☎ 94-424 00 11, 🖹 423 20 39) C/Ledesma, 10-bis, 2°, 48001 Bilbao. **Banoa (Barcelona)** (☎ 93-318 96 00, 🖹 318 00 37) Ronda de Sant Pere, 11, àtic 3ª, 08010 Barcelona. **Expo Mundo** (☎ 03-412 59 56) Diputacion, 238 Stco, 08007 Barcelona.
● **Sweden Aeventyrsresor** (☎ 08-654 1155, 🖹 08-650 4153, email info@aventyrsresor.se) Fleminggatan 68, PO Box 12168, S-102 24 Stockholm. **Himalayaresor** (☎ 08-605 5760) Box 17, S-123, 21 Farsta.
● **Switzerland S.S.R.** (☎ 01-242 30 00) Backerstr. 52, CH 8026, Zurich. **Suntrek Tours** (☎ 01-387 78 78) Birmensdorferstr. 187, CH-8003 Zurich.

Trekking agencies in the USA

North American trekking agencies quote land-cost only (ie not including flights to Nepal) but are generally of a high standard. They range from a few days in the Annapurna foothills for US$900 to US$1500-2300 for the Circuit (28 days). Treks that include some climbing cost from US$2500 to more than US$3500. Some US companies sell cheaper 'no frills' trekking vacations for British or Australian trekking agencies.

● **Above the Clouds Trekking** (☎ 508-799 4499, 🖹 797 4779, email sconlon@world.std.com) PO Box 398, Worcester, MA 01602.
● **Adventure Center** (☎ 510-654 1879, ☎ 800-227 8747, 🖹 654 4200) 1311 63rd St, Suite 200, Emeryville, CA 94608 – agents for Explore (UK).
● **Geeta Tours & Travels** (☎ 312-262 4959) 1245 West Jarvis Ave, Chicago.
● **Geographic Expeditions** (☎ 415-922 0448, ☎ 800-777 8183, 🖹 415-346 4435) 2627 Lombard St, San Francisco, CA 94123.
● **Himalayan Travel** (☎ 800-225 2380, 🖹 203-359 3669) 2nd Floor, 112 Prospect St, Stamford CT 06901 – agents for Sherpa Expeditions (UK).
● **Journeys International** (☎ 313-665 4407, ☎ 800-255 8735, 🖹 665 2945, email info@journeys-intl.com) 4011 Jackson Rd, Ann Arbor, MI 48103. Also includes some treks specifically for families.
● **Mountain Travel & Sobek Expeditions** (☎ 510-527 8100, ☎ 800-227 2384, 🖹 510-525 7710, email info@mtsobek.com) 6420 Fairmount Ave, El Cerrito, CA 94530. Wide range of up-market treks.
● **Overseas Adventure Travel** (☎ 800-221 0814) 349 Broadway, Cambridge MA 02139 offer a number of treks in this area.
● **Safaricentre** (☎ 310-546 4411, ☎ 800-223 6046, 🖹 546 3188, email info@safaricentre.com) 3201 N Sepulveda Blvd, Manhattan Beach, CA 90266 – agents for Exodus (UK).

● **Wilderness Travel** (☎ 510-558-2488, ☎ 800-368 2794, 🖹 510-558 2489, email info@wildernesstravel.com) 1102 9th St, Berkeley, CA 94710.

Trekking agencies in Canada

● **Canadian Himalayan Expeditions** (☎ 416-360 4300, ☎ 800-563 8735, 🖹 416-360 7796, email treks@chetravel.com) 2 Toronto St, Suite 302, Toronto, Ontario M5C 2B6. This is one of the few Canadian companies that run their own treks, rather than acting as agents for other companies.

● **Travel Cuts**, also agents for Exodus (UK), have offices in **Edmonton** (☎ 403-488 8487) 12304 Jasper Ave, Edmonton, Alberta, T5N 3K5, **Toronto** (☎ 416-979 8608) 187 College St, Toronto, Ontario M5T 1P7 and **Vancouver** (☎ 604-689 2887) 501 602 West Hastings St, Vancouver BC, V6B 1P2.

● **Trek Holidays**, agents for Explore (UK), have offices in **Calgary** (☎ 403-283 6115, 336 14th St NW, Calgary, Alberta T2N 1Z7), **Edmonton** (☎ 403-439 9118, 8412 109th St, Edmonton, Alberta T6G 1E2), **Toronto** (☎ 416-922 7584) 25 Bellair St, Toronto, Ontario M4Y 2P2 and **Vancouver** (☎ 604-734 1066, 1965 West 4th Ave, Vancouver BC V6J 1M8.

● **Worldwide Adventures Inc** (☎ 416-221-3000, 🖹 416-221-5730, from USA ☎ 1-800-387-1483) 36 Finch Avenue, West Toronto, Ontario, Canada M2N 2G9 – agents for World Expeditions (Australia).

Trekking agencies in Australia

● **Adventure World** has branches in **Adelaide** (☎ 08-231 6844, 7th floor, 45 King William St, Adelaide, SA 5000), **Brisbane** (☎ 07-3229 0599, 3rd floor, 333 Adelaide St, Brisbane, Qld 4000), **Melbourne** (☎ 03-9670 0125, 3rd floor, 343 Little Collins St, Melbourne, Vic 3000), **Perth** (☎ 09-221 2300, 2nd floor, 8 Victoria Ave, Perth, WA 6000) and **Sydney** (☎ 02-9956 7766, toll free 008-221 931, 73 Walker St, North Sydney, NSW 2059).

● **Ausventure** (☎ 02-9960 1677, 🖹 9969 1463) Suite 1, 860 Military Rd, (PO Box 54) Mosman, NSW 2088. This long-established adventure travel company offers a comprehensive range of treks.

● **Classic Adventures** (☎ 02-9264 5710) Level II, 456 Kent St, Sydney. Agents for Mountain Travel & Sobek Expeditions (USA).

● **Exodus Expeditions** (☎ 02-9552 6317) 81A Glebe Point Rd, Glebe, NSW 2037 – agents for Exodus (UK).

● **Outdoor Travel** (☎ 03-9670 7252, 🖹 9670 3941) 382 Lt Bourke St, Melbourne, Vic 3000 – agents for Sherpa Expeditions (UK).

● **Peregrine Adventures** is a Nepal specialist with branches in **Melbourne** (☎ 03-9662 2700, 🖹 9662 2422, 2nd floor, 258 Lonsdale St, Melbourne, Vic 3000) and **Sydney** (☎ 02-9241 1128, 5th floor, 58 Pitt St, Sydney, NSW 2000) and offers a good range of treks.

● **Peregrine Travel** (08-223 5905) 192 Rundle St, Adelaide, SA 5000.

● **Summit Travel** (☎ 09-321 1259) 1st floor, 862 Hay St, Perth WA 6000.

● **Sundowners** (☎ 03-9600 1934, 🖹 0 3-9642 5838, email: rail@sundowners.com.au) Suite 15 , 600 Lonsdale St, Melbourne, Vic 3000, are agents for Encounter Overland (see UK).

● **World Expeditions** (☎ 02-9264 3366, ☎ 1-800 811 469, ▤ 9261 1974) 3rd floor, 441 Kent St, **Sydney** NSW 2000. Branches also in **Melbourne** (☎ 03-9670 8400, ▤ 03 9670 7474) 1st Floor, 393 Little Bourke St, Melbourne Victoria 3000 and **Brisbane** (☎ 07-3216 0823, ▤ 07-3216 0827), Shop 2, 36 Agnes St, Fortitude Valley, Queensland 4006. The main competition for Peregrine Travel. As well as range of standard treks, some climbing expeditions are offered.

Trekking agencies in New Zealand
● **Adventure World** (☎ 09-524 5118, 0800-652 954, ▤ 520 6629) 101 Great South Rd, Remuera, PO Box 74008, Auckland – agents for Explore (UK).
● **Suntravel** (☎ 09-525 3074, ▤ 525 3065), 407 Great South Rd (PO Box 12-424), Penrose, Auckland – agents for World Expeditions (Australia).
● **Venture Treks** (☎ 09-379 9855, ▤ 770 320) PO Box 37610, 164 Parnell Rd, Auckland – agents for Sherpa Expeditions (UK).
● **Himalaya Trekking** (☎ 06-868 8595, email: treks@clear.net.nz, www.trailblazer-guides.com/trek-nepal/), 54a Darwin Rd, Gisborne. Tailor-made treks and trekking peak expeditions.

Getting to Nepal

BY AIR
Carriers that fly into Nepal include the national airline Royal Nepal, Transavia (Netherlands), Gulf Air, Qatar Airways, Austrian Airlines, Singapore Airlines, Thai, Pakistan International, Indian Airlines, Bangladesh Biman, Aeroflot, Druk Air (Bhutan) and China Southwest Airlines. Royal Nepal, Indian Airlines and Thai operate international flights daily and the other airlines each average two flights a week. Necon, a private Nepali airline, has several flights a week between Kathmandu and Patna, and will soon also have flights to Calcutta.

Kathmandu is the only international airport in the country.

From the UK
● **Airlines and routes** The **shortest** route is on Royal Nepal's direct London-Kathmandu flight with short stops in Frankfurt and Dubai. Modern Airbuses are used and they're maintained in Europe. The flights are fully booked months in advance for the high (Oct/Nov) season. The **cheapest** flights are with Aeroflot and Bangladesh Biman but changing planes in Moscow or Dacca will add hours to the journey time. Usually each operates only one flight a week and delays are all part of the service. Biman may require you to stay overnight in Dacca on the return journey. If so you should ensure that your ticket includes hotel accommodation or they may try to charge you at the airport. Flying **via India** is now less popular since the num-

ber of airlines flying into Kathmandu has increased as has the price of the Delhi-Kathmandu sector (see below). In the high season, however, this may be your only option. Note that in December and January fog in the Delhi area may lead to the closure of the airport and subsequent delaying of flights.

● **Travel agents and prices** For up-to-the-minute prices check the travel pages of the Sunday newspapers or magazines like *Time Out* since prices vary considerably according to the season. As well as phoning several travel agents, it's sometimes worth trying airlines or their main agents direct: **Aeroflot** (☎ 0171-493 2410), **Transavia** (☎ 01293-596650), Brightsun Travel (☎ 0171-565 7979), 4 New Burlington St, London for **Royal Nepal**.

Sample return London-Kathmandu fares are currently £350-381 on Aeroflot, £370-499 on Biman, £520-588 on Qatar, £552-588 on Transavia, £576-711 on Gulf, £430-640 on Royal Nepal and £529-598 on Pakistan.

Recommended travel agents to try include: **Quest Worldwide** (☎ 0181-547 3322, 4/10 Richmond Rd, Kingston, Surrey KT2 5HL); **Trailfinders** (☎ 0171-938 3366, 42-50 Earls Court Rd, London W8 6EJ; ☎ 0161-839 6969, 58 Deansgate, Manchester M3 2FF; ☎ 0141-353 2224, 2 McLellan Galleries, Sauchiehall St, Glasgow, ☎ 0117-929 9000, 48 Corn St, Bristol BS1 1HQ); **Travel Cuts** (☎ 0171-255 2082, 295 Regent St, London W1); **STA Travel** (☎ 0171-361 6262) and **USIT Campus Travel** (☎ 0171-730 8111 or 0131-668 3303).

From USA & Canada

The Sunday newspapers are a good source of information for cheap flights from North America. Travel agents to try include **STA Travel** (branches in many cities), and in California **Overseas Tours** (☎ 800-323 8777, 475 El Camino Real, Rm 206, Millbrae, CA 94030) have been recommended. Most flights go via Bangkok and many require an overnight stop there. Expect to pay from about US$1200 round trip to Kathmandu from the West Coast, US$1600 from the East.

In Canada try **Travel Cuts** with branches in Edmonton (☎ 403-488 8487, 12304 Jasper Ave, Edmonton, Alberta, T5N 3K5); Toronto (☎ 416-979 8608, 187 College St, Toronto, Ontario M5T 1P7) and Vancouver (☎ 604-689 2887, 501 602 West Hastings St, Vancouver BC, V6B 1P2).

From Australasia

Cheapest routes are also via Bangkok and cost A$1600-2000 return. Travel agents to try include **STA Travel** (☎ 02-9212 1255, 1 Lee St, Railway Square, Sydney) and **Suntravel** (☎ 09-525 3074, PO Box 12-424, Penrose, Auckland).

From Asia

● **India** You can fly into Kathmandu from Delhi (£86/US$142) on Royal Nepal or Indian Airlines daily, from Varanasi (£45/US$71, four flights a week) Calcutta (£58/US$96, six flights a week) and Mumbai (£130/US$210, twice weekly). Student/youth discounts of 25% are applicable. From

Kathmandu Necon has three flights a week to Calcutta (£60/US$100) and Patna (£45/US$75).

● **Tibet** The Lhasa-Kathmandu flight (£140/US$228) on China Southwest Airlines might be convenient if you're visiting Nepal via China. There are flights both ways on Tuesday, Thursday and Saturday.

● **Thailand** Prices on Bangkok-Kathmandu flights are currently around £130/US$220.

● **Singapore** The cheapest flights are £190/US$310.

● **Hong Kong** Prices are from £190/US$310 to Kathmandu.

OVERLAND

● **From the UK** The classic route to Kathmandu is, of course, the overland route. Doing it yourself is still possible (via Bulgaria, Romania and Hungary to by-pass European hot spots around Bosnia). The UK operator, Encounter Overland (see UK trekking agencies above), offers an 11-week package in purpose-built trucks for £1525. Dragoman (☎ 01728-861133, 🖹 01728-861127, www.dragoman.co.uk) is another overland operator.

● **From India via Sunauli/Belahiya** The most popular overland route to Nepal is via Gorakhpur and the Sunauli/Belahiya border post. On this route you could bypass Kathmandu entirely (although it's a fascinating city well worth a visit), and catch a direct bus to Pokhara from the border. Beware of ticket touts in Delhi, Varanasi and Gorakhpur who will try to sell you 'through' tickets to Kathmandu or Pokhara. Everyone has to change buses at the border anyway so there's no such thing as a 'through' ticket. Doing things yourself gives you a choice of bus from the border and is cheaper.

It's best to travel by train from Delhi to Gorakhpur (14^1/2 hours, about £3/US$5 in 2nd class). The bus journey between Varanasi and Gorakhpur (Katchari bus station) takes 6^1/2 hours. Buses to Sunauli go from Gorakhpur's other bus station, near the railway station. If you want to catch the day bus to Pokhara or Kathmandu to arrive at the border in time you'll have to take the 5.00 am bus from Gorakhpur which reaches Sunauli in three hours. There are, however, many other Gorakhpur-Sunauli buses throughout the day.

Visas (US$25 for 30 days) are available at Sunauli. The border post is staffed from dawn to dusk, although you're allowed to walk through at night to stay in the cheap hotels on the Nepalese side (better than the choice on the Indian side). Don't continue into Nepal without getting your passport stamped next day or there may be serious problems when you try to get a trekking permit in Kathmandu or Pokhara.

From Sunauli, buses to Kathmandu (£1.25-2/US$2-3.50, taking 12 to 14 hours) leave between 5am and 9am for the day service. Night buses depart between 3.30pm and 8.30pm. The best day bus to get is the government 'Sajha' bus but this leaves only from Bhairawa (4km from Sunauli) at 6.30am and 7.15am for Kathmandu. Buses to Pokhara (£1-1.50/US$1.50-2.50, 8 to 10 hours) leave Sunauli from 5am to 9am and 3.30pm to 8.30pm.

● **From India via Raxaul/Birganj** The overland route through crowded and polluted Raxaul/Birganj is less pleasant and involves travelling via Patna in India. The bus journey between Patna and Raxaul takes 5 hours. Visas are available at the border. There are buses from Birganj to Kathmandu (£1.25/US$2, taking 10 to 12 hours) and Pokhara (£1.25/US$2, 9 to 11 hours). Buses to Kathmandu travel via Narayanghat and Mugling rather than the shorter (and much rougher) Tribhuvan Highway via Naubise.

● **From India via Kakabhitta** The Darjeeling to Kathmandu route goes via Kakabhitta. Parts of the road can be washed away during the monsoon. Buses from Kakabhitta to Kathmandu (£3.50/US$6) take 16 to 19 hours.

● **From Tibet** Chinese regulations governing the movements of foreigners in Tibet have always been in a state of flux; sometimes it's tour groups only, sometimes independent travellers. If regulations are relaxed a regular Lhasa-Kathmandu bus service may be initiated. There are regular overland tours between Kathmandu and Lhasa, easy to organise in Kathmandu (see p40). This is also becoming a popular mountain biking route. (For more information see Trailblazer's forthcoming *Mountain Biking in Tibet*).

Budgeting

It's hardly surprising that Nepalis consider Westerners to be made of money. Just one night in the Club Shangrila suite in the Hotel Yak & Yeti in Kathmandu (£370/US$600) would cost the average Nepali three years' wages. Alternative accommodation is, however, available from as little as £1.30/US$2, so your holiday money can go a long way if you want it to.

❏ **Economise but don't penny-pinch**

Many tea-house trekkers are travellers spending several months in Asia and trying to make their money last as long as possible. On a very tight budget, it would be possible to get by on around £3/US$5 per day, as some travellers do. Among them, however, you will always meet the ones that seem to have lost sight of the fact that they are on holiday. Every transaction becomes an aggressive exercise in seeing just how little they can pay. I once met a couple who were trekking because it was cheaper than staying in Kathmandu and, sharing plates of rice and bargaining even for their accommodation, they'd come to hate Nepal and the Nepalis. No doubt the feelings were mutual but the local people remained polite and good tempered.

If you're travelling on a very short shoestring give yourself occasional splurges and you'll find the trip much more enjoyable. Stay in dormitories and eat a basic diet for a few days then reward yourself with a private room and a slice of apple pie or a beer. Taking along as little as £60/US$100 extra, the price of a few CDs in the West, could make all the difference to your holiday.

Costs in Kathmandu

Budget hotels tend to be rather better value in Nepal than in India and it's possible to get a very basic room for just £1.30/US$2, or £3/US$5 for a double with attached bathroom. In a more up-market hotel a comfortable double with attached bathroom and constant hot water would be £6-12/US$10-20.

In most Kathmandu restaurants you'll pay around £2-3/US$3-5 for an evening meal. Compared to food, beer is an expensive item at £1/US$1.50 a bottle, about the same as a main dish.

Apart from the hotels and restaurants, there are other drains on your resources in Kathmandu. In Thamel, the travellers' quarter, the streets are lined with shops selling a tempting array of souvenirs from woollen sweaters to prayer wheels. There are also some excellent bookshops here.

Costs on the trek

Few lodges charge more than £0.70/US$1.20 for a night although there are now several up-market places in the region charging £4/US$6.50 and a five-star resort being built above Jomsom.

Since everything has to be brought in by porters, food prices depend on how far a village is from the main road. Some sample prices for food in lodges are: daal bhat £0.60-1/US$1-1.50; porridge, omelette or apple pie £0.50/US$0.75 each; small bar of chocolate £0.30-0.60/US$0.45-0.90; cup of tea £0.04/US$0.07; Coke £0.30-0.60/US$0.45-0.90. A daily budget of £5/US$8 should be adequate if you quench your thirst with water you've purified yourself, tea or the occasional Coke rather than with beer, which costs around £1/US$1.50 in the hills. Employing a porter will add £3-6/US$5-10 to your daily costs if arranged locally.

Your overall budget

Average daily budgets for shoestring travellers will work out at £5-10/US$8-16. Although this will be what you get by on for most days, you should take considerably more with you to allow for unforeseen circumstances (for doctor's fees or a flight if you are ill, for example). You should also allow for any side trips (river-rafting or jungle safaris – see p39) which you might want to add on.

When to go

Before going on a journey, it is customary to consult an astrologer about the proper time for departure. The traveller takes some rice, one betelnut and one coin in a piece of cloth to ensure a successful journey. If, for any reason, he is unable to depart, this bundle is sent out of the house at the auspicious time determined by the astrologer.
Kesar Lall *Nepalese Customs and Manners*

The Annapurna region is one of the few trekking areas in Nepal where year-round trekking is not only possible but also enjoyable. The northern part of the region receives little of the monsoon rain since it's shielded by the Annapurnas and other ranges.

Mountain-viewing is a prime reason for going trekking, so it's not surprising that the most popular trekking seasons correspond to when the Himalaya are at their clearest and most dramatic and the weather is neither too cold nor too wet. The average monthly number of visitors to the Annapurna region (based on figures for 1995-7) is as follows:

January (2145)	May (2478)	September (4279)
February (2642)	June (873)	October (10,939)
March (6558)	July (1077)	November (7299)
April (5506)	August (1330)	December (3761)

SEASONS

While Nepal has four seasons corresponding to the winter, spring, summer and autumn of Europe or North America, the pattern of rainfall is very different. About 70% of the total annual rainfall occurs in the monsoon season between June and September.

October and November
The post-monsoon season is the most popular time to go trekking. The atmosphere has been flushed clean by the rains leaving the mountains stunningly clear and the weather is still warm. Above 3000m/9843ft, however, the temperature will usually drop below freezing at night. The drawback is the fact that from October until the end of November the trails are very crowded and lodges fill up early in the afternoon.

December to March
Early December is quieter than November, though cold at higher altitude. From mid-December to late February is the coldest time. The Thorung La, the 5400m/17,769ft pass on the Circuit, may be closed by snowfalls for days at a time between January and March. If you plan to attempt a crossing in this season, ensure you are in a group of at least five people with adequate

❏ AVERAGE TEMPERATURES

Kathmandu (1336m/4383ft)

Month	Jan	Feb	Mar	Apr	May	Jun	Jul	Aug	Sep	Oct	Nov	Dec
min °C	-3	-2	2	5	9	11	18	13	12	7	2	-2
max °C	22	27	30	33	37	33	33	32	32	32	27	25
min °F	27	28	36	41	48	52	64	55	54	45	36	28
max °F	72	81	86	91	99	91	91	90	90	90	81	77

Pokhara (833m/2733ft)

Month	Jan	Feb	Mar	Apr	May	Jun	Jul	Aug	Sep	Oct	Nov	Dec
min °C	3	2	7	9	12	15	20	19	15	11	6	3
max °C	23	28	32	35	37	33	33	33	34	31	28	25
min °F	37	36	45	48	54	59	68	66	59	52	43	37
max °F	73	82	90	95	99	91	91	91	93	88	82	77

Gorkha (1200m/3937ft)

Month	Jan	Feb	Mar	Apr	May	Jun	Jul	Aug	Sep	Oct	Nov	Dec
min °C	3	4	7	10	11	14	17	15	12	9	8	5
max °C	22	26	32	34	34	34	33	32	31	29	28	24
min °F	37	39	45	50	52	57	63	59	54	48	46	41
max °F	72	79	90	93	93	93	91	90	88	84	82	75

Jomsom (2800m/9186ft)

Month	Jan	Feb	Mar	Apr	May	Jun	Jul	Aug	Sep	Oct	Nov	Dec
min °C	-4	-2	2	3	5	10	12	11	9	3	0	-3
max °C	13	14	14	22	25	27	27	27	25	22	16	14
min °F	25	27	36	37	41	50	54	52	48	37	32	27
max °F	55	57	57	72	77	81	81	81	77	72	61	57

Chame (2670m/8760ft)

Month	Jan	Feb	Mar	Apr	May	Jun	Jul	Aug	Sep	Oct	Nov	Dec
min °C	-4	-1	1	5	5	8	7	7	7	5	0	-5
max °C	10	14	15	22	22	23	23	22	20	19	15	12
min °F	25	30	34	41	41	46	45	45	45	41	32	23
max °F	50	57	59	72	72	73	73	72	68	66	59	54

As a rule of thumb, temperature decreases by 2°C/3.5°F for every 300m or 1000ft of altitude gained. The highest places where you are likely to spend the night on a tea-house trek are at Thorung Phedi (4450m/14,600ft) on the Circuit and at Annapurna Base Camp (4130m/13,550ft) in the Sanctuary. In November at these altitudes you can expect temperatures at night to fall to minus 10°C or below.

supplies in case you get stranded, and take local advice. Each year somebody dies up here either because they get caught in a storm or because they were overcome by the effects of the altitude (see p240) and were unable to descend on their own. The lodges in the Annapurna Sanctuary stay open as long as the path up is not blocked by snow. Avalanche danger is greatest on this route in the spring. Information about conditions is available in Chomrong. Between mid-March and mid-April is the best time to see the rhododendrons flowering in the forests around Ghorepani. The display is spectacular, whole hillsides aflame with the scarlet, pink or white blooms.

April and May

This is the second most popular trekking season and an ideal time to do the Annapurna Circuit. The high passes are usually free of snow and the mountain views are still clear in April although by May they're becoming increasingly hazy and may be obscured by the odd afternoon cloud. At higher altitudes, however, the skies are clear and the temperatures pleasant: May is a rather under-trekked month in Nepal.

As the heat builds up on the plains with the approach of the monsoon, trekking at lower altitudes becomes very uncomfortable and you may sweat profusely. If you'll be trekking for several days at these lower altitudes bring one or two packets of oral rehydration (the Merck brand in Nepal is most drinkable) to replace the salt lost.

June to September

The monsoon reaches the Annapurna region in mid-June and continues into September.

Trekkers have been put off coming to Nepal at this time by reports of torrential downpours, landslides and plagues of leeches. This is certainly true of the lower altitudes – the Pokhara area boasts the highest rainfall in the country and the rhododendron forests around Ghorepani are infested with leeches – but the higher, northern region is very different. Geographically, this area could really be included in Tibet; it lies in rainshadow, protected by the mountains from the force of the monsoon. Monthly precipitation figures (rainfall) at the height of the monsoon average 800mm in Pokhara but only 50mm in Jomsom and 60mm in Marpha.

Trekking in this season has a number of things to recommend it. You meet few other trekkers on the trails and as the only foreigner in the lodge you're given special attention by the lodge-owners. There is an abundance of flowers and plant life, revitalised by the rains. This is the time of pilgrimage and festival. The annual horse race in Muktinath usually takes place in August and draws people from all over Mustang and Manang.

If you can afford to fly to Jomsom, you can avoid the lower altitudes and the monsoon. Flights to Ongre (Manang), however, are suspended during the monsoon. See p31 for some itineraries.

❏ **Senior trekking**

'In our fifties, we were proud to discover from the police checkposts that we were the oldest couple trekking independently. For really enjoyable senior trekking we suggest:

    1. Don't carry anything. Employ a porter or a porter-guide.
    2. Walk with a stick and take your time.
    3. Make frequent stops – a real 'tea-house' trek!

Lilli Eriksen and Torben From (Denmark)'

Route options

The popularity of the Annapurna region with trekkers is entirely under-standable. Amongst some of the most dramatic scenery in the world there are trekking routes to suit all seasons and levels of fitness.

The main trekking routes in the Annapurna region follow the two major river valleys (the Kali Gandaki and the Marsyandi) and the trail into the Annapurna Sanctuary via Ghandruk and Chomrong. As well as these main routes there are many alternative trails and short cuts offering trekkers numerous possibilities. The options are even greater for those with camping equipment who can explore some of the rarely-trekked high altitude routes.

Planning your route

Most people are constrained by time. A common mistake when route plan-ning is to try to pack in too much. Your trek, which should be a holiday and escape from the rigid schedules of work or study, then becomes a race against time. It's far better not to trek every day but have some rest days, not only to allow yourself to become acclimatised if you're walking at altitude but also to appreciate fully the places you're passing through.

Don't forget to allow for at least two nights in Kathmandu or Pokhara to collect your trekking permit and get ready for your trek, plus extra days if you're flying to or out of Jomsom or Ongre (Manang) in case planes are delayed.

THE ANNAPURNA CIRCUIT (16-21 DAYS)

This is the region's classic long-distance trek for which you'll need an absolute minimum of 16 days. Three weeks would be safer and more enjoy-able. The route follows two river valleys, crossing between them over the Thorung La, at 5416m/17,769ft the highest pass on this trek. The best sea-sons for doing the trek are October to December and mid-March to May.

Clockwise or anti-clockwise?

Most people do the Circuit in an anti-clockwise direction because there's only limited accommodation (and then only during the trekking season) between Muktinath (about 1600m or 5300ft below the pass on the western side) and Thorung Phedi (about 966m or 3170ft below the pass on the east-ern side). Crossing between the two is a long day whichever way you come but less strenuous from east to west. One advantage of doing the trek clock-wise is that you'll be travelling against the flow, rather than with the same people each day. Outside the main seasons, though, this is a positive disad-vantage on the dangerous pass. Safety in numbers.

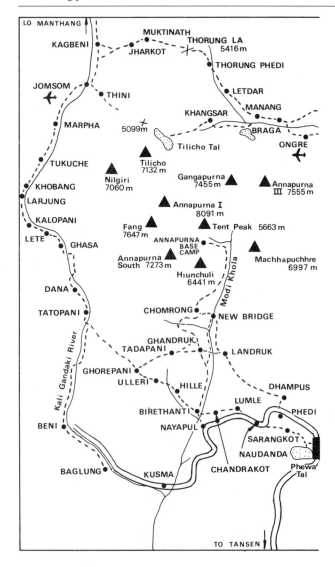

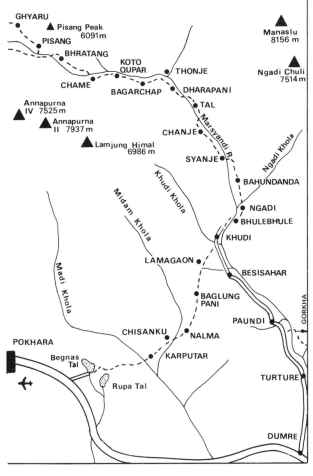

The Annapurna Region

The route

The traditional start of the trek is Dumre, a five-hour bus ride from Kathmandu along the road to Pokhara, although it's possible to walk from Begnas Tal (near Pokhara) to Khudi, adding another three days to the circuit. Few trekkers pass this way as the lodges are fairly basic and there are some steep climbs early on in the trek but the views are superb. See p226. The other alternative to Dumre is to walk from Gorkha (see p222). Most people go via Dumre, from where trucks and buses run up the rough track to the roadhead at Besisahar/Khudi. There are now even direct buses between Kathmandu and Besisahar. Trekkers follow the Marsyandi River up to the Manang Valley and Manang town, where they spend a day or two acclimatising before continuing to cross the Thorung La.

Muktinath, the first village west of the pass, is in a side valley leading to the Kali Gandaki River valley. The temples here have attracted both Buddhist and Hindu pilgrims for hundreds of years. Passing through the region's capital at Jomsom, trekkers follow the valley to Tatopani where most climb up the ridge to Ghorepani. By continuing along the river to the roadhead at Beni it's possible to avoid the climb, although you will miss the superb view from Poon Hill. The lodges along this route are fairly basic, though.

From Ghorepani the alternatives are to descend to Birethanti (you can catch a ride on a bus or taxi to Pokhara from the road nearby) or cross the rhododendron forests to Ghandruk (and Chomrong for the Sanctuary) reaching Pokhara via Landruk and Dhampus.

Pros and cons

Varying in altitude between 445m/1460ft and 5416m/17,769ft, this is a strenuous trek passing through a tremendous range of ecological zones from sub-tropical to alpine. It is also culturally diverse and you'll meet Hindu Gurung and Magar people in the south, Buddhist Manangbhot and Thakali in the north. The fact that it's a long trek is another plus since it takes a few days to get into the rhythmn of trekking. Since it's a circuit, there's no need to backtrack.

THE ANNAPURNA SANCTUARY (7-12 days)

For those with less time the trek into the natural amphitheatre amongst the Annapurnas, known as the Sanctuary, offers stunning mountain views.

The trek requires a minimum of seven days but it's really worth allowing extra time and to take alternative routes back to Pokhara. In the winter the route into the Sanctuary may be blocked by snowfalls but as long as trekkers are getting through, a few lodges stay open; as they do during the monsoon. A maximum altitude of 4130m/13,550ft is reached on this trek.

The route

From Pokhara it is a short bus or taxi ride to the beginning of the trek. There are several routes in via typical Nepali villages with abundant accommodation for trekkers and superb mountain views, a pleasant introduction to trekking in Nepal. The village of Chomrong is the gateway to the Sanctuary and has some excellent trekkers' lodges. Between Chomrong and the Annapurna Base Camp (4130m/13,550ft) is a string of lodges purely for the benefit of trekkers; there used to be no permanent habitation above Chomrong. At Annapurna Base Camp you are surrounded by impressive peaks and, in particular, the dominating face of Annapurna I. To leave the Sanctuary you must return to Chomrong down the same trail, after which there are a similar number of options for returning to Pokhara.

All routes begin from either Nayapul (a ¼-1 hour bus or taxi ride from Pokhara, then a 20-minute walk to Birethanti), or Phedi (a 35-minute bus or taxi ride from Pokhara followed by a 2-3 hour climb to Dhampus).

Then it's a question of getting to Chomrong. The **quickest but least exciting route** is from Birethanti via Syauli Bazaar and Himal Qu (New Bridge), perhaps a day and a half from Pokhara going up, and a mere day's walk if you're in a hurry to get back to Pokhara.

The other three options all offer a more cultural experience and beautiful mountain panoramas. The **longest route** is to begin with the Ghorepani/Poon Hill trek to catch the glorious sunrise vista that includes Dhaulagiri, Annapurna South and Machhapuchhre, then continue via the picturesque village of Ghandruk to Chomrong. Alternatively from Ghorepani there is a marginally **more direct route** to Chomrong. For a slightly shorter trek in, the route via Birethanti and Ghandruk to Chomrong is popular, the well-appointed lodges of Ghandruk and views from Ghandruk and Kimrong Danda being highlights.

The last option is **Phedi – Dhampus – Landruk – Jhinu Danda – Chomrong**. The mountain panorama from Dhampus is superb, making this a popular route for either the start or end of the trek. The lodges, while good, are on a somewhat smaller scale than those at Ghorepani and Ghandruk.

Pros and cons

The dramatic mountain scenery is the reason for doing this trek. Standing in the middle of the Sanctuary, surrounded by towering snowy peaks, ranging from 6000-8000m (20,000ft to 26,000ft), is a truly awe-inspiring experience.

Against this though, you get neither the cultural nor the environmental diversity of the Circuit or the trek to Muktinath. In fact above Chomrong there is little in the way of cultural interest since all accommodation is purely for trekkers but the views once you reach Base Camp are compensation enough.

Altitude sickness and snowfall are factors to consider on this trek. The route above Chomrong is subjected to occasional avalanches. Although there have been no deaths for many years, there is a small risk. During October, November and into December, the Sanctuary is generally snow-free and so there is little or no risk of avalanches. If, however, you are unlucky enough to be hit by a heavy storm, the avalanche risk rises. Winter brings on the snow. If the falls are light the lodges stay open while if drifts build up they are closed until someone opens up the trail again. In spring to the end of April expect snow in the Sanctuary; and expect to be trekking on it for a day or two, along a well-forged although often slippery trail. This is the period of highest avalanche risk, too.

The trek is surprisingly strenuous so unless you are fit and relish being independent, taking a porter or porter-guide is sensible. No matter which route you take, there are lots of ups and downs and, once above Chomrong, some exposed slippery sections of trail. Route finding is easy, and all the lodge owners speak English so you don't need a guide.

THE JOMSOM TREK (12-16 days)

This popular trek follows the old trade route along the Kali Gandaki River, part of the Circuit trek described above. The fact that this has been a trade route for hundreds of years means that the system of tea houses is well-developed. The friendly Thakali people who inhabit the area in the northern half of this trek are renowned for being accommodating hosts, ready to turn their hands to anything to satisfy the culinary desires of their guests.

Jomsom has an airfield with daily flights by plane or helicopter to Pokhara and Kathmandu so you can cut several days off this trek and save backtracking. Be prepared for delays, though; flights do not operate when it is cloudy or windy.

The route

From Pokhara, you take a bus, truck or taxi to Nayapul, near Birethanti. Don't let the hard climb which follows to Ghorepani put you off this trek as it's otherwise easy. You descend from Ghorepani to the Kali Gandaki at Tatopani, famous for its hot springs by the river. Alternatively, you can take a bus or taxi from Pokhara to Baglung or Beni and walk up the Kali Gandaki to Tatopani.

The trail follows the river into the Buddhist villages of the north via the world's deepest valley between the 8000m+ peaks of Dhaulagiri and Annapurna I. The surroundings change dramatically, the country becomes much drier and the river bed widens. There are some very pleasant places to stay here. Marpha, the Thakali village surrounded by apple orchards and just south of Jomsom, must be the cleanest village in the whole of the Annapurna region.

From Jomsom, Kagbeni is a half day's walk north and is as far up the Kali Gandaki as you can go without a costly permit for Lo Manthang (see p37). From Kagbeni most trekkers walk up the side valley to Muktinath. Allow an extra 3-4 days for the return trip from Jomsom.

Pros and cons

The cultural diversity, good views, excellent tea-house accommodation and the fact that, apart from the climb up to Ghorepani, this is an easy trek all contribute to the popularity of this route. Its main drawback, in fact, is that it can be very crowded in October, November, March and April.

If you're not flying back from Jomsom, on the return journey you can avoid backtracking the whole way by continuing along the Kali Gandaki from Tatopani to Beni.

THE MANANG TREK (7-12 DAYS)

While the Jomsom trek is established as a trek in its own right, a similar route and style of trek on the other side of the Thorung La has yet to be recognised. Perhaps the arduous bus trip to Besisahar has something to do with this, although this can be avoided by walking in from Begnas or Bandipur; allow 2-3 extra days.

Starting from Besisahar in the fertile middle hills, the route passes through Hindu villages with rice paddies and buffalo. A series of formidable gorges, although with a wide path through them, takes you behind the Annapurna Massif. Here the houses have Tibetan-style flat roofs and the Manangi women wear the Tibetan *ungi* or *chuba*. Above, icy peaks pierce the sky.

You can fly from Ongre airport between Pisang and Manang, about eight days' walk up the valley or you could explore around Manang to turn this into a satisfying 8-12 day trek. Flights between Pokhara and Manang cease during the monsoon or if there's snow in the valley. The airfield and surrounding country is at approximately 3300m, and so walking in and flying out makes far more sense.

Pros and cons
As with the Jomsom trek, there is an outstanding variety in the cultures and landscape. The lodge accommodation is good, although not quite to the Jomsom trek's sizzling steaks standards. Close to Manang there are two route options, the standard route between Pisang and Manang, and the less trekked high route; once at Manang there are plenty of side trips possible. This side of the Annapurna Circuit is far less busy, even during peak season, than the Jomsom side.

There are only two disadvantages: the limited number of flights from Manang's Ongre airport and the rough bus ride to Besisahar.

SHORT TEA-HOUSE TREKS (3-9 DAYS)

There are a number of short treks that can be undertaken from Pokhara any time between late September and May. Since they cover low to middle altitudes they can be followed even in January or February, at the height of winter. During the monsoon, however, these trails receive the full force of the rains; they are hot and humid and since they pass through perfect leech habitat (rhododendron forest) they are not much fun at this time of the year.

Ghandruk Circuit (4-5 days)
For this popular short trek, take a bus or taxi to Nayapul, a short walk from Birethanti. The route follows the Modi Kola and climbs to the prosperous

Gurung town of Ghandruk. To reach Landruk across the valley a steep descent is required. Return to Pokhara via Dhampus and a bus or taxi from Phedi. There's no shortage of accommodation (including the luxury lodges above) on this short trek and some good views towards the Annapurnas, particularly from Dhampus, Landruk and Ghandruk.

Poon Hill (3-4 days)

This viewing point just above Ghorepani is a popular place to catch the sunrise panorama, with superb views of Dhaulagiri (8167m/26,794ft) and the Annapurnas. In spring the rhododendrons are spectacular. It takes two days to reach Ghorepani from Pokhara, via Birethanti, and a day to return.

Ghorepani-Ghandruk Circuit (6-7 days)

This trek combines the above two short treks, going via Birethanti to Ghorepani then through the rhododendron forests to Tadapani and Ghandruk. You can return to Pokhara via Birethanti (saving a day) or via Dhampus.
● **Chomrong extension (+2 days)** If you can afford another couple of days, it's well worth continuing to Chomrong from Ghandruk for even closer views of the Annapurnas. The lodges in upper Chomrong turn out some of the best trekkers' meals in the region.

Return flights to Jomsom or Ongre/Manang (minimum 4 days)

Flying in and out is one way to spend as much time as possible in these interesting northern areas. There are numerous day walks in both these valleys but the altitude would preclude anything too energetic for the first day or so. With several airlines now offering flights to Jomsom the area is developing fast and standards in some of the lodges are high.

Luxury tea-house trekking

The building of four up-market lodge-hotels, *Laxmi Lodge* in Birethanti, the *Sanctuary Lodge* just outside Birethanti, *Himalaya Lodge* in Ghandruk and *Basanta Lodge* in Dhampus means that this little circuit from Pokhara can be now be made with the comforts of tiled bathrooms with lashings of hot water, comfortable beds with clean sheets and cosy sitting-rooms equipped not only with roaring fires but also with copies of the *Tatler* and *Hello* magazine. Laxmi Lodge is usually reserved for clients of Foreign Window (see p12, and in Kathmandu ☎ 471630) and the other lodges for clients of Ker & Downey (☎ 416751 in Kathmandu). Outside the high season, however, passing trekkers can rent rooms (about £6-12/US$10-20) when the trekking companies are not using the lodges.

The up-market **Jomsom Mountain Resort** (☎ 427150 in Kathmandu, 🗎 427084, email; soi@wlink.com.np, www.south-asia.com/soi) above Jomsom is set to open in late 1999 or early 2000.

(Opposite) Faces of Nepal. Top: Young monks from the monastery near Ngawal (see p209). **Bottom left:** Gurung man (see p174). **Bottom right:** Cheerful lodge owner, Dovan (see p184). (Photos: Jamie McGuinness).

SIDE TRIPS

Dhaulagiri Ice-fall (1 day from Larjung)

This day-trip up to the high altitude yak pastures (3800m/12,467ft) by the ice-fall below Dhaulagiri can be made from Larjung on the Kali Gandaki. There are superb views across the deep valley to the Annapurnas. See p150.

Tilicho Tal – tents required (3-4 days from Khangsar)

The trip up to this high altitude lake (5000m/16,404ft) and back to Khangsar, near Manang, may be completed in three days but only if you're very well acclimatised.

It's possible to continue down from Tilicho Tal to Thini and Jomsom via the Mesokanto La (5099m/16,729ft). Since there's nowhere to stay along the way this is not a viable alternative to the Thorung La unless you're well-equipped and have a guide who's been this way before.

EXPEDITION-STYLE TREKS (5-12 DAYS)

If you are willing to spend £12-21/US$20-35 a day, there are many more trekking options than you might at first suppose. The following treks are not covered in detail since you will need to organise them through a trekking company. Normally a company will send a sirdar (guide) and crew who are familiar with the route. A few of these treks can also be attempted just with camping gear and a porter-guide to carry some gear. Trekking this way you have to be ambitious and should have some Nepal trekking experience to understand what you are letting yourself in for.

Nepali trekking companies normally charge £12-15/US$20-25 per person per day for full service (expedition style) trekking. This should include all transport from Pokhara, permits as required but not necessarily the ACAP fee, and all food: three-course meals cooked by a kitchen crew, accommodation in tents, and porters to lug all this gear around. Basically you should have to pay only for soft drinks and rum, if so inclined, and tips for the crew.

Most companies and guides organise everything fairly efficiently but their one weak point is medical knowledge. The compact *Himalayan First Aid and Survival Manual* (available from KEEP in Kathmandu, see p112) is a useful book to take along.

Panchase (4-7 days)

The new road to Baglung and Beni, while cutting out the first couple of days of the Annapurna Sanctuary and Jomsom treks, has opened up the Panchase region for 'soft' treks. Essentially you begin from either Damside, Pokhara

---

(Opposite) Top: Bridge below Tatopani (see p144). Mule caravans are still used to transport goods along the Kali Gandaki between Pokhara and Lo Manthang. You should always give way to them by standing on the inside (mountain side) of the trail. Never try to cross a suspension bridge at the same time. **Bottom:** Bus on a rough section of the road between Dumre and Besisahar (see p191; photo: Jamie McGuinness).

or several kilometres along the paved road to Tansen and climb west to Panchase, a 2500m-hill with a superb panorama of the entire Annapurna range and a good chunk of the Dhaulagiri and Manaslu ranges, too. To end the trek you descend via the Baglung-Beni road and return to Pokhara. Treks of four to seven days can be arranged, passing through villages as yet unused to trekkers. There are no lodges although small shops sell soft drinks and beer.

Sikles Eco-trek (5-7 days)
This delightful loop north of Pokhara has been one of Pokhara's little secrets. It is a cultural trek that visits one of the largest Gurung villages in Nepal and, as with anywhere in the Annapurna region, there are magnificent mountain panoramas too.

ACAP has been working to prepare this region for the onslaught tourism before too many groups arrive. Now there are a series of environmentally sound camp-sites, trained local guides available, village cultural programmes and handicraft manufacturing, in addition to ACAP's ongoing integrated community development programmes. Since the eco-camp-sites generate only a small income the next step will be to assist locals to set up environmentally sound lodges. So expect this route to slowly develop into a tea-house route. See p237 for a description of the trek.

The Royal Trek (4 days)
So-called because Prince Charles trekked this way in the 1980s, the Royal Trek is a four-day, low altitude circuit from Pokhara east to Begnas Tal with night stops at Kalikathan, Shaklung, and Chisopani. Tea-house accommodation is basic; most people who do this walk are with guided trekking groups.

Mardi Himal (7-9 days)
Surely all the best treks must have been discovered and trekked out by now? Not so! The trek to the base of Mardi Himal is a fine ridge walk with classic views including Machhapuchhre, Hiun Chuli and Annapurna South, Annapurna IV and Annapurna II. From the high point you can also see Annapurna I and into the sanctuary.

Beginning from Dhampus you soon leave the tea-house trail for Shireko Danda, a ridge used only by herders. After climbing out of the forest there is a series of three camping places that lead you right under Mardi Himal, a 5587m peak at the base of Machhapuchhre. After a day exploring, possibly to 5000m, you return to Pokhara by leaving the ridge for Siding, a little-visited village, which is a day away from the Pokhara-Beni road.

ACAP are planning to assist the locals to turn this into an eco trek with managed camp-sites. This trek is currently only possible using an experienced trekking company who know the area well. Good local knowledge is vital not only for route finding but also for locating water sources. There are also some rather long, tough walks between camps. Another problem is the rapid ascent to altitude, which few companies take into account. Encounter (in the Kathmandu Guest House courtyard) are the most experienced operators of this trek. Their eight-day trek (ex-Kathmandu) costs US$325.

North Annapurna Base Camp (18-21 days)
This trip to the Base Camp of the French expedition that conquered Annapurna in 1950 takes 5-6 days from Lete, through superb country that supports blue sheep and snow leopard. The views across the valley to Dhaulagiri are magnificent but you'll need a guide who has been this way before as the trail is difficult to follow.

Khyar Tal/Annapurna South Base Camp (14-18 days)
Although this is not a strenuous trek, perhaps falling into the moderate category, there are a few long ascents and descents that will test your knees. The trek, however, needs a very experienced guide and careful planning (particularly from the point of view of the porters and the kerosene they will need) as you spend many days away from villages.

There are great views of Dhaulagiri across the valley, the Niligiris up the valley and even views of Machhapuchhre. And, of course, being at Annapurna South's base camp, the mountain itself looms over you.

Peregrine, the Australian trekking company (see p16), were among the first to lead treks up here.

Around Manaslu (17-23 days)
Similar to the Annapurna Circuit in the days before tea houses, this is a classic trek. Beginning in the fertile middle hills from either Gorkha or Dhading-Arughat, the path slowly climbs, occasionally on exposed narrow trails, to the rain-shadow region behind the Manaslu massif. Here the culture is Tibetan, flat-roofed houses and *gompas*. An overnight side trek to one of the base camps brings you face to face with groaning glaciers and the eighth highest mountain in the world.

After the long crossing of the spectacular Larkya La, a 5115m pass, the trail drops to Thonche-Darapani on the Annapurna Circuit for the last couple of days' walk out to Besisahar.

The area was opened in 1991, and only to group treks at that. Permits cost US$90 for peak season and US$75 for off peak for the special region, plus US$5 per week for the non-restricted section. In an effort to minimise the environmental and cultural damage a liaison officer is also required to accompany the group, and this can only be organised through a trekking company, well in advance. Since the costs of the liaison officer are borne by the trekking company, this trek tends to work out most economically only for groups larger than six or so people.

Around Dhaulagiri (16-21 days)
● **Route** One of Nepal's toughest and most dangerous treks, the highlight is simply the fact that you are passing through terrain which seems only marginally less inhospitable than Mars. The stark barrenness of Upper Hidden Valley is beaten only by the stupendous panorama from the 6035m

Dhampus/Thapa viewpoint. Over the 5360m French Col, Dhaulagiri rears up and the valley is flanked by glaciers. Below the rocky and uninviting Dhaulagiri Base Camp the route (for there is no real trail) is on a glacier. Rock debris gives way to ice, then some nasty knife-edged ridges traversing gaping crevasses. Just when you think you can breathe more easily another glacier blocks the valley meaning a tricky crossing of steep moraine slopes.

From Italy Base Camp on the far side the trail is a delight, so small that you wouldn't know it was there unless you were standing on it. What with bridges and narrow traverses worthy of an Indiana Jones movie the surprises don't end here: even from Boghara, the first village, the trail is exposed enough to scare the life out of anyone who suffers from vertigo. A day's walk brings you to main paths and in 1-3 days, depending on which trails you take, you reach Baglung and Pokhara.

● **Planning** Although there is no true mountaineering involved it should only be attempted by trekkers familiar with extreme rocky alpine environments. The trek has shocked many expecting something similar to the Annapurna Circuit – going without a guide is for adventurous mountaineers only. Since you spend extended time at high altitudes it should be attempted only when snow-free, from late September to December or perhaps in May. Hidden Valley is perpetually cold, at least -15°C in October and -20°C in November at night.

Altitude sickness is a real concern. It is more common for groups to attempt the trek clockwise but every group I have seen has had some dangerous, occasionally fatal AMS problems. Following standard 300m a day acclimatisation guidelines would mean sleeping three more nights on the glacier, in addition to the standard two nights at Italy Base Camp – basically impossible. So the better way to trek is anti-clockwise, after having acclimatised by crossing Tilicho or the Thorung La.

Many trekking companies say they can organise this trek but few understand what is involved, and porters have died because of their ignorance. To run a safe trek you must ensure the sirdar, a sherpa and at least a couple of porters have been there several times. Porters must be provided with warm trousers and jackets. The sirdar and a sherpa or two should have plastic boots in case there is snow, and spare pairs of shoes. All the crew must have tents to sleep in (and 40 porters need more than one dining tent). They should also have two blankets at minimum, sleeping pads and an extra tarpaulin. Porters must be in top condition so the trekking company should provide them with fuel and food after leaving the last village, something companies are loth to do. There is no firewood above 4000m and porters often don't take enough

❑ **Further information**
More information about the Around Dhaulagiri, Tilicho, Dhorpatan Circuit and Churen Himal treks can be found at: **www.trailblazer-guides.com/trek-nepal**

food or fuel, dangerously weakening themselves. If conditions are perfect, all these preparations will be just enough. If it snows you'll wish you had taken more. The alternative is to take porters from Marpha to Hidden Valley then send them back and continue around with only a sherpa who knows the route well and carrying all your own equipment – and hope that you don't get a surprise two-metre fall of snow!

Dhorpatan Circuit (11-13 days)
Between Beni and the hill station of Tansen is a rewarding cultural trek, the Dhorpatan Circuit. If you begin from Beni or Baglung, after walking through picturesque villages over a couple of days you camp near the top of the Jalja La (3250m/10,663ft) for a Dhaulagiri-Annapurna sunrise.

The forest leading down to Dhorpatan is particularly beautiful with mature pine, spruce, cedar and rhododendron and a sparkling stream. When Tibet was invaded by the Chinese in 1959 Dhorpatan was set up by the International Red Cross as a refugee base and there are two small Tibetan villages here, including a Bon Po monastery.

As you turn south the villages surprise with their variety. A drawn out although mostly pleasant climb leads to Thamgas where it is a rough day's journey to Tansen. Avoiding this climb means several more days of walking along a tractor trail to Ridi Bazaar (not recommended). Tansen, also called Palpa, is beautiful historic town connected by paved road to Pokhara and to Kathmandu.

Churen Himal (16-18 days)
The route is similar to the Dhorpatan Circuit but in the middle you take a detour to Churen Himal Base Camp, a beautiful valley that is like the Annapurna Sanctuary, except that it's currently visited by less than 25 trekkers a year! After the last village, Gurja, there are several possible routes in and out of the base camp region, including one remote route to Dolpo. In the alpine valley the views are stunning, a ring of no less than five 7000m/23,000ft mountains.

The Mustang Trek (14-18 days – groups only)
Tantalisingly sealed off from foreign trekkers until 1992, the upper reaches of the Kali Gandaki River above Kagbeni are now open for business – but at a price. Government restrictions have imposed not only a US$700 (£430) entry fee (for the first ten days, US$70 per day thereafter) but have also stipulated that only organised groups arranged through a trekking agency and complete with guide, porters and liaison officer will be allowed in. There can, however, be as few as just one member in the 'group'.

Most groups fly from Kathmandu to Jomsom before trekking through Kagbeni into north Mustang. The barren landscape is similar to that around Kagbeni. High winds race up the valley for much of the day weathering the sandstone into weird shapes. The trek passes through villages, each of which, like Kagbeni, has a crumbling castle and a Buddhist temple, to Lo Manthang, the region's capital. The return route is back the same way. Only

1000 permits are issued each year. The drawback is the high cost and the fact that you can't do this as a tea-house trek. The less adventurous may find the wind annoying since driving sand permeates everything.

More comfortable accommodation should now be available in Lo Manthang with the opening of the **Mystique Himalayan Resort**, which claims to be able to organise helicopter flights from Pokhara to Lo Manthang. The 'resort', more a small hotel, has seven rooms – and hot and cold running water in the bathrooms. For more information contact Mystique Himalayan Resort (☎ 427150 in Kathmandu, 🖹 427084, email: soi@wli nk.com.np, www.south-asia.com/soi) Lo Manthang, Mustang.

TREKKING PEAKS

Around the Annapurna Sanctuary are four peaks that may be climbed with trekking peak permits. They are Mardi Himal (5588m/18,333ft), Hiun Chuli (6441m/21,132ft), Tent Peak (5663m/18,579ft) and Fluted Peak (6501m/21,329ft).

Accessible from the Manang Valley are three other trekking peaks: Pisang Peak (6092m/19,987ft), Chulu East (6558m/21,516ft) and Chulu West (6420m/21,063ft). It's likely that Thorungtse (6032m/19,790ft) and Khatung Kang (6484m/21,273ft) above the Thorung La, and Dhampus Peak (6013m/19,728ft) may soon also be approved as trekking peaks.

For more information see p235.

❏ **OTHER ACTIVITIES**
Nepal now offers a lot more than just trekking. Unless your schedule is tight, these activities don't need to be planned in advance, just remember to allow some extra time.

Chitwan National Park wildlife safari (3-4 days)
Chitwan National Park is one of Asia's premier game parks, a mix of jungle, grasslands and river plains teeming with wildlife, including the endangered **royal Bengal tiger**, the rare **Gangetic dolphin** and the much more common **one-horned rhino**. Safari Asian style is quite different from African. The game, although abundant, is often more elusive. Also it is better hidden in the long elephant grass and jungle undergrowth, hence the advantage of spotting by elephant-back, from canoes and from *machans* (hides or blinds). However, you'll see lots of game and there's a special thrill finding it in its natural environment.

There are two ways of enjoying Chitwan: staying inside the park or outside. Sauraha, the travellers' haunt outside the park, is the cheaper but less satisfactory alternative; the elephant ride to go rhino spotting is short so most game spotting is done on foot (and by climbing trees if a rhino charges) or by jeep. And in the cosmopolitan village, you miss the absolute serenity of the morning and evening jungle. Inside the park, the wildlife resorts (packages from £85/US$140) provide a secluded, peaceful, relaxing and comfortable place to stay. The activities are well planned and the service is superb. Each has its own fleet of dugout canoes, jeeps and elephants who are handled by guides who know the wildlife's habits and who can usually spot the game long before you do. The resorts make the Chitwan Experience a wonderful way to begin or end a holiday in Nepal. If you're around in early December, Tiger Tops (🕾 +977-1-414075, email: info@tigermountain.com) hosts an annual **elephant polo tournament**.

Bardia National Park (4-8 days)
Lost in Nepal's Wild West, Bardia is almost undiscovered compared to Chitwan, only because it is either inconvenient or expensive to get to. Here four- or five-day safaris penetrating well into the park are better. Access is from Nepalganj, a £60/US$99 flight (one way) or a gruelling 14-18 hour night bus journey. From Pokhara, flights cost £37/US$60; the bus journey is as long as from Kathmandu.

Other more remote parks are **Kaptada National Park**, a middle altitude forest plateau which can only be trekked into (seven to 14 days total) and the **Royal Suklaphanta Wildlife Reserve** which is close to Mahendranagar. The reserve is a grassland area with the occasional tiger and wild elephant and is rich in rare swamp deer. It's an exhausting 30 hours by bus or £86/US$142 for a flight from Kathmandu.

Rafting (2-12 days)
While Nepal is famous for its mountains it should also be world-famous for its white water. Huge mountains mean big, steep rivers which are perfect for rafting and kayaking. For thrill-seekers no trip to Nepal would be complete without a white water expedition. Almost every trek in Nepal could be rounded off with a rafting expedition. Costs are £9-40/US$15-65 per day.

For a cheap and gentle introduction try the Trisuli. Almost every rafting company run trips on this river (two to four days) for most of the year. If you know you will enjoy the thrills and spills go straight for a river with a higher scare factor. The Bhote Kosi (2 days) and the Marsyangdi (5 days) are steep, technical and fun.

For the ultimate experience, try the massive waters of the Karnali (eight to nine days plus three travelling) and the Sun Kosi (eight to nine days plus two travelling), which have rapids that will make even the coolest cucumber gulp in disbelief. Another world-class river is the exhilarating Tamur (Kanchenjunga region) with its magic trek in and 130 rapids in 120km. For a shade off full throttle consider the cultural Kali Gandaki (three days out of Pokhara).

There's also kayaking: Kayak Clinics come highly recommended – just ensure the instructors are qualified.

The high water season, for those with no fear, is late September-early October and May. Trips run into November then begin again in March and taper off by late May. Wherever you go, safety should be paramount. Take a look at Peter Knowles' *Rafting: a consumers' guide*, available in Kathmandu. There are only three Thamel companies to run big rivers with; **Ultimate Descents**, **Equator Expeditions** and **Himalayan Encounters**.

For more information on all the rivers of Nepal see Knowles' & Allardice's excellent *White Water Nepal* and also check Adventure Whitewater's Web site: **www.adventure.whitewater.com**.

Mountain biking (1-4 days)
The hills around the Kathmandu valley have many roads. Most of these should be called four-wheel drive tracks, though for some even this title is fanciful. However they are perfect for mountain biking. Trips can be organised through **Himalayan Mountain Bikes** or **Dawn till Dusk** in Thamel. A minimum of two, sometimes four, people is required.

❑ OTHER ACTIVITIES (cont)

Cycling/motor-biking around the valley

Cycling used to be the most pleasant way to see Kathmandu but now with the dust and pollution few people cycle there for pleasure. However, once outside the city limits it's a different story; consult a detailed map of the valley for ideas. Clunky Indian mountain bikes (better kept on tarmacked roads) cost £1.20-2.50/US$2-4 a day while motorbikes go for around £6/US$10 a day plus petrol.

Mountain flight

During the peak season highly rated mountain flights around the Annapurna Circuit (£37/US$60) operate out of Pokhara. From Kathmandu there's also an Everest viewing flight (£60US$99). Although most of the airlines operate mountain flights, deciding which to take depends on the planes in operation – some can go higher or faster than others. Buddha Air's new Beech 1900D's are currently the best options. If the sky is clear, however, any domestic flight will usually give you spectacular mountain views if you sit on the appropriate side of the aircraft.

Balloon flight

The latest adventure activity to lift off in Nepal is hot air ballooning (£120 US$195). Piloted by a colourful Australian, the hour or so flight is exhilarating, peaceful and somewhat random; you land where the gods have taken you. Contact **Balloon Sunrise Nepal** (☎ 424157 in Kathmandu).

Canyoning

The latest activity for those wanting an adrenalin fix is canyoning: wet and wild exploring and abseiling down small creeks with plenty of waterfalls. **Borderland Resort** (☎ 425836 in Kathmandu) are the pioneers.

Visiting Tibet

If you already have a Chinese visa, you can usually cross the border as an individual. On the other side, since there are (officially) no buses, you often have to hire a landcruiser (minimum £37/US$60 per person) to Shigatse. This also gets around random permit problems. The easier and quicker way is to book one of the eight-day fixed departure tours in Kathmandu. These drive to (or from) Lhasa stopping at most points of interest along the way. The budget versions cost £320-380/US$520-600, including the £140/US$228 flight back, with departures Saturdays and Wednesdays. They run from March through to mid-November. There are four or five operators in Thamel with little to distinguish them. Most trekking and travel companies organise through them too.

Visiting Bhutan

The Land of the Thunder Dragon is a particularly rewarding destination. The friendliness of the people and the smooth organisation come at a price; around £120/US$200 a day whether trekking or travelling. Visits take time to arrange; a minimum of two weeks but starting at least three months in advance is better.

A second trek?

Trekking can be addictive! Around 20% of trekkers do it again in the same holiday. Trekkers also have one of the highest tourism return rates in the world; an amazing number of people just keep coming back year after year.

Other Himalayan trekking guides from Trailblazer include: *Trekking in the Everest Region*, *Trekking in Langtang, Helambu & Gosainkund* and *Trekking in Ladakh*.

What to take

The basic essentials

How much you take obviously depends on the type of trek you'll be doing, how high you'll be going and the season but, nevertheless, almost everyone seems to take far too much.

The key to sensible packing is to take just what you'll need to make yourself comfortable enough to enjoy the trek. What constitute the bare necessities varies from person to person and assessing your own needs is the difficult bit.

Independent minimalists on a short low altitude trek (Pokhara to Poon Hill to Ghandruk to Pokhara, for example) get away early or late in the season with just a day-pack containing water bottle and change of clothes. Travelling this light would be impossible in winter and would not be recommended in the main trekking seasons when lodges may not have enough quilts to go round. Most people, however, consider a sleeping-bag and a little more than just a change of clothes essential on a tea-house trek. If you're on an organised trek, companies usually provide a list of things you should bring.

In Kathmandu and Pokhara it's possible to rent down jackets, backpacks and sleeping-bags. These can also be bought there, new and second-hand but don't believe all the labels – some of the ruck-sacks are fakes, though perfectly serviceable all the same. Some climbing equipment is also available.

What to pack it all in

Deciding what to pack your belongings in depends on your style of trekking but most people will find it comes down to three containers – backpack/large hold-all, small day-pack and a hold-all to leave in Pokhara or Kathmandu. If

---

❏ **Pack in plastic**
Even in the trekking season there's a small chance of a rain shower. There's nothing more miserable after a day in the rain than a night in a damp sleeping-bag. With your gear packed into plastic bags this is entirely preventable. I once met a meticulous organiser who had packed everything into colour coded plastic bags labelled 'bedroom' (sleeping bag), 'dressing-room' (clothes), 'bathroom' (washing-kit/medical) and 'canteen' (trail snacks) – just slightly over the top but she did always seem to know where everything was and it all stayed perfectly dry.

A heavy gauge plastic bag to line the backpack will protect against dust (on the road from Kathmandu or Dumre) and the odd shower of rain. It's also worth having a second strong bag to help protect your pack from nimble-fingered baggage-handlers on the flight out to Nepal. Most check-in counters are able to supply a roll of strong tape to secure it.

you'll be carrying your pack yourself or arranging your own porter then it's worth buying a good quality, internal frame **backpack**. Get one bigger than you think you'll need so you don't have to compress everything into it.

If you're on an organised trek a hold-all is as good as a backpack, since it'll probably be tied to the back of a mule or put in a porter's *doko* (basket). If the hold-all does not have a lock sew on a small hoop at the zip end so a padlock can be attached. This is enough to discourage light fingers.

A **small day-pack** is vital for valuables (cameras etc) that you wouldn't want to leave in your room when you come down to eat in your lodge. During the day it can be packed into the top of your backpack. On an organised trek a day-pack is essential for carrying your camera, water-bottle and anything else you may need while walking.

Most people find it useful to leave a **hold-all** at their hotel in Kathmandu or Pokhara, containing a change of clothes and other things they don't need while trekking. Hotel owners are usually happy to store things free of charge as long as you come back to stay with them after your trek.

Sleeping-bag

A good-quality bag is essential since, although some lodges do have quilts, they're usually in short supply in the high season, and they're often of dubious cleanliness.

A down-filled bag is preferable to a synthetic one because it is lighter and can be rolled up tighter so it takes up less space in your pack. If you're trekking off-season between mid-May and early September a light sleeping-bag (one- or two-season) is sufficient; a thick bag would be too warm.

Some people like to bring a sleeping-bag liner, made from a folded sheet sewn up on two sides. This is easily washed and helps keep the bag clean; it also makes it warmer.

Unless you're planning to spend some nights outside you won't need a sleeping-mat or insulating-pad. It's true that the mattresses on the beds in the lodges are often not quite the 'Supa Dunlopilow Spong' advertised outside but you'll be tired enough not to notice this.

Footwear and foot care

Overtaken on the trail by Nepalis in flip-flops (thongs) or even barefoot, trekkers may feel overdressed in big hiking-boots but for soft Western soles good footwear is vital. The condition of your feet will have a direct effect on your enjoyment of the trek. What you need is a pair of boots that will support your feet properly and keep them dry and blister-free. If you're buying new boots do so well before you leave to allow time to wear them in. Walking with blisters is no fun and may become so uncomfortable that you are forced to give up your trek.

● **Choosing boots** Many people get by in just a pair of trainers, but this is not recommended, especially if you're carrying your own pack. Apart from the chance of twisting your ankle, trainers cannot keep your feet warm and dry in snow. Crossing the Thorung La with the possibility of sudden snowstorms, there's the risk of frostbite which could result in the amputation of toes. Choose a boot that offers **good ankle support**, especially important if you're carrying your own pack. They needn't be heavy; there's a wide range of modern boots. A leather boot treated to make it water-resistant is better than a Gore-tex or Sympatex boot. Ensure that there is enough room around the toes for steep descents.

● **Socks** In middle- or heavy-weight boots, wearing thin silk socks under thicker boot-socks can help prevent blisters. With close-fitting modern light-weight boots this is not necessary as long as you wear good quality hiking socks.

● **Foot care** It's important to keep your feet as dry as possible since this also helps stop blisters forming. Since your feet will sweat as you walk you should take off your boots and socks during your lunch break and let them dry in the sun.

Wash your feet and change your socks regularly. See p244 for information about how to deal with blisters.

● **Extra footwear** A pair of trainers as backup to your boots is a luxury you'll probably only wish to indulge in if someone else is carrying your pack. A pair of **flip-flops** (thongs) is well worth taking, however. They're light and you can wear them while your boots are drying off in the middle of the day, for washing in and even in the evening with a pair of socks if necessary, though this looks pretty daft. Some people bring down booties for evenings at high altitude. Who cares what you look like as long as you're warm?!

Clothes

Since most treks in the Annapurna region take you through a wide range of altitudes, you need to have clothes to cope with a corresponding range of temperatures. On the day you cross the Thorung La on the Circuit trek, for example, in November the temperature could fall as low as -10°C/14°F dur-

---

❑ **Old clothes needed by Kathmandu charities**
If you have a little space in your luggage there are a couple of worthy local charities that would be very grateful for some old clothes.

Kumbeshwar Technical School (☎ 536483) in Patan was set up to cater specifically for the very low caste groups. It incorporates a small orphanage, a primary school and a technical school where carpet weaving and carpentry are taught. High quality sweaters are on sale in the showroom here.

Child Workers in Nepal (CWIN) is a charity working for the rights of children and the abolition of child bonded labour (16% of children in the country are bonded labourers). They also run a 'Common Room' to support the 1000 children who live on the streets of Kathmandu. Clothes are always needed; children's clothes are best but they can alter adults' clothes. They can also make use of any medicines you may have left after your trek. CWIN (☎ 271658) is near the Soaltee Holiday Inn Crowne Plaza in Kalamati.

ing the night at Thorung Phedi and reach +15-20°C/59-68°F by the time you reach Muktinath the next day.

The accepted principle of wearing a number of thin layers of clothing rather than one thick one applies as much in the Himalaya as in the Yorkshire Dales. Air is trapped between the layers helping to insulate you from the cold and as you warm up the layers can be shed one by one.

● **Jacket** A good thick jacket, preferably down, is essential in the autumn, winter and spring. Although you won't need it during the day when the sun's shining, the temperature plummets as soon as the sun sets. On very cold nights you may even need to wear it inside your sleeping-bag.

● **Jersey/fleece top** One or other is essential. The thick Tibetan sweaters sold in Kathmandu and Pokhara are warm but very bulky.

● **Trousers/pants & skirts** Cotton trousers are sold in the tourist shops in Kathmandu and Pokhara and these are ideal for trekking. Poly-cotton travellers' clothing of the sort sold by Rohan is also good since it dries quickly but it's expensive. Thick trousers, jeans especially, are not a good idea as they restrict movement and are difficult to dry. If it's cold you can wear a couple of pairs of light trousers or some thermal underwear. Long skirts are better than trousers for women because they are more culturally acceptable and also useful as a screen if there are no bushes to crouch behind.

● **Windproof/down trousers/pants** Windproof over-trousers are useful at altitude and take up little space in a pack. In winter down trousers are worth considering.

● **Shirts/blouses** Light cotton shirts with long sleeves and collars are best. Many people take T-shirts and end up with burnt necks in the fierce sun. I take two or three shirts, and a T-shirt to wear at night or under a shirt during the day if it's cold.

❏ **Watch what you wear**

Foreigners should take care over what they wear in Nepal as it can have a profound effect on the way Nepalis relate to them.

For Nepali men, shorts are generally a sign of the low status labourer, so you'll probably see only porters wearing them among the Nepalis. On the more popular tourist routes it's generally acceptable for Western men to wear shorts, although you'll be accorded higher status in a pair of long trousers. Far more serious than the long trousers vs shorts issue for men is shirtlessness. Men should always wear a shirt.

Nepali women never show more than their ankles. I once wore a plain cotton skirt that came to just below my knees and they all thought I'd forgotten to put my skirt on, and that this was just my petticoat! However, along the more popular routes Nepalis have got used to seeing Western women in shorts (as long as possible, no short shorts) but you'll probably not notice until you wear a skirt that the reception they give you is much warmer. **Tara Winterton** (UK)

● **Underwear** Three changes of whatever you usually wear is fine. In the winter thermal underwear or thick tights are essential and, if you feel the cold, worth bringing in the autumn and early spring seasons, too.

● **Socks** If there's enough room in your boots to wear thick socks over thin, then bring two pairs of thick and two or three pairs of thin. Otherwise three pairs of thick socks is enough.

● **Hat** A sun hat with a wide brim is important protection against the heat during the day. A woolly hat or balaclava is essential in winter and at altitude and useful on cold evenings in the trekking seasons.

● **Gloves or mittens** Cheap woollen gloves are available in the tourist shops in Kathmandu and Pokhara and are essential during winter and the trekking seasons.

● **Swimsuit** This is useful for hot springs and for swimming. Both sexes should also wear a T-shirt if the bathing-spot is in a public place although for women it's better to do as local women do and wear a sarong.

● **Towel** This can be difficult to dry so bring only a small one. A tea-towel works well enough and can be pegged to your pack to dry as you trek. One trekker recommends taking a large chamois cloth, as used for cleaning car windows.

● **Rain/wind gear** Don't worry about trying to equip yourself with fully waterproof clothing. Even during the monsoon it rarely rains for more than a few hours and people simply dash into the nearest tea house to wait for it to pass. A plastic cycling poncho or tailored pack-cover will keep your backpack dry but Nepalis use the big heavy-gauge plastic bags available in most village shops.

Some people recommend buying one of the big black umbrellas available in Nepal. As well as keeping off the occasional shower, a sturdy umbrella can also be used as a walking-stick and sunshade.

If you're going to be spending some time at altitude a wind-cheater is useful protection against cold winds. Most people on the Circuit trek get by with just a thick jacket, though.

Toiletries

A well-equipped washbag doesn't have to be bulky. Take only the balms and lotions you really need to be comfortable but in the smallest (plastic) bottles available. Bring a bar of **soap** in a plastic soap container. You won't be washing your hair much so a few of the **sachets of shampoo** sold in Kathmandu and Pokhara are better than a big bottle. The smallest tube of **toothpaste** is fine for a trek.

Tampons are available only in Kathmandu or Pokhara so are better brought from home. Likewise, don't expect to be able to obtain in Nepal the brand of **condom/contraceptive pill** you may be using.

Loo paper is available along tea-house trekking routes, though expensive. If you can't face the water-and-hand method then keep a **lighter** in the same bag as your loo paper to burn it after use. Some people recommend bringing **'Wet Ones'** (pre-moistened towelettes).

If you want to sleep in Kathmandu, **ear-plugs** are recommended as defence against the barking dogs. **Sun-screen** is essential protection against the powerful sun at altitude. **Lip balm** is useful in the dry atmosphere of the Kali Gandaki Valley.

Medical kit

There's no need to drag around a vast chest of medicines that you don't really know how to use. Self-diagnosis is not recommended unless you're off the beaten track and have no alternative. If you're doing a standard tea-house trek, basic health facilities are available in some of the villages. At Manang the Himalayan Rescue Association has a health post staffed by Western volunteer doctors during the trekking season. The problems that most commonly affect trekkers are discussed in the health section (see p239).

Take along **paracetamol** for headaches and **aspirin** for inflammation of the joints; both can be used as general painkillers. The only drugs you really need to take on a tea-house trek are best purchased in Kathmandu or Pokhara (no prescriptions necessary): **Diamox** (10 tablets) for altitude sickness – if you're doing the Circuit or Sanctuary treks, **Tinidazole/Tiniba** (10 tablets) for giardia, and **Norfloxacin** for diarrhoea. See the health section (p239) for dosages.

Plasters/bandaids and **antiseptic cream** are needed for dealing with cuts. If you get blisters **Second Skin**, the gelatin film, is the best cure. In the UK, it's available only in climbing/hiking shops. Bring a **bandage** for sprains. **Knee supports** can be a real boon for the long descent over the Thorung La or down from the Sanctuary. **Throat lozenges** and **Lemsip** can be useful as colds and sore throats are not uncommon.

For lower altitudes, Kathmandu and Pokhara, **insect repellent** is recommended. To be really effective it should contain at least 30% diethyltoluamide (deet). Jungle Formula contains 40% and is widely available in the West; 100% deet is harder to find. If you're taking **anti-malarials** (see p54) don't forget these. Since they can also cause nausea, take them at night with or straight after food.

All travellers to developing world countries should have an **anti-Aids kit** containing sterilised syringes, needles and suture materials that might be needed in an emergency. These kits are sold by travel clinics and at some pharmacies in the West. If you're going on a long low-budget trek **multi-vitamin tablets** may be a good idea.

You must not drink untreated water in Nepal so bring some form of **water purification kit**. See p240 for details. Bottled mineral water is available but you can't always be sure it is pure. Also the plastic bottles in which it is supplied are creating a serious litter problem.

General items

A good pair of **sun-glasses** is necessary in summer as well as in winter when the sun on the snow is particularly bright. Note that snow reflects up to 75% of ultra violet light. If you wear **contact lenses** note that some people have problems with the soft variety – check with your optician. Don't forget your **cleaning solution** which should be kept in your sleeping-bag at night if there is a chance of its freezing. A **torch/flashlight** is essential. Best is a head-torch but a small pocket torch will do. Candles are provided in lodges so you don't need to bring these with you but you will need **matches** or a **lighter**.

Other items that may be useful: a **penknife** (Swiss Army knife is best), **clothes-washing liquid** (biodegradable; see also p90), a few **clothes pegs**, **sewing-kit**, **games** such as Travel Scrabble, pocket chess or a pack of cards and a **camera** (see below) with adequate supplies of **film**. Leave the walkman behind and listen to the sounds of the river, the forest insects and the thundering avalanches.

Some trekkers find a **walking stick** helps take the weight off knees during steep descents. Rather than pillage the dwindling forests for a suitable stick bring a **ski pole** with you or use a strong umbrella.

A litre-capacity **water-bottle** is essential. The Swiss-made blue aluminium ones are best since, filled with boiling water, they can double as a hot water bottle. They need to be covered with a sock, though, or you'll burn yourself. Since it's been boiled, the water can then be drunk in the morning. You should do this only when it's very cold since boiling water for drinking, rather than purifying it with iodine, wastes valuable firewood.

Most people keep a **diary** while they trek. Overdosing on fresh air and exercise seems to concentrate the mind; writing comes easily providing a record of your trek that will give pleasure long after you've left Nepal.

Ideas for gifts

● **For Nepalis** Don't load up with sweets and ball-point pens to answer the children's begging calls. Although playing Father Christmas may make you feel good it can have detrimental effects upon the recipients, decreasing their self-worth and leading to a picture in the child's mind of all things good coming from and being to do with the West, rather than from their own country. There will be occasions, however, when you wish you had something to give. Obviously what you take with you will need to be small and light: a few souvenir ball-point pens from your country, even some small toys (simple things purchased in Kathmandu may never have been seen by hill children), postcards of your country's more famous sights.

● **For Westerners** If you have expatriate friends working in Nepal there are several things they might appreciate. In the last few years, however, numerous foreign goods and foodstuffs (French wine, cheese, chocolate etc) have become available, although they are quite expensive. Find out if there's anything they particularly need (replacement part for an appliance, for example) before you arrive. A recent 'wish' list from a Kathmandu expatriate included real English bacon, dental floss, Bendicks Bittermints, and assorted baby gear. Herbal teas go down well, as do bottles of good wine and other luxury items. Glossy Western magazines and the Sunday papers are also well received.

Provisions

Since the tea houses in the Annapurna region are probably the best in Nepal a varied enough diet is available and it's not necessary to bring any food. You may, however, wish to take a few 'comfort foods' with you such as **Marmite, Bovril** or **Vegemite** (decanted from their heavy glass jars). Marmite is, however, now available in Kathmandu; and Mars Bars are on sale along all the major trails in Nepal. **Kendal Mint Cake** is worth bringing with you; it gives you a good boost on long climbs. You can get **peanut butter** in the lodges but many people bring their own to put on cream crackers sold in village shops. You can also buy little boxes of **glucose powder** (an instant energy restorer) at these shops.

Most trekkers treat the water they drink with iodine. The unpleasant taste that this leaves can be neutralised with vitamin C tablets or masked with **fruit drink powder**. These must not be added until the iodine has purified the water.

Some people even lug small bottles of **champagne or wine** to the top of the Thorung La for a celebratory drink. At 5416m (17,769ft) the effects are certainly interesting!

Money

In banks, you get a better rate for **travellers' cheques** than for cash and your money is obviously far safer in this form. Bring cheques from a well known company such as Thomas Cook or American Express. The better-known currencies are all accepted except New Zealand dollars.

The major **credit cards** are accepted in many hotels, restaurants and shops in Kathmandu and Pokhara. You can get instant cash advances (in Nepalese rupees cash or US$ travellers' cheques) on cards at some banks.

Black market exchange rates are about 5-10% above bank rates. Large denomination **US$ bills** are best but you won't be helping Nepal's balance of payments by changing money this way.

A **money-belt/pouch** is a useful way to carry your money safely while you're travelling around Nepal. Most people find them too hot to wear while trekking, though, and put them into their pack on the trail. Don't put them in a side pocket or anywhere where they could easily be removed.

Photographic equipment

Most travellers will want to bring a camera with them. Kodak, Fuji, Agfa and Konica print film is widely available in Nepal and some brands of transparency film are stocked. It's better to bring your own film with you; then you know it hasn't spent several days in the sun in transit. Bring more film than you think you'll need – 100ASA is best as the light is bright. Try to

❏ **Panorama cameras**
One of the problems with photographing mountains is that the printed result can be disappointing. With a standard lens you can't show the powerful sweep of mountains that are visible in many parts of the Annapurna region; with a wide-angle lens you may get all the mountains in the picture but they will be mere dots. I'd recommend one of the lightweight disposable makes of 'panorama' or 'stretch' camera which produce long prints (approximately 3 ½"x10"/100mmx 250mm). The lens and shutter speed are fixed so good light is essential but that's rarely a problem in Nepal. They are expensive (about £9 in the UK with developing a further £9) but worth it as the results can be breathtaking – all four Annapurnas in one stunning photo!   **Heather Oxley** (Italy)

avoid letting your film go through the X-ray machines in airports in Asia even if the notices tell you it's perfectly safe.

A spare set of batteries is essential, especially if you're trekking in the cold. If they go dead in the cold, however, they can be rejuvenated by warming them up in your hand or pocket.

If you're looking for a new camera, Kathmandu seems to be taking over from Singapore and Hong Kong as one of the cheapest places in the world to buy one. Don't expect a wide range, though.

RECOMMENDED READING

Background reading will make your trip all the more enjoyable and much has been published on Nepal and the Annapurna region. The best place to buy books on Nepal is Kathmandu where there are several excellent bookstores. There are also many second-hand bookshops and book exchanges in Kathmandu and Pokhara.

Guidebooks

Lonely Planet's *Nepal* is the best general guide to Nepal with good coverage of the whole country. There's also the *Rough Guide to Nepal* and Moon Publications' *Nepal Handbook*. Photography in the APA's *Nepal Insight Guide* is excellent. For treks other than those covered in this book the best general trekking guide to the whole of Nepal is *Trekking in Nepal* by Stephen Bezruchka, now in its sixth edition. This American doctor has been visiting Nepal since 1969. Lonely Planet's *Trekking in the Nepal Himalaya* gives useful overviews of the main treks in Nepal. For those attempting trekking peaks there's Bill O'Connor's *Trekking Peaks of Nepal*, better on some peaks than on others.

First aid manual

Everyone going on a trek should buy a copy of *The Himalayan First Aid and Survival Manual* by Jim Duff and Peter Gormly. Small, light and packed with information that could save a life in an emergency, it's available from KEEP in Kathmandu or direct: Dr J Duff, PO Box 53, Repton NSW 2454 Australia.

Flora and fauna

ACAP publishes *A Popular Guide to the Birds and Mammals of the Annapurna Conservation Area* by Carol Inskipp, an excellent little guide available in Nepal. *Himalayan Flowers and Trees* by Dorothy Mierow and Tirtha Bahadur Shrestha has numerous photographs to help identification of plants.

Ornithologists should try to get hold of a copy of *Birds of Nepal* by RL Fleming but this is now out of print. There's also *A Birdwatcher's Guide to Nepal* by Carol Inskipp, the Collins *Handguide to the Birds of the Indian Subcontinent* and S. Ali's *Field Guide to the Birds of the Eastern Himalayas* (OUP).

Other books

Maurice Herzog's *Annapurna – Conquest of the First 8000-metre Peak* is a classic and, unlike some mountaineering adventures, very readable; the French expedition made an attempt on Dhaulagiri before conquering Annapurna. Chris Bonington's *Annapurna South Face* describes the technically more difficult climb of the face of Annapurna that you can see from the Sanctuary.

The Snow Leopard by Peter Matthiessen charts the author's journey from Pokhara to Dolpo with naturalist George Schaller. It's more a journey of self-discovery as far as the author is concerned.

In Kathmandu you may be able to buy the reprint of Giuseppe Tucci's *Journey to Mustang*, an account of the expedition made in 1952. Even if you're not going all the way to Lo Monthang it's interesting for the descriptions of Kathmandu, Pokhara and the lower Kali Gandaki. *Mustang – A Lost Tibetan Kingdom* is Michel Peissel's account of the journey made in the 1960's. His biography of Boris Lissanevitch, *Tiger for Breakfast*, gives an good idea of what the country was like when the first tourists arrived and explains how a former dancer with Diaghilev's Ballet Russe came to be running Nepal's first international hotel.

HW Tilman, the mountaineer who led the 1938 attempt on Everest, was one of the first Westerners to travel in the Annapurna region. His very readable *Nepal Himalaya* is reprinted in *The Seven Mountain Travel Books*.

David Snellgrove's *Himalayan Pilgrimage* is an interesting account of travel in this area in the mid 1950s. For his research into Buddhism, the author visited virtually every monastery and temple in the region. *Annapurna Circuit: Himalayan Journey* by Andrew Stevenson details a more recent trek in the area.

Dervla Murphy's *The Waiting Land – A Spell in Nepal* is an interesting description of what Pokhara was like in the mid 1960s, before it was linked to the outside world by a road. The author was working with Tibetan refugees here. In *Thirty Years in Pokhara*, Dorothy Mierow describes the many changes that have taken place in this town.

In *Nepali Aama: Portrait of a Nepalese Hill Woman*, Broughton Coburn translates the life story of the elderly Gurung woman who was his landlady when he lived in Danda, a village south of Pokhara. They make a pilgrimage to Muktinath together. It's a charming book, full of universal truths and excellent photographs.

Charlie Pye-Smith's *Travels in Nepal – The Sequestered Kingdom* is both an entertaining travelogue and an analysis of the success (and often failure) of aid programmes in the country. It includes an account of a trek from Jomsom to Pokhara.

MAPS

Annapurna (1:100,000), published by **Schneider**, known for their accurate maps of the Everest region, is sometimes available in Kathmandu (£10, US$15). In London, Stanfords (☎ 0171-836 1321) can supply the map by mail order. You should also look out for new 1:50,000 topographical series of maps currently in production by the **Nepal Survey Department** with assistance from Finland (FinnAid) and due to be published in 2000. The surveys were done more recently than those for the Schneider map, contours are shown for every 40m. In the UK they will be able to be ordered from bookshops through the distributor, Cordee.

Locally-produced maps are available in Kathmandu for under £2/US$3. They are marketed under a variety of names, *Pokhara to Jomsom Manang (Round Annapurna Himal)* for example, and inaccurate even though they may be headed 'New Improved Latest Edition' (plus next year's date!). Most people make do with one of these maps and in conjunction with the route maps in this book, they're good enough. More expensive is the *Annapurna Conservation Area Map*, a full-colour map with contours, or Nepa Maps' *Annapurna*. All these maps are at the same scale: 1:125,000.

For smaller areas, **Himalayan Map House (Nepa Maps)** have a good series that includes *Pokhara-Jomsom-Muktinath* (1:75,000), *Pokhara to Ghandrung* (1:50,000) which also includes Chomrong, Ghorepani and Tatopani, and *Pokhara to Annapurna Base Camp* (1:50,000). They cost £2-4/US$3.50-7. They also produce *Deep Sky of Nepal*, an astronomical map that is well worth taking on your trek. The skies here are among the clearest

---

❏ **Useful Web sites**

For updates to this guide check **www.trailblazer-guides.com**.

Other sites which can be helpful for planning a trip include the following:
- The Nepal section at **www.south-asia.com**.
- Nepal Information Center at **www.uni-mainz.de/~baadj000/nepal.htm** for links to 600 Nepal sites - and to hear the Nepal National Anthem!
- There are numerous guest houses and local trekking companies advertising on **www.catmando.com**.
- The best online health information is on CIWEC Clinic's section on Kathmandu's concise page: **www.bena.com/nepaltrek/ciwec/immune.html**.
- At Lonely Planet's site (**www.lonelyplanet.com**), you can leave messages for other travellers on their 'Thorn Tree'.

in the world and it's interesting to know what stars you're looking at.

Karto Atelier produce the best maps to *Kathmandu* and *Pokhara* and also an excellent full colour map to the Pokhara/Dhaulagiri/Mustang/Annapurna Manaslu area at 1:250,000.

The *Annapurna Sattrek Map, Nepal*, published by Cartoconsult, Austria, is an enhanced satellite image map. It gives the best idea of the extent of the valleys and mountains but at a scale of 1:250,000 is not much use for trekking.

Health precautions and inoculations

There is always a greater risk of getting ill when travelling to a country where levels of hygiene are far below those in the West. These risks can, however, be considerably lessened by ensuring you're in reasonable physical shape when you arrive; by being aware of the dangers and by taking the relevant precautions (see p239). Check carefully that your inoculations are still valid.

WHO SHOULD AVOID HIGH ALTITUDE TREKS?

Most people of all ages with a reasonable level of fitness will have no difficulties trekking but the altitude on some treks in this area will create problems for certain groups. People with chest or heart diseases or high blood pressure should get the advice of a doctor who may recommend that they do not ascend above a certain altitude.

Children are more susceptible to altitude sickness than adults so should not be taken above 3000m or 10,000ft. Young adults (in their teens or early twenties) are also more susceptible and extra days should be allowed for acclimatisation.

If you are on any special medication you should seek the advice of your doctor before trekking to altitude. The greatest danger to these people (asthma sufferers and those with diabetes, for example) is losing their medication but with due care this needn't be a problem.

PRE-TREK PREPARATIONS

Getting fit – before or during your trek?

Although most people hit the trail without any training it makes sense to do some preparation, especially if you usually lead a sedentary existence. Ideally you should start about three months before you go and do something to emulate what you'll be doing in Nepal: walking up and down hills with a pack on your back. Any form of exercise is better than nothing. The dedicated urban-dwelling health freak will find a convenient block of flats, at least 20 storeys high, and spend several evenings a week walking up and down the stairs with a pack full of paving-stones. Most people don't bother, simply taking it very easy for the first few days to get fit as they trek.

Visit your dentist
Since dental care in Nepal is in its infancy you should ensure that your teeth are in order before you leave.

INOCULATIONS

No inoculations are listed as official requirements for foreigners visiting Nepal unless they are flying in from Africa or South America, in which case a yellow fever certificate is required. You would be particularly imprudent, however, not to get yourself vaccinated against several diseases listed below.

Travel clinics are usually better informed than your local doctor. Up-to-the-minute health information and an on-the-spot vaccination service is available in London at **Nomad Travellers Store & Medical Centre** (☎ 0181-833 4114, STA Travel, 40 Bernard St, WC1N 1LJ). Note that in the UK few vaccinations are now available on the NHS and NHS prices for some inoculations may actually be higher than those at the travel clinics above. It can pay to shop around. You should be given a record book in which your inoculations are listed. Although it's much better to have all the required inoculations before you arrive in Nepal, most can be obtained in Kathmandu.

Note that some inoculations cannot be given at the same time and in some cases boosters may be necessary four to six weeks apart. Check the situation a couple of months before you leave to ensure you will have time for full courses if necessary.

● **Tetanus** A vaccination is vital if you've not had one in the last ten years. If you then cut yourself while travelling you won't need another.

● **Infectious hepatitis** Infectious hepatitis (or hepatitis A) is a disease of the liver that drains you of energy and can last from three weeks to a couple of months. It's spread by drinking infected water, and by using utensils or eating food that has been handled by an infected person.

Gamma globulin injections are the usual form of vaccination and give a certain amount of protection for two to six months, depending on the strength of vaccine used. To be effective for as long as possible they should be given just before departure. Havrix is the more expensive vaccine now also being offered. The full course (three injections) is given over a 6-month period but protection lasts 10 years.

● **Meningitis** The inoculation is recommended. There have been some cases of the disease amongst Westerners in Nepal.

● **Typhoid** The disease is caught from contaminated food and water and the inoculation is recommended for travel to Nepal.

• **Japanese Encephalitis** Recommended if trekking in the monsoon.

● **Rabies** There is a minimal risk of being bitten by an animal carrying this often fatal disease (the risk is probably greatest in Kathmandu itself) and you may wish to consider the vaccination but the course of three injections is expensive. If you are unlucky enough to be bitten in Nepal a series of injections is available only from the CIWEC clinic in Kathmandu.

● **Others** Most people in the West will have been vaccinated against **diphtheria**, **tuberculosis** (TB) and **poliomyelitis** in their childhood. Check your medical records. Note that a **cholera** shot is only worth considering if you're travelling to or through an area where an epidemic has broken out; the vaccine gives very little protection.

Malaria prophylaxis

This mosquito-borne disease that is debilitating, occasionally fatal and on the increase, occurs in Nepal only at elevations below about 1000m/3280ft. This, therefore, excludes Kathmandu and the Sanctuary and Jomsom trekking routes. Although Pokhara is below 1000m the town is malaria free. The first few days of the Circuit trail from Dumre are below this elevation and there may be a very slight risk but it is higher in the Terai, the lowland area which includes Chitwan, particularly during the monsoon.

If your travels in Nepal are an extension of a holiday in India, if you're doing the Circuit between May and September or if you're also visiting Chitwan and other lowland areas you should certainly take anti-malarials. Some trekkers may want to take anti-malarials at other times of the year, too, though this is not really necessary.

The parasite (carried by the *Anopheles* mosquito) that causes malaria is resistant to chloroquine, so you may need to take two kinds of tablet, usually Chloroquine/Maloprim (two tablets once a week) and Paludrin/Proguanil (two tablets daily). Start the course one week before you go and continue for 4-6 weeks after you leave. Lariam (Mefloquine), taken only weekly, is a more recent alternative but it has more adverse side effects.

Whether you decide to take anti-malarials or not you must try to avoid being bitten by mosquitoes since some insects also carry **dengue fever**, and there's also a chance of bites becoming infected if you scratch them. Note that if you change planes in a malarial zone (eg Delhi where the airport is infested with mosquitoes) there's a risk of contracting malaria. *Anopheles* mosquitoes operate only at night when you should cover your legs and arms, use a powerful insect repellent and a mosquito coil (available in Nepal). Once you get up into the mountains you leave the mosquitoes behind.

TRAVEL & HEALTH INSURANCE

You may not need to use it but insurance is definitely very sensible to have. Beware of credit card companies that advertise free travel insurance if you book a flight with them. You will find that you're covered only for what you've paid for on the card (your flight).

For further information on health matters see p239.

PART 2: NEPAL

Facts about the country

The country is wild and mountainous, and is little frequented by strangers, whose visits the king discourages. **Marco Polo**

GEOGRAPHICAL BACKGROUND

Sandwiched between India and China, Nepal is roughly rectangular in shape, 500 miles long by 125 miles wide (800km by 200km). With a total area of 147,181 square km it's about the same size as England and Wales combined, or Florida.

Although Nepal's geographical claim to fame is indeed the Himalaya (eight out of ten of the world's highest peaks are here) there is a tremendous range in elevation across the country. Everest, the top of the world, stands at 8848m/29028ft while the lowest place in Nepal, the town of Kechanakawal, is a mere 70m/230ft above sea-level.

Mountains, valleys and plains
Nepal conveniently divides into three distinct regions, running as east-west bands across the country:

● **Himalayan region** The world's longest range of mountains stretches almost 5000 miles (8000km) across Asia and along the top quarter of Nepal. The Nepalese section of the Himalaya includes eight of the world's fourteen Eight-thousanders (as mountaineers refer to peaks over 8000m/26,247ft).

● **Middle region** Lying between the Himalaya and the southern lowland, the middle region comprises mountains and hills, river valleys and basins, including the Kathmandu and Pokhara Valleys. It covers about half the country. Running parallel to the Himalaya are the Mahabharat, rising to 4877m 16,000ft and the Siwaliks (or Churia) ranging from about 600m to 1500m (2000ft to 5000ft).

● **The Terai** Along the southern border with India is the lowland plain known as the Terai, covering a little under a quarter of the country. Once a dense subtropical forest, much has now been cut down to make way for settlers and provide firewood and building materials for both India and Nepal. Some of the remaining forest areas, such as Chitwan, have been set aside as national parks. Almost 60% of the country's cultivated land is in this area, its fertility enriched by the alluvial soil washed down annually from the mountains to the Terai.

Rising peaks, deepening valleys
The Himalaya were formed by the collision of the Asian and Indian continental plates, the Indian plate forcing up the edge of Tibet on the Asian plate. This collision is still continuing today, at the rate of a few mm each year, resulting in landslides, erosion and mountains that are still rising. Quite how fast the Himalaya are growing is difficult to say since not all peaks are pushed up at the same rate. The annual growth rate is estimated at between 1mm and 3mm (up to one eighth of an inch).

These are also the youngest mountains in the world and geographers are especially interested in the fact that they don't form the watershed. This is further north on the Tibetan plateau which is why the major rivers that flow through Nepal into India's Ganges have their sources north of the Himalaya, cutting south through deep valleys. On the Jomsom trek you follow the world's deepest valley, the Kali Gandaki, and at one point you stand almost 3 miles (4.8km) below Dhaulagiri and Annapurna I. Several of these valleys form ancient trade routes with Tibet.

CLIMATE

Dramatic variations in temperature
With variations in altitude of nearly 8000m/26,247ft, climatic extremes from sub-tropical to alpine are to be expected.

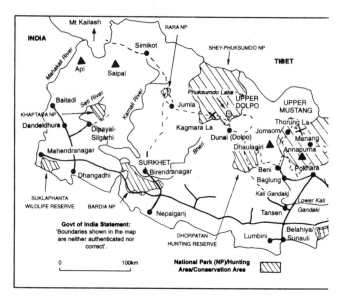

In June on the Terai the temperature can rise as high as the mid-40s°C (around 110°F). Winter temperatures in the mountain towns of Jomsom and Jiri (Everest region) fall well below zero °C (32°F) each night but can rise to 20°C/68°F in the middle of the day. Trekkers start and end the day in thick jackets but can eat lunch in shirt-sleeves.

Kathmandu's climate is pleasant year round, with average temperatures ranging from 18-30°C/65-86°F during the day and 2-19°C/36-66°F at night.

Rainfall

The climate of the southern half of the country is affected not only by altitude but also by the monsoon. Up to 80% of the total annual rainfall is during this June to September season.

The monsoon, which affects the whole sub-continent, is caused by the land and sea heating up at different rates. It reaches eastern Nepal in the first week of June, and the west about ten days later. The monsoon clouds sweep up to the Himalaya which act as a barrier, denying areas to the north more than a sprinkling of rain.

The wettest area in Nepal is the Pokhara Valley with a mean annual rainfall of 4000mm. Most of this falls during the monsoon. Kathmandu's mean annual rainfall is 1400mm.

See p22 for Nepal's trekking seasons.

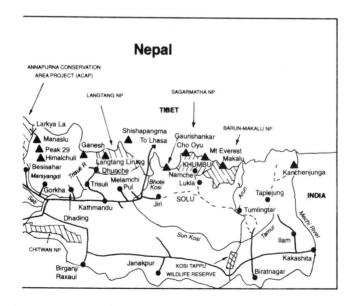

HISTORICAL OUTLINE

Out of the Tethys Sea

On the trek to Jomsom, you may be lucky enough to find an ammonite, a fossilised mollusc, amongst the pebbles of the wide Kali Gandaki Valley. Thousands of these 180-million-year-old fossils have been found, clues to the submarine origins of parts of Nepal as the floor of the Tethys Sea. Around 55 million years ago the north-bound Indian continental plate drifted into the Asian plate and since then has been lifting up the southern edge of Tibet, creating the Himalaya.

The Kathmandu Valley

The first evidence of humans in Nepal dates back to about 200,000 years ago, when the Kathmandu Valley was a lake.

An ancient Newari myth tells of the monk, Manjushri, draining the Valley by creating the Chobar Gorge. This he did single-handed, with two slashes of his sword. Many of the world's myths and legends seem to have been triggered by some catastrophic event that really did happen and this is no exception. Scientists have shown that about 10,000 years ago the rim of the Kathmandu Lake ruptured at Chobar, allowing the water to drain out, leaving a fertile valley.

Early history

Among the earliest known rulers of the Kathmandu Valley were the Kirati, from whom the Rai and Limbu people of eastern Nepal claim to be descended. The Kirati had their capital in Matatirtha, west of modern Kathmandu in the second half of the first millennium BC.

Other centres were springing up on the Terai at around this time. It was in one of these lowland kingdoms, Lumbini, that Prince Siddhartha Gautam, who was to become the Buddha, was born in 543BC. Buddhism developed in India and spread into surrounding parts of the sub-continent, particularly under the Indian emperor, Ashoka. Several of the stupas (Buddhist religious monuments) he built around Kathmandu in the 2nd century BC can still be seen.

The Lichhavi

The Kirati were replaced by the **Lichhavi** around 200 AD. With their capital near Pashupatinath in Kathmandu, the Lichhavi dynasty orchestrated a golden age of art and culture, fuelled by trade with states to the north and south of the Valley. Their legacy to modern Nepal is the pagoda style of architecture, extensive stone carving (some of the work at Pashupati-nath dates from this time) and the caste system. Although Hindu, the Lichhavi were tolerant of other religions and this, too, has been passed down to the present day.

By the 9th century the Lichhavi had been overpowered by the **Thakuri**, invading from the Terai. The next 300 years are known as the Nepalese Dark Ages but, as with the European Dark Ages, art and learning continued to prosper in the monasteries and temples. The **Khasa** controlled the western area of the country including Pokhara, in an empire that stretched west as far as Kashmir.

The Malla Dynasty

This period in Nepal's history was a second Golden Age, a renaissance of art and architecture under the Malla kings (1200-1768). The palaces and temples of the Durbar Squares in Kathmandu, Patan and Bhaktapur date from this time.

The name Malla, meaning 'wrestler', is said to have been coined by King Ari Deva who was in the ring when his son, the first Malla, was born. This was, however, a title used by other kings at the time, including the Khasa.

Jayasthiti Malla (1382-95) was one of the greatest reformers in the history of the country, with a penchant for bureaucracy that led to the restructuring of Nepalese society on an orthodox Hindu framework. Thirty-six main castes, which included Buddhists as well as Hindus, were created in a system that is still observed by many Nepalis today. He unified the four main city states in the Kathmandu Valley: Kathmandu, Patan, Banepa and Bhaktapur.

Centralised control reached its peak under **Yaksha Malla** whose empire extended into India, west to the Pokhara Valley and east to Sikkim. On his death in 1482, Kathmandu, Patan, Banepa and Bhaktapur were split between his heirs. Competition between them seems to have been no bad thing as far as the rich architectural heritage from this time shows; but the feuding led to the disintegration and weakening of the Malla kingdom over the next 200 years.

The unification of Nepal

By the 18th century Nepal was again just a large collection of independent kingdoms. In the Terai and lower hills these were in the hands of Rajput princes ousted from India. The hilltop kingdom of Gorkha was the domain of the Shah dynasty to which the reigning King of Nepal belongs. In 1743 the King of Gorkha, **Prithvi Narayan Shah**, set off on a pilgrimage to Varanasi. He took the opportunity to restock his arsenal while there and on his return took the town of Nuwakot in 1744 to begin the slow conquest of the Kathmandu Valley. Kirtipur fell in 1764 after a siege of six months. For wounding the king's brother all the inhabitants (except musicians and children) were punished by having their noses removed.

The last of the Malla kings of Kathmandu, Jaya Prakash Malla, sought help from the British East India Company who sent a force of over 2000 soldiers. The Gorkhalis provided the British with a display of bravery they never forgot. Only a third of the British force returned and the Gorkhalis were left with a rich hoard of weapons.

In 1768, Prithvi Narayan Shah took Kathmandu without a struggle on the eve of the Indra Jatra festival (still held to mark the end of the monsoon) and became the acknowledged founder of modern Nepal.

Wars with Tibet and Britain

The territorial aspirations of the Shah dynasty led to further expansion and a number of embarrassments. In 1792, with the help of China, Tibet managed to halt Nepal's northern advance and Nepal was burdened with annual tributes to China that lasted 120 years.

In the south there was confrontation with the British East India Company, this time more successful from the point of view of the British. By the **Treaty of Segauli** in 1816 Nepal was forced to relinquish claims to parts of the Terai and to accept a permanent British ambassador, or Resident, in Kathmandu. So impressed were the British with the fighting skills of their enemy that they began recruiting Nepalis immediately, beginning a tradition of Gurkha regiments that continues in the British and Indian armies to this day.

❏ The Gurkhas

Forming what is probably the world's most famous fighting force, the tough Nepali hill men who fill the Gurkha battalions within the British and Indian armies are renowned for their bravery and resilience. Stories of their fearlessness have been sending shivers down the spines of every enemy they've faced since recruitment began in 1815.

During the Falklands Conflict, it is said that rumours were circulating through Argentinian ranks that the Gurkhas were not only tough fighters but that the extent of their ruthlessness included decapitation of their victims (with the famous khukri) followed by ritual cannibalism! In June 1983 when it was leaked that Gurkhas would be used in an assault on an outpost near Port Stanley, the Gurkhas arrived to find that the enemy had fled.

Since Britain began recruiting the soldiers of the disbanded Gorkhali Army nearly two centuries ago these 'Gurkhas', as they came to be known, have served in every conflict that has involved Britain or India. In World War I, 200,000 Gurkhas served; 250,000 in World War II. When India became independent in 1947 six of the ten Gurkha regiments remained with the Indian Army; the others becoming part of the British Army.

Gurkha wages, pensions and payments for associated services (eg frequent charter flights for families of Gurkhas going on leave or returning from Nepal) were, until recently, the country's largest source of foreign currency. They are still a vital source of earnings, accounting for about 20% of Nepal's GNP.

There are now about 100,000 Gurkhas in the Indian Army, 4000 in the British Army. When the Hong Kong base was closed in 1997 as the colony reverted to China, Gurkha numbers fell by 2500. There are currently two infantry battalions, one based in Britain and the other in Brunei, where one battalion is already on loan to the Sultan.

In Britain the army is having difficulty in finding enough British recruits – despite a £17.5 million advertising campaign. In Nepal they are swamped with applicants. Since the fitness test used for British recruits is too easy for Nepalis tougher tests have been devised. They must complete the $1\frac{1}{2}$ mile run in $9\frac{1}{2}$ minutes, $1\frac{1}{2}$ minutes less than the test used for British soldiers. In Nepal, the 1998 recruitment tests attracted 36,000 young hopefuls – for just 230 places with the British Gurkhas.

The Kot Massacre

By the 19th century, the power of the Shahs had been weakened by internal conflict and palace intrigue. The Queen was planning to seize power from the King and was furious when one of her allies was murdered. She asked **Jung Bahadur Rana**, a young general, to avenge her. He took her at her word and arranged the murder of 55 of the top officials who had gathered for a meeting in the armoury in Durbar Square, in what became known as the 'Kot Massacre'.

The Ranas – Nepalese Borgias

Following the Kot Massacre, Jung Bahadur made himself prime minister and took most of the power away from the throne. He was wise enough to preserve the monarchy since the people believed the king to be an incarnation of the Hindu god Vishnu. The office of prime minister (and therefore the reins of power) became hereditary within the Rana family, with the monarchy mere puppets for the next 104 years.

The country's new rulers did virtually nothing to advance the lot of the Nepali peasantry, their main legacy being the bizarre collection of whitewashed palaces that litter the capital. If these vast neo-classical wedding-cake buildings look out of place in the eyes of the Western tourist, they must have seemed almost extra-terrestrial to the Nepalese in the 19th century. This architectural fashion was started by Jung Bahadur after his European tour in 1850. He visited England and had an audience with Queen Victoria; his visit to the opera at Covent Garden is said to have made more of an impression on him.

Restoration of the monarchy

The policy of isolationism that had always been a characteristic of the country's rulers began to break down in the 20th century. Although the borders were effectively sealed against outsiders, more than a quarter of a million Gurkhas travelled abroad to fight in the two world wars, bringing back new ideas as well as foreign exchange.

Discontent with the Ranas was growing, not only amongst the Nepali people but also among the many members of the Rana family who did not hold positions of power. The Nepali Congress Party was formed under BP Koirala in 1946, in India, backing **King Tribhuvan**, virtually a prisoner in his palace in Kathmandu, as the figurehead.

On 6th November 1951 the King managed to escape to the Indian Embassy in Kathmandu, where he was granted asylum. The forces of the Nepali Congress Party attacked the country from India, gaining control of most of the Terai. An agreement was reached with the help of Indian prime minister, Nehru, and Tribhuvan returned to a hero's welcome in Kathmandu on 15 February 1951. A coalition government comprising the Nepali Congress Party and the Ranas was installed with the promise of free elections in 1952.

Panchayat system

The promised elections didn't materialise until 1959, after Tribhuvan had died. The Nepali Congress Party swept the board with almost three-quarters of the seats and BP Koirala became prime minister.

The new King Mahendra was less keen on this experiment with democracy than were his people. In 1960 he took matters into his own hands, jailing BP Koirala and dissolving parliament on allegations of corruption. In its place he installed the *panchayat* system, which he considered more appropriate to the country with its largely illiterate population. Panchayat (council of five), involved sending locally elected representatives to a district council, which in turn elected a representative to the national assembly. Ultimate power remained with the king who chose the prime minister and cabinet.

1979 Referendum

On the death of his father in 1972, the reins of power passed to **Birendra**, who is still the reigning monarch. The new king, educated at Eton and Harvard, began his reign with a crackdown on corruption. This had little effect and discontent grew, erupting in riots in 1979. Still convinced that the panchayat system was the most appropriate form of government for Nepal, he held a national referendum. Fifty-five per cent of the votes called for its retention but there were widespread allegations of vote rigging.

The 1980s

During the last decade of real power for the monarchy, the prisons filled up with political dissidents. Newspapers were strictly censored and journalists imprisoned without trial. The king became increasingly distanced from the people, who, having successfully removed the Ranas 30 years before, were now being ruled by another form of autocracy. The Ranas still held many of the highest positions of power, particularly in the army. The queen, also, is a Rana. It appeared that the gods, too, were displeased with the situation. In 1988, 1200 people died in a devastating earthquake in eastern Nepal and in 1989 a temple in Patan collapsed.

Democracy in the 90s

The democracy movement was given added impetus in February 1990 when the Nepali Congress Party and the Nepal Communist Party campaigned together for the lifting of the ban on political parties. The leaders were arrested but there were democracy rallies and strikes across the country.

By April the movement reached a dramatic final stage. An uprising in Patan was followed on 6th April by a demonstration of over 200,000 people in front of the palace in Kathmandu. The police began by beating the people back and, when a demonstrator climbed on to the statue of King Mahendra and symbolically removed his sceptre, the shooting began. At least 100 people (and probably as many as 300) lost their lives. Their martyrdom, combined with pressure from the West, forced the king to lift the ban on political parties and appoint an interim government to oversee the change to a constitutional monarchy similar to Britain's.

'Vote for Tree'

The 1991 elections, the first for over 30 years involved a large amount of political graffiti. Since many of the voters were illiterate each party chose a symbol (tree, spade, cow, sun etc). The Nepali Congress Party (the tree) defeated the United Marxist-Leninist Party (the sun) but by only a narrow margin. The Maoist Masale Party was popular in the Pokhara area.

Given that the collapse of communist states in eastern Europe was a major catalyst for the democracy movement in Nepal, it seems surprising that communist parties had such support in these first elections. Part of this may be attributed to the fact that people have always considered that the Nepali Congress Party is too pro-India. Nepalis have an ingrained fear of foreign domination that stems from the 1814 war with the British and accounts for the long policy of isolationism.

Broken promises

When things go wrong Nepalis shrug their shoulders and say 'Ke garne' – literally, 'What to do?'. No doubt many must have thought that once the monarch had been removed from power all would be well. They must have had the same hopes back in 1951 when they got rid of the Ranas. But nothing seemed to have changed. Corruption was rife at all levels of government office (as it still is today). The promised rise in living standards never came and it was not long before the people lost confidence in their new government. The opposition parties were quick to take advantage of this, stirring up riots in which several people were killed. The government itself was torn by internal dissent and Nepal's second general election was called 18 months early, in November 1994. The communists took power, ruling in a coalition government under the leader of the United Marxist-Leninist Party, Man Mohan Adhikari.

In September 1995 Adhikari's party lost a vote of no-confidence in parliament. A tripartite coalition government composed of the Nepal Congress Party, the right-wing Rastriya Prajatantra Party and the pro-India Nepal Sadbhavana Party, was sworn in under prime minister Sher Bahadur Deuba.

A decade of democray

As Nepal reaches the end of its first decade of democracy the pattern of short-lived coalitions and changing prime ministers continues. Some parties, such as the Communist Party of Nepal (Maoists), have taken matters into their own hands, declaring a **People's War** in 1996 that involves strikes, hostage taking and civil disobedience. Maoist insurgency has claimed the lives of more than 80 people but the violent backlash from the police has also been condemned by Amnesty International.

The country is currently ruled by two parties, the Communist Party of Nepal (Marxist-Leninist) under Sahana Pradhan and the Nepal Congress led by **Girija Prasad Koirala**, who is also the current prime minister.

A **general election** is due to be called in November 1999 but it's likely that this will take place earlier in 1999.

ECONOMY

Nepal is one of the world's poorest countries in terms of average per capita income. Almost half of the population earns an average of just £50/US$82 per year. The overall per capita income is only £130/US$210 per year.

It's said that in a country where over 80% of the people work as subsistence farmers outside the cash economy, per capita income figures don't mean all that much. It's certainly true that most people manage to feed their families off the land producing a surplus that is used to buy tea, sugar, salt and clothes but in many cases this is a small surplus, where it exists at all. Although very few starve to death in Nepal many people (and up to 70% of children) are undernourished. Along the comparatively affluent Annapurna trekking routes you will not see much evidence of this. Nevertheless, with a rapidly rising population putting ever increasing pressures on the environment, the situation is likely to get worse rather than better.

Agriculture

Less than 20% of Nepal is cultivatable yet it employs 81% of the population and produces 40% of the GNP. Most farmers own their own plots of land but these are generally very small. Tenant farmers must hand over half their crops as rent.

A trek up the Kali Gandaki will take you through most of the crop regions of Nepal. Rice is grown on the Terai and up to about 2000m (6562ft), wheat and maize up to about 2500m (8202ft). Other crops include barley, millet, sugar cane, jute, oil-seed, tobacco and potatoes.

There are orchards of apple, peach and apricot at about 2500m (8202ft) in the Annapurna region but, as with rice on the Terai, distribution of any surpluses produced is a problem. Whilst some of the mountain regions suffer from a shortage of food in the winter months, Nepali rice from the Terai is sold to India.

Industry

The manufacturing industry employs only about 5% of the labour force but accounts for 21% of GNP. The largest industries in terms of employees are carpet-making, weaving and tile- and brick-making. On the Terai there are factories producing soap, cigarettes, beer, cloth and cement, and processing jute, grain and oil-seed.

Tourism

In 1995 (the most recent year for which statistics are available), 354,000 tourists visited the country. Of these, 36% were Indians, 64% from other countries. Tourism earned the country US$88 million, accounting for 30% of Nepal's foreign exchange earnings but each year about half of this money leaves the country to pay for the foreign goods that tourists demand.

(**Opposite**)   Rice terraces near Bahundanda (see p200). With 81% of Nepalis living off the land, every fertile space must be utilised. (Photo: Charlie Loram).

Energy resources

Over 80% of the country's fuel requirements are provided by fire-wood. Consequently forest cover has been reduced from 60% in 1951 to little more than 30% now. Deforestation is a very serious problem that can only worsen as the population rises. In 1984 a US$24 million forest development programme was begun. Although Nepal has to import all its petroleum products several companies are at present prospecting for oil in the South-East.

One abundant Nepali resource that can be harnessed to provide energy is water. Several hydroelectric projects have been built but it's estimated that less than 0.3% has yet been utilised. Most of these projects, however, are large, expensive and sometimes environmentally damaging. The potential for valuable foreign currency earnings through the sale of electricity to countries like India is undeniable. Several micro-hydro schemes have been successfully set up in the hills (a number in the Annapurna region) but, however it's produced, few Nepalis can afford electricity.

See p88 for advice on how to limit your environmental impact.

DEFENCE

Nepal is a member of the United Nations and the Colombo Plan. In 1975, King Birendra declared the country's neutrality by proclaiming Nepal a 'Zone of Peace'. India has rejected this since it contravenes a longstanding mutual aid defence treaty between the two countries.

The army comprises the royal guard, seven infantry brigades, one air squadron, and engineer, artillery, signals, transport and parachute battalions. The air force operates three transport planes and four helicopters (also used for mountain rescues). The armed forces employ 40,000 people and 27,000 in the paramilitary police force.

See p60 for information about Gurkha regiments.

EDUCATION

There have been considerable advances in education in the last 45 years but by Western standards there is still a long way to go. The country's literacy rate stands at 40%, and the literacy rate of men is more than twice that of women: 55% to 23%.

Primary education of a sort has been provided free by the government since 1975. It's pretty miraculous that the children manage to learn anything in the classroom since most of the learning seems to be achieved by rote chanting. Almost half the teachers have no proper training and pupil-teacher ratios are about 40:1. There are about 1,960,000 boys and 1,300,000 girls in

---

(**Opposite**) The private chapel in the Red House Lodge, Kagbeni (see p162), contains a large gilt image of the Red Buddha Amitabha. **Previous pages:** The village of Jharkot (seen from below Muktinath) sits on a spur overlooking the valley.

primary education; the disparity in numbers caused by parents keeping their daughters away from school to help in the fields. The ratio of boys to girls in secondary education is similarly discouraging: 190,000 boys to 100,000 girls. There are now four universities: Tribhuvan University in Kathmandu with a second campus in Pokhara, Kathmandu University, Mahendra Sanskrit University (solely for the study of Sanskrit) and Purbanchal University.

HEALTH

Health care in Nepal is still in its early stages of development. Although Bir Hospital, the country's first, opened in 1890, it was not until 1960 that the Ministry of Health was established. There are now about 13,700 people for every doctor, compared to 6500 in Indonesia, 2100 in India, 580 in the UK and 420 in the US. In the entire country there are fewer than 5000 hospital beds. Most health care is through health posts staffed by local workers trained in both Western and ayurvedic medicine.

Infant mortality is approximately 75 deaths per 1000 births – a third of what it was thirty years ago but still unacceptably high compared to the 6-8 per 1000 rate in the West. Cleaner water supplies, vaccination programmes and oral rehydration powders have helped reduce this rate.

Life expectancy, at 58 years for men, 57 for women, is amongst the lowest in the world.

THE PEOPLE

In 1951 Nepal's population was just eight million people but, rising at a fast 2.5%, it's now 23.7 million. Basic health care and cleaner water supplies

---

❏ **Development programmes and foreign aid**

Nepal abounds in foreign aid programmes. Playing on his country's position between two giants, India and China, King Mahendra allowed Nepal to be wooed by almost any foreign power willing to pour money into the country. Foreign aid now amounts to over US$400 million annually, which is about 35% of foreign exchange earnings and comprises up to 30% of the government's annual budget.

Development schemes of every kind have been thrust upon Nepal: everything from massive hydro-electric projects to small tree-planting schemes in villages. They vary widely in their efficacy but the more successful programmes now seem to be the small-scale ones initiated by the people themselves. With the large projects, substantial amounts of foreign aid get pocketed long before they reach the projects. Development has become very big business here with many owing their lucrative jobs to foreign agencies.

One of the most successful development projects is the Annapurna Conservation Area Project (ACAP), established in 1986 to provide resource management and sustainable development in a tourist area (see p87).

Charlie Pye-Smith's *Travels in Nepal* gives an excellent assessment of some of the aid programmes operating in the country in the late 1980s, including projects in the Annapurna region.

have led to this disturbingly high growth rate. As has now been discovered in many developing world countries education, not just the provision of free contraceptives, is the key to controlling the population explosion in Nepal.

Ethnic patchwork

Nepal comprises at least 35 different peoples with unique cultures and languages, although 58% of the population now describe themselves as 'Nepali', according to information from the Central Bureau of Statistics. Most of these people are also Hindus. Brahmins and Chhetris (see p68), the higher Hindu castes, are not ethnic but cultural groups very different from the lower castes.

● **People of the Terai** After Nepalis, there are three main groups on the Terai. The **Maithili** constitute Nepal's next largest group: 11% of the total population. The **Bhojpuri** constitute 7.6% and the **Tharu**, one of the country's few indigenous groups, 3.6%.

● **Newar** The indigenous Newar make up about half the population in the Kathmandu Valley but only 3% of Nepal's overall population. The buildings in Durbar Square bear witness to a long and rich cultural history of these craftsmen and merchants. Bhaktapur, near Kathmandu, is a largely Newar city. The Newar are Hindu and Buddhist, and many follow a mixture of the two. They have over 80 caste divisions and their own calendar.

● **Tamang** This group of people originated from the north. Constituting 3.5% of the population, they live in the middle hills in central and eastern Nepal and work as porters and farmers.

● **Gurung & Magar** Living in the southern area of the Annapurna region, the Gurung (see p174) farm the higher slopes and the Magar the lower. Most Gurkha recruits come from these two groups.

● **Thakali** This small but prosperous ethnic group (see p155) comprises a number of villages along the Kali Gandaki. The Thakali controlled the old trade route up the river to Tibet and have a well-deserved reputation for running the best travellers' lodges in Nepal.

● **Manangbhot/Manangba** The inhabitants of the Manang Valley (see p206), in the Annapurna region, are traders with links as far away as Hong Kong. They speak a Tibeto-Burman language and are Buddhists. The Manangba are just one of the many *bhotia* (mountain people originally from Tibet) in Nepal.

● **People of the east** The **Sherpa** are the most famous of Nepal's ethnic groups. From the Solu-Khumbu (Everest) region, they've been so closely linked with mountaineering and the trekking industry that their name now stands for almost any Nepali who works on an organised trek.

The **Rai** and **Limbu**, known collectively as the **Kirat**, the descendants of Nepal's earliest inhabitants, are also from the east, in the lower hills.

RELIGION

Nepal describes itself as a Hindu Constitutional Monarchy. Official statistics state that 89.5% of the population is Hindu, 5.3% Buddhist, 2.7% Muslim, 2.4% Shamanist and Animist, 0.1% Jain and 0.04% Christian. Since being Hindu and Nepali-speaking can confer greater employment opportunities and higher social standing, it's likely that there are more Buddhists and fewer Hindus than these figures suggest. The long tradition of religious toleration has led to a blurring of distinctions, especially between Hinduism and Buddhism. You'll see Buddhist prayer-flags fluttering over a Hindu temple and statues of Hindu gods in Buddhist gompas (monasteries). In fact, many Hindu deities have their Buddhist counterparts.

Hinduism

The most complex of all religions is also the most tolerant – in Nepal, at least, if not in India. In theory, Hinduism accepts all other beliefs as true and allows for forms of worship which range from simple animism to deepest philosophy. Its many paths even include *tantra* which maintains that enlightenment can come through absolutely anything in life; and that includes drink, drugs and sex.

Central to Hindu beliefs is reincarnation, the belief that all living things go through a series of rebirths which lead eventually to *moksha*, salvation in the form of escape from the cycle and unity with the Creator. What determines whether you're reborn in the next life as a flea or a wealthy landowner is *karma*. Good and bad karma are the direct result of good or bad actions during your lifetime.

The Hindu caste system still has a profound influence on the lives of most people in Nepal. It was actually extended by the Malla king, Jayasthiti, to bring Buddhists into this rigid form of social control. The main Hindu castes are the **Brahmins**, the priestly caste (some Brahmins are still priests but many are now employed in the civil service), **Chhetris** (warriors and rulers), **Vaisyas** (traders and farmers) and **Shudras** (artisans). Below them are the **untouchables** (butchers, tailors, sweepers and those who carry out other menial tasks).

The Hindu pantheon has three main gods, Brahma the creator, Vishnu the preserver and Shiva the destroyer and god of reproduction. Most Hindus are Vaishnavites (followers of Vishnu) or Shaivites (followers of Shiva). On the Jomsom-Muktinath trek you may meet a *sadhu* (see p97), Shaivite pilgrim (carrying a trident as the symbol of Shiva) on a pilgrimage to Muktinath.

Other popular deities include Saraswati (Brahma's consort and the goddess of science and wisdom), Kali or Durga (Shiva's blood-drinking consort, the goddess of death), Rama and Krishna (the seventh and eighth incarnations of Vishnu) and Hanuman (the monkey god).

Buddhism

In its purest form Buddhism isn't actually a religion since it's concerned not with gods or the saving of the soul but with personal enlightenment dependent solely upon the works of the individual. Buddhism grew out of Hinduism in the 5th century BC and shares with Hinduism the belief in reincarnation. For Buddhists, however, escape from the cycle of rebirth brings *nirvana*, the extinguishing of self and desire.

The Buddha was born Prince Siddhartha Gautam in 560BC in Lumbini, southern Nepal. Overcome by all the suffering and pain in the world, he tried to find the reasons first in philosophy, then as an ascetic submitting himself to a round of tough penances. These included sitting on thorns, sleeping by rotting corpses and eating a diet so low in calories that he is reputed to have been able to feel his backbone when he grasped his stomach. He became so weak that one day, walking along a river near Bodhgaya in India, he fainted and fell into the water. Coming to he decided that enlightenment was not to be found in extreme deprivation. He restored himself with a good meal and sat down under a tree (the famous bodhi tree) to meditate.

● **The Middle Way** In his meditation, it was revealed to the Buddha that human desires cause people to be locked into the eternal circle of rebirth. Only when people cease to desire can they escape this cycle of suffering and achieve final peace. He realised that he couldn't have achieved enlightenment before because it was what he desired. He realised that extremes of self-mortification and self-indulgence were not the answer; the 'Middle Way' is the path to enlightenment. This involves mastering the four noble truths (that all life is suffering, that desire is the cause of all suffering, that it is possible to escape from this state and achieve nirvana, and that this can be done by following the Eight-Fold Path of right views, right thought, right speech, right action, right livelihood, right endeavour, right mindfulness and right concentration).

● **Buddhist sects** Soon after the Buddha's death in 480 BC, a schism occurred amongst his disciples that eventually divided Buddhism into two main camps, Theravada and Mahayana; but there are now many sects within these. **Theravada Buddhism** ('the tradition of the elders') is closer to the Buddha's original teachings that enlightenment comes through your own endeavours, not through divine interference. Also known as Hinayana (the 'Lesser vehicle'), it's followed in Sri Lanka and the countries of SE Asia.

❏ **Om mani padme hum**

The most famous *mantra* (prayer chant) of the Tibetan Buddhists is 'Om Mani Padme Hum', which means 'Hail to the Jewel in the Lotus', the jewel being the Buddha. It's believed that the more times this magical phrase is prayed, the greater protection against evil it affords. Enterprising worshippers have come up with some novel ways to do this. **Prayer flags** printed with the mantra release its magical powers into the winds. **Prayer wheels** contain the mantra on lengths of paper and come in a range of sizes from small portable models to huge painted drums. These must always be turned clockwise. The mantra is also carved onto rock faces and **mani stones**, which can be seen piled up into walls along the trails in the northern part of the Annapurna region.

Mahayana Buddhism is entirely different. It's much more like a religion with a colourful pantheon of enlightened beings known as *bodhisattvas*. The Buddha himself is seen as a divine being, just one of a number of Buddhas who've come down to earth (and some who have yet to come) to help everyone achieve nirvana. Buddhism was given a much wider appeal because converts did not have to give up their old gods; they could continue to worship them as bodhisattvas.

Tibetan Buddhism or Lamaism is the main form of Buddhism practised in Nepal. When Mahayana Buddhism reached Tibet in the 7th century, it absorbed the deities of the native religion, Bon. Lamaism emphasises the importance of magic and the reciting of magical phrases from *tantras* (manuals) to achieve certain ends; it's often referred to as Tantric Buddhism. Tantrism was formerly popular also in Hinduism, and it taught that there are two parts to each deity, male and female. It was thought that a mystical union with one or other part of the deity was possible by mortals through sexual excess. In the 11th century, Tibetan Buddhism was purged of these extreme tantric elements by the monk, Marpa.

In Tibetan Buddhism, spiritual teachers are known as *lamas* and live in the gompa (monastery) that is usually attached to the temple. In the course of Tibetan history these lamas achieved greater power than the kings. There are four main orders of monks. The **Nying-ma-pa** (the Ancient Order or Red Hat school) was founded in the 8th century by the monk Padmasambhava (also known as Guru Rinpoche), who spent some time in Nepal. Most of the Buddhists in the mountain regions here are followers of this order. The **Sakya-pa** and **Kagyu-pa** (founded by the reforming monk Marpa) have few adherents in Nepal, although there are monasteries of the Sakya-pa sect in the north Annapurna region. The **Geluk-pa** (Yellow Hat school) is led by the Dalai Lama, the exiled Tibetan leader who now lives in India. Many of his followers came to Nepal after the invasion of Tibet by China in 1959.

Newari Buddhism, as practised in the Kathmandu Valley, is not derived from Tibetan Buddhism but from earlier influences from the south. The religion of the Newars is an interesting mixture of Hinduism and Mahayana Buddhism. Their Buddhist priests do not live in monasteries but marry and belong to a hereditary caste.

Bon-po is a sect which mixes pre-Buddhist beliefs with religious practices close to Buddhism. There are not many adherents in Nepal but Lupra, a small village up a side valley near Jomsom, has a Bon-po gompa.

Animism

Even older than the established religions in Nepal is a belief in the forces of nature which are able to affect human beings. The sun, the moon and the stars, mountains, rocks and rivers are all thought to have an *anima* (spirit) which needs to be placated or a delicate balance will be upset that will lead to some human misfortune. Particularly amongst the mountain people, there are still **shaman**, or faith-healers (*jhankri*) who intervene between the deities and mortals, especially when the latter are ill.

Practical information for the visitor

VISAS AND TREKKING PERMITS

Visas are required by all foreigners except Indian passport holders and as well as a visa every trekker is required to have a trekking permit. Visas are most easily obtained on arrival at the airport or border (US$25 for a 30-day visa, US$15 for 15 days – both single entry). A double entry 30-day visa costs US$40, and there's another option: a 60-day multiple entry visa for US$60. Visas are also obtainable from Nepalese embassies abroad (see p234) but prices vary from country to country. In the UK, a 30-day visa currently costs £20 and takes 24 hours to process. One passport-sized photo is the official requirement; they don't seem to insist on this if you're getting your visa on arrival at the airport but sometimes do at the border.

Visa validity and extensions
Visa extensions are available in Kathmandu and Pokhara and cost the equivalent in rupees of US$1/£0.60 per day for a total of 120 days. One photo is required. It's sometimes possible to get an additional 30 days in special circumstances. In any one calendar year no tourist may stay longer than 150 days.

Nepalese visa regulations and prices are subject to frequent changes. At one time you used to have to show bank receipts to prove you had cashed a certain amount of money through legal means (ie not the black market) in order to gain a visa extension. Although this is no longer the case you might be wise to keep keep all currency exchange receipts.

If you overstay the period on your visa you will be charged the regular extension fee plus 100%.

Trekking permit and ACAP entry permit
A trekking permit may be obtained only in Nepal, at the offices of the Department of Immigration in Kathmandu (see p112 for new location) or Pokhara. You must first be in possession of a visa valid for at least as many days as the trekking permit. Charges start at the equivalent in rupees of US$5 per week for the first month, US$10 per week thereafter. Permits are processed the same day but the offices are closed on Saturday. If you are stuck in Jomsom and need an extension to your trekking permit it's sometimes possible to get one from the District Officer.

As well as the trekking permit, trekkers in the Annapurna region are also required to pay an **ACAP entry fee** (currently Rs1000) which goes directly to the Annapurna Conservation Area Project. You can get this at any of the ACAP offices on the trek or from the National Parks Office in Kathmandu.

LOCAL TRANSPORT

● **Air** Since 1991, when the new government permitted the formation of private airlines, visitors have been offered alternatives to the national carrier, Royal Nepal Airlines (RNAC). They still have the largest number of routes and planes but the new airlines have provided much needed back-up on the popular routes. For the mountain routes STOL (Short Take-Off and Landing) planes, such as the Twin Otter, Pilatus Porter, Beech and Dornier are used. Taking off and landing in these tiny planes can be a most exhilarating experience.

For tourists, ticket prices are quoted in US$ and must be paid for with hard currency. Locals pay considerably less than foreigners but on popular flights tourists get precedence. Tickets can be bought for the same price from a travel agent as from the airlines companies. Check that the travel agent is not adding on a service charge; they get a commission from the airlines.

● **Bus** Long distance local buses are cheap and uncomfortable; night buses pure torture. Unless you're really strapped for time it's far better to take a day bus; the views are spectacular.

There are three kinds of bus: cheap **private buses** which operate from the bus stations; government-run **Sajha** buses which leave from their own bus stops; and the more expensive **tourist buses**, some of them even air-conditioned.

The two former are similarly-priced but Sajha buses, Mitsubishis (part of a Japanese aid package), tend to be a little faster than the Indian Tatas run by private companies. Tourist buses are more comfortable and have the advantage of leaving from the tourist areas in Kathmandu and Pokhara. Packed with like-minded foreign trekkers, they're not much of a cultural experience. Note that in Pokhara, the taxi mafia has ensured that buses go only as far as the bus station and don't take you to the hotel area. They do, however, allow the buses to leave from the hotel area in the morning.

● **Taxi** The battered troupe of elderly Toyotas that for many years constituted Nepal's taxi fleet has been joined by some newer vehicles. As well as the black and yellow cabs there are several other taxi companies. All taxis

---

❑ **Flying in 1957**

With seven domestic airlines and 44 airports around the country Nepal's air network is somewhat more developed than when Dorothy Mierow first flew to Pokhara in 1957 but it appears to have lost none of its charm:

'The airplanes (DC2s) had benches with bucket seats on both sides which could be folded up when the plane was transporting goods. Passengers were weighed as well as baggage, then the baggage was piled up in the aisle and tied down with a long rope from one end to the other. We took our seats, fastened our seat belts and held onto the rope in front. ... Walking over the baggage, the steward collected the tickets from the passengers during the flight.

Thirty Years in Pokhara **Dorothy Mierow**

have meters although the drivers are reluctant to use them for tourists. Some foreigners establish a price with the driver before getting in. Instead you could try offering Rs10-20 on top of the meter price or just get in and wait until you've got a short way down the road before threatening to get out if the driver doesn't turn the meter on.

● **Auto-rickshaw** These Indian-built Bajaj three-wheelers of Italian descent should be about 25-50% cheaper than taxis. They have meters but the advice above also applies since drivers are even less keen to use them than are taxi drivers. From time to time the meters need recalibrating and you may be asked to pay what's on the meter plus a certain percentage. Check the current situation at your hotel.

● **Tempo** Larger versions of auto-rickshaws, tempos have cramped bench seating in the back for up to eight people. They follow fixed routes and can be flagged down anywhere along them. Fares are only a few rupees.

● **Cycle-rickshaw** Environmentally friendly but bargaining is required before you climb in. Tourists have pushed prices up so that they're not much cheaper than auto-rickshaws.

● **Motorbike** A number of places in the tourist areas of Kathmandu and Pokhara have started motorbike rental. This costs around £6/US$10 per day for a 125cc Indian-built Kawasaki. Helmets are also available and are vital, given the appalling state of both the roads and the hospitals.

● **Bicycle** Renting a bike is a good way to get around Kathmandu or Pokhara and there are numerous rental shops. Heavy Indian Heros cost around £0.60/US$1 per day. Mountain bikes are also available, for £1.20-2.50/US$2-4 per day. Try for a discount if you're renting for more than a day or two.

Check your bike's tyres, brakes, bell and lock before cycling off. You will be held responsible if your bike is stolen so take particular care with mountain bikes.

LANGUAGE

Nepali is the national language of Nepal but it is the mother-tongue of less than 60% of the population. It's a Sanskrit-based language similar to India's Hindi. There are two other important languages on the Terai, Maithili (spoken by 11% of Nepalis) and Bhojpuri (7.6%). Newari, a rich Tibeto-Burman language, is spoken by only 3% of the population. Languages spoken in the Annapurna region tend to be of the Tibeto-Burman group and include Gurung (which has several dialects but no script), Magar, Thakali and Manangba as well as Nepali. Many other languages are spoken in Nepal.

Along the main trekking routes you'll always find someone who knows at least a few words of English but you should try to learn some Nepali phrases (see p250).

ELECTRICITY

Only 14% of the population has access to electricity but some villages in the mountains are supplied by low voltage micro-hydro schemes. Bulbs glow rather than burn brightly and recharging batteries is difficult which fortunately discourages people from dragging their camcorders too far into the mountains.

In Kathmandu and other towns on the national grid the voltage is 220V, 50Hz. Sockets are of the old, round pin variety (2, 5 and 15 amp) as formerly used in Britain.

The little gadget (decorated in Heath Robinson style with dials, switches and lights) that you may see beside fridges in Nepal is a voltage regulator. It's necessary to protect against frequent power surges that would otherwise overload the circuitry.

Power cuts are frequent so a torch/flashlight is vital.

TIME & DATE

Nepal time

Nepal is 5 hours 45 minutes ahead of Greenwich Mean Time (GMT) which (to show the country's independence, no doubt) is 15 minutes ahead of India. Time calculations for the following cities are:
● London: -5 hours 45 minutes (Oct to Mar); -6 hours 45 minutes during British Summer Time (Apr to Sep)
● New York: -10 hours 45 minutes
● Los Angeles: -13 hours 45 minutes
● Sydney: +4 hours 15 minutes
● Auckland: +6 hours 15 minutes
● Lhasa: +2 hours 15 minutes (Oct to Mar); +3 hours 15 minutes (Apr to Sep)

Date

The Nepalis may be just a few minutes ahead of the Indians as far as the time goes but they're halfway through the 21st century according to their calendar. The official calendar is based on the Bikram era (**Bikram Sambat** or BS) and is 56 or 57 years ahead of the Gregorian calendar used in the West. The new year begins on 13 April and thus 1999 AD is 2055 BS until then, 2056 BS thereafter until 12 April 2000 AD.

The months run from the middle of months in the Gregorian calendar. They are Baisakh (Apr-May), Jestha (May-June), Asadh (June-July), Shraaun (July-Aug), Bhadra (Aug-Sep), Aswin (Sep-Oct), Kartik (Oct-Nov), Mangsir (Nov-Dec), Pous (Dec-Jan), Magh (Jan-Feb), Phalgun (Feb-Mar) and Chaitra (Mar-Apr). They vary in length from 29 to 32 days.

Religious festivals and many other ceremonies, including weddings and death anniversaries follow a **lunar calendar**. Months are 28 days long and are made up of a 'light' fortnight (Sukla Pachhi – when the moon is waxing) followed by a 'dark' one (Krishna Pachhi – as it wanes).

Date-keeping is further complicated by many of Nepal's communities operating their own systems. The Newar year starts around the end of October and is 880 years behind the Gregorian calendar. New Year's Day comes in February for the Tibetans.

HOLIDAYS AND FESTIVALS

Office hours
Saturday is the day off during the week when all offices are closed, including the Department of Immigration where trekking permits are obtained. Business hours are from 10am to 5pm (to 4pm from mid-Nov to mid-Feb), Sunday to Friday, although many offices close at 1pm on Friday. Embassies are closed on Saturday and Sunday.

Festivals
With the rich patchwork of cultures and religions in Nepal, there's a festival going on somewhere at least every other day. The main season for festivals, however, comes in August and September as the monsoon withdraws.

The main festivals which are celebrated in Kathmandu or the Annapurna region are listed below. Since almost all are determined by the lunar calendar they occur on a different day each year. The Ministry of Home Affairs issues a list of the 25 official holidays at the beginning of each year.

● **Dasain** (Durga Puja) is the biggest of Nepal's festivals, lasting at least 10 days and beginning at the end of September or early October. The whole country grinds to a halt as people return to their villages for family reunions and feasts. It's a Hindu festival, which celebrates the triumph of good over evil, symbolised by the victory of the Hindu Rama over Ravana and the goddess Durga over Mahisasur, the devil who took the shape of a buffalo. Consequently numerous buffalo (and goats, sheep and cockerels) lose their heads during the eighth and ninth days of the festival and the roads literally flow with blood. Every form of transport, from the cycle-rickshaws of Thamel to Royal Nepal Airlines' Boeing 727s, has its wheels doused with sacrificial blood to bring good luck for the year ahead.

● **Tihar** (Deepavali) lasts five days and usually falls in November, two weeks after Dasain. It's known as the 'Festival of Lights' after the thousands of oil lamps that are lit in windows to welcome Lakshmi, the goddess of prosperity. Children go singing door-to-door for coins, houses are cleaned, sisters perform pujas for their brothers and everyone pujas the local cow.

● **Losar**, the Tibetan New Year, falls in February. If you're in Kathmandu at this time, Baudha is the place to be. On the fourth day thousands of Tibetans converge on the stupa for prayers.

● **Shivaratri** is celebrated in February at Pashupatinath in Kathmandu. It's a day of ritual bathing and puja that attracts Hindus to this Shiva temple from as far away as India.

● **Holi** If you're in any Hindu area in March you can't escape this boisterous spring festival. It involves tossing buckets of water over everyone and 'playing colours' (throwing handfuls of coloured powder). Westerners (particularly women) are a favourite target so put on your old clothes, stock up with bags of powder and water squirters and keep your camera covered.

● **Bisket Jatra** is Nepalese New Year's Day, which falls in April. Main celebrations are in Bhaktapur and then in Thimi the following day.

● **Raato Machhendranath** The god Raato ('Red') Machhendranath is the protector of the Kathmandu Valley, worshipped by both Hindus and Buddhists. Held in April or May to ensure that the monsoon will reach the Valley, this festival lasts at least a month. An image of the god is pulled on a huge chariot through the streets of Patan in a smaller version of the Jagannath procession that takes place in Puri in India.

● **Buddha Jayanti** is the birthday of the Buddha, celebrated in May. Conveniently, it's also the anniversary of his enlightenment and death. In Kathmandu the main celebrations take place at Swayambhunath but there will be pujas at most Buddhist temples.

● **The Dalai Lama's birthday** is on 6 July, celebrated particularly by Tibetans.

● **Janai Purnima** falls in August on the full moon of Shraaun and is centred on the Kumbeshwar temple in Patan. High caste Brahmins and Chhetri change the sacred red thread (*janai*) that they wear over their left shoulder and under their clothes. The festival also attracts shamans. The **Gai Jatra** ('Cow Festival') follows the next day, to honour those who have died within the last year.

● **Teej**, celebrated in August/September, is a women's festival that begins with a feast and is followed by a day of fasting. Husbands are honoured and women take ritual baths at Pashupatinath in Kathmandu to cleanse themselves from the 'sin' of touching a man during menstruation.

❏ **Puja**

A *puja* (act of worship) can be anything from a quick prayer to a festival of several days but offerings of some sort are usually involved. Hindus offer flowers, food and coloured powders and light incense and butter lamps. They receive a *tika* (a red mark on their forehead) as a blessing from the deity. Hindu pujas to mark the year's most important festivals require animal sacrifices (formerly human sacrifices) and at Dasain thousands of buffalo and goats are beheaded.

Buddhist pujas are rather more humane. Juniper is burnt as incense, mantras (see below) are chanted and prayer wheels are spun. Lamas are sponsored to say prayers and invoke the blessing of the gods on certain people. In Manang, on the Annapurna Circuit trail, there's a lama who will perform a puja to get the gods to help you over the Thorung La.

● **Indra Jatra** This important festival marks the end of the monsoon in September. It lasts eight days and in Kathmandu there are mediaeval pageants and masked dances. Prithvi Narayan Shah conquered Kathmandu to unify Nepal during Indra Jatra in 1768 and this historic event is remembered during the festival.

An important part of the festival is the appearance of the Kumari, the 'living goddess' (see p114), in Durbar Square. She rides in a chariot to greet the image of the god Bhairab in Hanuman Dhoka, whereupon beer flows from a pipe between his teeth. To get a sip of this brings good luck. On the last night of the festival the Kumari places a tika on the forehead of the King to give him the right to rule for the next year.

MONEY

Currency
The Nepali rupee (Rs) is issued in banknote denominations of Rs 1, 2, 5, 10, 20, 25, 50, 100, 500 and 1000 and coins of Rs 1, 2, 5, 10, and paise coins of 5, 10, 25 and 50 paise. There are 100 paise in a rupee. As in India, people won't accept damaged notes so check your change to make sure you're not being slipped some. If there's a hole in the note it does not matter.

Foreign exchange
When changing money at a bank keep the exchange certificate you are given. It's worth ensuring you're given some small change although on the main trekking routes during the season lodge owners are usually able to break larger bills for you. Rates do not vary greatly between banks but they're a little better at the lesser-known Nepali banks (eg Nabil Bank) than at branches of Western banks (Grinlays). At the foreign exchange offices in Thamel rates are less good. Travellers' cheques usually attract a slightly better rate than cash, about 2% more.

Black market rates are less attractive than they once were – now only about 5% higher than at the banks. The black market tends to be centred on the carpet shops and, surprisingly, dealers accept travellers' cheques as well as cash in major currencies. The best rates are for US$50 and US$100 bills. Note that using the black market helps the Indian carpet sellers get their profits out of the country but does nothing to reduce the national debt of Nepal.

❏ Rates of exchange	
Euro 1	Rs75
US$1	Rs67
UK£1	Rs110
Can$1	Rs45
Aus$1	Rs43
DM1	Rs38
FF1	Rs11
CHF1	Rs50
NG1	Rs34
IndRs1	Rs1.60

International banks in Nepal
Nepal-Grinlays, Standard Chartered and American Express all have branches in Kathmandu. Nepal-Grinlays will give instant cash advances on a Visa or MasterCard for as much as your credit agreement with these companies will stand, as will numerous other banks.

Tipping

Not a tradition in Nepal, tipping has come to be expected in the top hotels and restaurants. A service charge of 10% is, however, sometimes included in the bill. At smaller places tip 5-10% if the service was particularly good, although this is not necessary. Porters expect tips of about an extra day's wages per week trekked. If you're trekking with a group, the agency will usually offer guidelines on how much to tip.

Bargaining

This is expected when you're buying souvenirs, fruit or, to some extent, for hotel rooms out of season. Westerners are notoriously bad at it forgetting that it's as much a form of social interchange as a way to get the price down. They tend either not to bother and pay the asking price (in which case for things like fruit they drive up the price for the local people) or else they bargain too aggressively.

It's best to treat it as a game and not to try to force the seller down to the lowest possible price. When shopping for souvenirs, decide what your maximum price will be before you start bargaining. Don't offer more than 50% of the seller's initial price as your first bid. Only start bargaining if you're actually interested and never back out of a deal once you've both agreed on a price.

POST AND TELECOMMUNICATIONS

Postal services

Most travellers use the Poste Restante service at the GPO in Kathmandu and Pokhara to receive mail. Letters should be addressed with your surname underlined (or they may be mis-sorted), Poste Restante, The GPO, Kathmandu (or Pokhara). Since everyone is allowed to sift through the mail it's inadvisable to get anything valuable sent to you this way. American Express accepts mail for its clients.

When sending letters it's important to ensure they are franked or the stamps may be steamed off and reused. The numerous **communication centres** that have sprung up in the tourist areas sell stamps and take letters to the post office to have them franked. They can also receive mail for you.

Phone

The system now seems to work well, both within the country and for international calls. Local calls from a phone in your hotel room are usually free.

Fax

Sending and receiving faxes in Nepal is absolutely no problem. The communication centres are the most convenient places to use. Prices vary between them but it generally costs about £2/US$3 per minute (enough for a short fax). If you're trying to fax (or phone) into Nepal this is easiest to do when it's night-time in Nepal. The international dialling code for Nepal is 977; Kathmandu is 1 (01 within Nepal); Pokhara is 61.

Email

Cyber cafés have taken off in a big way in the tourist areas of Nepal. If you don't already have a free address with one of the companies such as hotmail, rocketmail or yahoo you can easily set this up in a cyber café in Kathmandu or Pokhara.

THE MEDIA

Newspapers and magazines

The English-language daily, the *Kathmandu Post*, is what to peruse over your porridge in the mornings but you'll be eating long after you've finished reading. You could then move on to the *Rising Nepal* once the mouthpiece of the monarchy and still adopting a squirmingly deferential attitude to the royal family; the ins and outs of palace life continue to reduce world news to no more than a few columns. The weekly *Independent* (Wednesday) can be a better read, and there's also the *People's Review* every Thursday.

Kathmandu's excellent bookshops also stock copies of the *International Herald Tribune, Asian Wall Street Journal* and *USA Today* plus international news magazines like *Time* and *Newsweek*. Pick up a free copy of *Nepal Traveller* at the tourist office at the airport. The bi-monthly environmental journal, *Himal*, has interesting articles.

The British Council Reading Room subscribes to many UK newspapers and magazines and is a good place to go if you want to know what the weather was like in Britain two weeks ago.

Radio and TV

Radio Nepal broadcasts the news in English at 08.00, 13.05 and 20.00 hours.

Short wave radio frequencies for the BBC World Service are 15310, 11955, 11750, 17795, 9740 and 5975. Voice of America broadcasts on 1575, 6110, 7205, 9700, 11710, 15205 and 17735. Lower frequencies generally give better results at night, higher ones during the day.

On Nepal TV, the news in English is at 22.00 hours. Satellite TV has caught on in Nepal and CNN, BBC World Service TV and Star TV are available in many hotels.

FOOD

Since Nepal is a cultural junction between the people of the north and the south, you might expect a wealth of culinary contrasts, as in Singapore which has a well-deserved reputation for the diversity of its food. In Nepal, however, the poverty of both the people and the ingredients means that for most of the population food is fuel not culinary art.

That having been said, the kitchens of Kathmandu and Pokhara have earned a reputation among travellers for being able to reproduce Western goodies like steak and chips, apple pie and chocolate cake. If you've been travelling round India for a while, you'll be very impressed by the food here. If you've just flown in from the West expecting Oriental delicacies you may not be quite so impressed but standards are rising fast. In Kathmandu you can now get really authentic pizza, genuine Irish stew and some of the best crème caramel east of Calais.

Vegetarians are well catered for in Nepal. Meat is an expensive delicacy for most Nepalis and is replaced by pulses (lentils in particular) and eggs. Cheese is sometimes available.

Daal bhat

The vast majority of Nepalis subsist on a couple of meals of *daal bhat* (lentils and rice) with *tarkari* (vegetables) each day, taken in the middle of the morning and in the early evening.

A good daal bhat is delicious. You're given a *thaali* (stainless steel tray) with a heap of boiled rice, a bowl of soupy lentils and a serving of curried

---

❑ Culinary expectations on the trek

● **Breakfast** Nepalis make do with a glass of sweet milky tea before hitting the trail early in the day. They'll stop for daal bhat between 10.00 and 11.00. If you've got a long day's walking ahead it's probably a good idea to start early after just a cup of tea, stopping for breakfast an hour or two later. Oat porridge, corn porridge, muesli (available with milk and diced apple), eggs (boiled, fried, poached, scrambled and as an omelette) all make a filling breakfast. Bread is rarely available, the alternatives being Tibetan bread (sweet, doughy and fried but good) and chapattis with jam, honey or peanut butter. A bowl of steaming porridge followed by an omelette placed between two chapattis makes an excellent breakfast.

● **Lunch** Although lodge owners will prepare the supper items listed below at any time in the day many trekkers prefer a light lunch. Noodle soup is one of the most popular items despite the fact that it comes out of a packet. It is, however, tasty and it's very quick to prepare so it uses little firewood. Vegetables are usually added to make it more interesting. Fried rice and chowmein are other popular lunchtime dishes; pancakes make a good pudding if you want one.

● **Supper** Most lodges have a good range of soups. Favourites include pumpkin, and garlic (although many cloves of garlic are used they're not strongly flavoured). There's also vegetable, and (usually from packets) tomato and chicken.

Meat is a delicacy that rarely appears on menus in trekking lodges although tinned tuna is sometimes available. Alternatives to daal bhat include pizzas, spring rolls, chopsuey, chowmein, Swiss rosti (potato, veg. and cheese), potatoes in a range of guises – mashed, boiled, lyonnaise, fried, au gratin – and Tibetan momos. Some of the more adventurous lodges even feature buritos, lasagne or miso soup on their menus.

Puddings included pancakes, apple pie, rice pudding, apple fritters, hot chocolate pudding or chocolate cake. Tibetan bread (fried) is good with honey or peanut butter.

The catering requirements of trekkers are placing a heavy strain on firewood resources in the Annapurna region. See p88 for information on how to limit your impact. Note that the three-course dinner is not part of the culture of Himalayan cuisine so don't expect your courses to come in any particular order and don't complain if you start with apple pie and finish with soup!

vegetables. You should wash your hands first (Nepalis do), pour some of the lentils over the rice, add some vegetables and eat with your right hand only. Use your thumb to push the food off your fingers and into your mouth. Most trekkers find eating without utensils difficult so spoons are provided. Daal bhat is an all-you-can-eat meal and your plate will be topped up until you've eaten your fill. It's also cheap, nutritious and filling – ideal trekking fuel. Some restaurants in Kathmandu and Pokhara serve up-market versions of daal bhat with many side dishes, some of them consisting of meat.

Other Nepali and Tibetan food

Rice is available along all the trekking routes in the Annapurna region but it is the staple diet for most Nepalis near the lower-altitude areas where it can be grown or cheaply portered. In the higher regions other grains take its place. Roasted flour made from millet, maize or, in the far north, barley, is made into *tsampa*. A versatile staple, it can be eaten on its own without cooking, mixed with Tibetan tea or made into porridge.

In the hills meat is rarely available but in Kathmandu and Pokhara chicken, goat and buffalo may be curried or may appear on tourist menus in a variety of guises including 'buff' steak. If you like biltong (jerky) you'll like *sukuti*, the Nepali/Tibetan equivalent. You may see it hanging in strings above the fire, being smoked. It's usually deep fried just before it's served and goes very well with beer or tumba (see below).

Tibetan food is popular and includes *momos* (meat- or veg.-filled pasta that are steamed), served with a chilli sauce. These are sometimes also fried; they're then called *kothay*. A favourite Tibetan soup is *thugpa*.

Cheese is good but not always available in the hills. It's made from the milk of buffaloes or naks (female yaks – the yak is the male). Many travellers eat yoghurt/curd although the containers this is stored in are far from spotless. Lassi is a delicious drink made from yoghurt but it's sometimes diluted with water and so not 100% safe. Order hot milk to ensure it's pasteurised.

Western food

Nepal's fame for apple pie and chocolate cake dates back to the 1960s when foreign volunteer workers encouraged the Freak Street lodge-owners in Kathmandu to provide them with a taste of home. Aunt Jane's Place, started by the wife of a Peace Corps volunteer, has now passed into history but was among the first of the budget restaurants serving Western food. What proves popular in one restaurant is quickly copied by most of the others and now it's possible to eat food that is at least recognisably Western along the main trekking routes in the Annapurna region.

You can get passable Nepali versions of pizzas on the trail and in Kathmandu and Pokhara menus feature pepper steaks, spaghetti bolognese, roast chicken and chips, lasagne, moussaka, quiche, tandoori dishes and even Mexican food (tacos, enchiladas and buritos). Standards in Kathmandu have risen considerably over the past few years and several places employ foreign chefs. There are now Italians, French, Germans, Irish and Thais concocting the dishes of their homelands in several restaurant kitchens in Kathmandu. Several excellent bakeries have opened, too.

Fruit and vegetables

Potatoes can be grown at high altitudes and are popular in the northern parts of the Annapurna region. They're small and tasty, served just with salt but sometimes also cheese. Vegetables include onions (onion omelettes are recommended), cauliflower, pumpkin and spring greens. In Kathmandu there's a far greater variety.

Fruit depends very much on what is locally available according to the seasons since distribution is costly. In the Annapurna region, apples, peaches and apricots are grown around Marpha and Chame and available in the summer and autumn. Mandarin oranges (*suntala*) are widely available in the winter and papaya and bananas can be found in Kathmandu and Pokhara throughout the year. Mangos and guavas are available during the monsoon.

DRINK

'Don't drink the tap water' is the number one health rule for Nepal (and most of Asia). Don't even use it to brush your teeth with. See p238 for a discussion of the methods of water purification.

Drinks that have been boiled or bottled are generally safe and as trekkers will lose a lot of liquid at altitude and through sweating they must ensure they drink large quantities. Tea (*chiya*) is the national beverage but it bears little resemblance to what some people might drink with their cucumber sandwiches. It's produced by boiling tea-leaves, milk and sugar together into a strong unappealing orange liquid. Luckily there are other options: black tea, lemon tea (delicious) and tea with milk but without sugar. It's available by the glass or in small, medium and large pots. Other hot drinks include coffee (Nescafé), milk, chocolate and even cappuccino. Tibetan tea should be tried, though few Westerners develop a taste for it. It's produced by churning hot tea, salt and butter together.

Bottled fizzy drinks include Coke, Pepsi, Mirinda Orange, Fanta (orange and lemon) and 7-Up, all cheaply produced under licence in Nepal under reasonably hygienic conditions. Plastic bottles of mineral water are available but you should ensure that the seal is intact or they may have been refilled with tap water. Because of the difficulty of disposing of the bottles, mineral water is not an environmentally-friendly alternative to purifying water yourself.

Alcoholic drinks include locally-produced beers. Star and Iceburg have now been joined by the better (and more expensive) Tuborg and San Miguel, brewed under licence. There's a large range of local spirits including Snowland gin, Khukri rum, Three Lions whiskey. *Chang* is home-brewed beer and *rakshi* a potent liquor made from rice or millet. When you visit Baudha in Kathmandu, you should try *tumba*, fermented millet mixed with boiling water and drunk through a straw. In Tukuche and Marpha local distillers produce powerful apple, apricot and peach brandies that taste great when you're trekking but seem a bit rough if you try them when you get home.

THINGS TO BUY

The souvenir shops in Kathmandu and Pokhara are stuffed full of carpets, crafts and knitware, some of it very well made but there's also some real tourist junk. It's best to do your shopping near the end of your trip, once you've had a chance to see what's available. Compare goods and prices in a number of shops and always bargain. The tourist shops in expensive hotels are not a good place for a bargain but they may have some high quality goods.

Read Jeff Greenwald's *Shopping for Buddhas* for an amusing portrait of Western consumers in Nepal. If it's real antiques you're after note that you need an export permit for anything that looks as if it could be more than 100 years old. For other antiques a receipt from the shop will suffice as long as it contains a detailed description of the item. You should be aware that your own country will probably have some restrictions on the value of goods you import duty-free.

● **Clothes and sweaters** Clothes shops sell the latest trekking fashions (including loose-fitting cotton trousers, which are recommended) and they also do a good line in embroidery. T-shirts are emblazoned with everything from 'Tintin in Tibet' to 'I love Kathmandu'. Woollen sweaters are a best buy. They're hand knitted in attractive colours but need careful washing as they lose their shape easily. Undyed Pasmina shawls, made from the highest quality wool, are expensive but luxuriously warm.

● **Carpets** The Tibetan carpet industry, started as a refugee relief programme in the early 1960s, expanded to become Nepal's largest exporter. The industry is, however, currently in recession following the banning of carpet imports by some countries owing to the use of child labour by certain companies. By the time you read this the export ban may have been lifted but it's difficult to see how the government can monitor the manufacturers to ensure child labour is not being used. Children are probably involved in the making of many other kinds of souvenirs sold in Nepal.

Prices vary according to the number of knots per square inch – from about 50 up to 100 for the best quality. They're usually made from wool and colours are mainly pastel hues but there also are some bright striped tiger rugs. Kashmiri traders have also opened shops in Nepal selling rugs in Kashmiri, Indian and Central Asian styles in silk or wool.

● **Thangkas** There are many shops specialising in these Tibetan religious paintings. They're bright, highly detailed and done on cloth but may not be quite as old as you're led to believe. Some thangka painters are also producing humorous modern paintings in this style. There are some good shops off Patan's Durbar Square as well as in Thamel and Pokhara.

● **Jewellery** There's a wide range of jewellery available but you have to know your gems or you could be fobbed off with glass. Silver filigree bangles, earrings and coral and turquoise necklaces are all popular. Strings of colourful beads are sold at the bead market in Kathmandu.

If you can afford it, you could have some earrings made up by a goldsmith in Kathmandu, Pokhara or even the Annapurna village of Tatopani (see p144).

● **Trinkets and other souvenirs** There's a wide range of interesting little souvenirs including attractive papier mâché boxes and vases in Kashmiri shops, puppets, masks, Nepalese caps and incense sticks. Nepalese tea also makes a good present.

Handmade paper is a traditional craft and you can buy block-print calendars, writing-paper and cards. There are also cloth covered notebooks and photograph albums with traditional-style black paper leaves.

The streets of Thamel are thronged with boys hawking Tiger Balm, flutes and khukris. Some sell 'Nepali padlocks'. Made from brass in the shape of animals, these make unusual little presents.

Thimi, near Kathmandu, is famous for its pottery and makes an interesting bicycle excursion but most pieces are too large and heavy to be convenient souvenirs.

SECURITY

The towns in Nepal are considerably safer than many cities in the West, even at night, although it might be wiser for women to go out in a group after dark.

Security in hotels is generally good but you shouldn't tempt staff by leaving valuables around. Bigger hotels have security boxes at reception; they'll also store anything you don't want to take trekking.

Beware of pickpockets in crowded places, especially on buses, and keep your passport, travellers' cheques and airline tickets in a pouch around your neck or in a moneybelt. A photocopy of the personal information pages in your passport will speed up the reissue process should you be parted from your documents. Remember to keep the receipt for your travellers' cheques separate from the cheques themselves or getting a refund could prove extremely difficult. Keep other valuables (cameras etc) with you at all times.

On the trail there's a greater risk from nature than from man and violent attacks on trekkers are rare but not unheard of – particularly in the woods around Ghorepani. It's not a good idea for men or women to trek alone and safest to walk in a group of three or four people. When crossing dangerous passes (the Thorung La, for example) it's imperative to get together a group of at least four people and to stick together. If one person falls ill or breaks a leg, one could stay with him or her and the others could go together to get help.

PART 3: MINIMUM IMPACT TREKKING

Minimum impact trekking

Nepal's trekking industry – the pros and cons

Tourism is a vital source of foreign exchange for Nepal. Directly or indirectly many Nepalis benefit from the increasing numbers of trekkers and tourists visiting the country even though most of the money they spend goes to just a few people: the trekking companies, the lodge owners and, of course, His Majesty's Government. How much of the money actually contributes to local village economies is debatable and one study places the figure as low as £0.14/US $0.20 out of the average £2/US$3 spent by a trekker each day. In a country where the annual average wage is just over £100 or

---

❏ THE MINIMUM IMPACT CODE

Developed by the Annapurna Conservation Area Project, this code of conduct summarises the steps trekkers should take to minimise their impact on the environment and cultures of this area:

● **Conserve firewood** Be self-sufficient in your fuel supply and make sure your trekking staff uses kerosene and has enough warm clothing. Make no open fires. Limit hot showers. If possible stay at lodges that use kerosene or fuel-efficient wood stoves and space heaters. Kerosene is available in Chomrong, near the Annapurna Sanctuary, and in Kagbeni and Jomsom.

● **Stop pollution** Dispose of all trash properly. Paper products, cigarette butts, toilet paper, food scraps etc should be burned or buried. Bottles, plastics and other non-biodegradable items should be packed out or deposited in rubbish pits if available. Use the toilet facilities provided. If none exist, make sure you are 20 metres away from any water source and carry a small shovel to bury wastes. Don't use soap or shampoo in any stream or hot spring. Supervise trekking staff to make sure they cover toilet pits and dispose of garbage properly.

● **Be a guest** Do not damage, disturb or remove any plants, animals, animal products or religious artifacts. Respect Nepali customs in your dress and behaviour. Women should not wear shorts or revealing blouses and men should always wear a shirt. Avoid outward displays of physical affection. Ask permission to take photographs and respect people's right to privacy. Begging is a negative interaction that was started by well-meaning tourists – please do not give anything to beggars. Don't barter for food and lodging. Encourage young Nepalis to be proud of their culture.

Above all, remember that your vacation has a great impact on the natural environment and the people who live off its resources. By assisting in these small ways, you will help the land and people of Nepal enormously.

Nepal is here to change you, not for you to change Nepal

US$160 and in a region that sees over 50,000 trekkers per year, however, this is not as inconsiderable as the statistic might suggest. Villages that are situated along the main trekking routes are generally more affluent than those that few trekkers pass through.

Much has been written about the negative effects of trekking. It is very true that trekkers place a far greater strain on local resources, firewood particularly, than do locals. According to ACAP, in one village on a main trail in the Annapurna region, up to one hectare (about 21 acres) of forest is cleared each year for use as firewood for the needs of trekkers. Forest clearance leads to soil erosion, already a major problem in the unstable Himalayan region. Trekkers make a significant contribution to the pollution problem with streamers of pink lavatory paper and plastic mineral water bottles. Far less obvious are the negative aspects of the cultural impact made by trekkers on local communities.

In the tourist boom of the 1970s and 80s it was realised that the pressures of visitors in popular areas like the Annapurna region could eventually destroy the very environment that attracted the visitors in the first place. Several organisations, the Annapurna Conservation Area Project in particular, have done sterling work in conservation education. Their advice is well publicised but, sadly, not always followed; some trekkers behave as if having paid their trekking fees and lodge bills this gives them the right to behave exactly as they choose. The oft-repeated 'Nepal is here to change you, not for you to change it' may sound trite but it is all too true: responsible trekkers should follow this maxim.

The main areas of concern are environmental, economic and cultural. The simple steps that can easily be taken by trekkers to lessen their impact on the delicate ecological balance in the Annapurna region are detailed below.

ENVIRONMENTAL IMPACT

Forest clearance

About 95% of Nepal's energy comes from firewood and the country's forests are being cleared at a rate of 3% per year. Reforestation projects cannot keep pace with this deforestation and the subsequent erosion that often occurs may make the land unusable. A rapidly expanding population and a reliance on firewood for fuel are the main causes of the problem but in a few localised areas, the Annapurna region in particular, trekkers may be more to blame than local people. It's been estimated that a trekker requires up to ten times the amount of firewood that a Nepali would need. Complicated meals are requested at odd times, hot showers are required immediately and boiled water may be demanded for drinking. In winter, trekkers may want a warm fire to sit around at night.

In a country that has tremendous hydroelectric potential, electricity would seem to be the answer to the problem. At present, most of the power generated in this way is either consumed in the Kathmandu Valley or sold to

❏ ANNAPURNA CONSERVATION AREA PROJECT (ACAP)

Origins

Set up in 1986 to help preserve this region in the face of the severe deforestation that was taking place to meet the needs of local people and trekkers, ACAP is a comprehensive programme of reforestation and forest management, alternative energy schemes, community development projects, wildlife studies and conservation education.

The ACAP region

This independent non-profit organisation opened its project headquarters in Ghandruk village in December 1986 to administer and protect an area of 2600 square km bordered on the west by the Kali Gandaki River, on the east by the Marsyandi and to the south by the Pokhara Valley. The area was extended in 1992 and now covers 7629 square km up to the border with Tibet to include the whole of Mustang and Manang districts. The project is directly funded by trekkers' contributions (the entry fee paid when applying for a trekking permit) and through its association with a number of international conservation organisations.

The ACAP approach – co-operation and integration

ACAP is currently regarded as one of the most successful conservation programmes in the country and its success is largely the result of a novel approach. Rather than establish the area as a traditional national park, relocating the inhabitants, it was decided that more could be achieved by co-operating with local people. The project's instigators were adamant that the concept of integrating the human and conservation needs of an area was a far better approach in a less developed country like Nepal where there is very little land that is not already occupied by people.

It was realised that trying to promote environmental conservation amongst very poor people would have little effect unless these people could see something in it for themselves. ACAP's initial drive was to help improve local living conditions to gain the respect and trust of the people. Sir Edmund Hillary, who founded the Himalayan Trust in the Khumbu region, was quick to realise that the projects that were most successful were those initiated by and for the villagers themselves. Like the Himalayan Trust, ACAP has provided the funding for schools, bridges, drinking water projects, health centres, micro-hydro schemes, reforestation projects, trail improvement and sanitation schemes. Local people must provide the labour if they want the projects to go ahead.

ACAP's conservation education projects have helped show local people, lodge owners and trekkers the importance of conserving firewood. Forests have been denationalised and self-regulation of forest resources is being revived with some success. Alternative energy sources have been developed and many lodges now have back-boilers or solar panels. Micro hydroelectric schemes have been established in some areas. Lodge management committees have been set up for each district within the ACAP area and these meet regularly to set prices for food and lodging in order to ensure a reasonable return for the lodge-owners and reasonable standards for trekkers. Training schemes in food preparation, the running of lodges and in basic English are held and the certificates awarded on completion of these courses adorn the walls of most lodges.

ACAP now has **visitor centres** in many of the villages in the Annapurna region. The main offices are in Ghandruk and Pokhara (☎ 61-21102, email: acap@kmtnc.mos.com.np) PO Box 183, Pokhara, Kaski.

India. There are a number of micro-hydro schemes in the hills but other than powering a few low-wattage cookers they're used mainly for lighting. It's been said that these lighting schemes may actually lead to a greater consumption of firewood since people are now able to stay up after dark and so keep fires burning for warmth.

In order to lessen your impact on the environment you should:

● **Have hot showers only at lodges with solar panels or back-boilers** Some lodges now have back-boilers installed in the cooking stove so that extra wood is not used to heat water. Other lodges have solar-panels for water heating that can be remarkably efficient (as long as you're not at the end of the queue for a shower). Patronise places like this if you want a hot shower and have a wash in a bucket of cold water in smaller places.

● **Order meals together and keep orders simple** Some of the complicated Western dishes that are requested by trekkers are far from fuel efficient, especially when they are ordered singly. Place your order for supper as soon as you arrive at a lodge so that the lodge owner can bulk dishes together. If you want something for pudding order this at the same time, even though you may prefer to wait until you've had your main course. Order simple things for lunch. Noodle soup is a good choice not only because it's fuel efficient but because it's very quick to prepare.

The Nepali staple of daal bhat is cooked in large quantities morning and evening, even in lodges largely patronised by Westerners. It's delicious, filling, cheap and arguably the most environmentally right-on dish you could choose.

● **Don't request boiled water for drinking** There are several perfectly good ways of purifying water (see p239) which render boiling unnecessary. If you treat water yourself you can also be absolutely sure that it has been purified, not simply warmed in a kettle. Micropur iodine tablets are available from the all the ACAP offices around the trek.

● **Put on extra clothes, not another log on the fire** Sitting round a fire toasting marshmallows on sticks may be all right in the West but in Nepal it's ecologically more sound to turn in early or put on extra clothes if you're cold.

● **Use kerosene if you're camping** Whilst most trekking companies now use kerosene for cooking for trekkers they do not provide such environmental luxuries for their porters who are forced to cook on fires. It's up to trekkers to lobby trek leaders and the trekking companies if this situation is to change. It has been calculated that to provide kerosene for everyone on the trek would increase the daily cost of a trekking holiday by only £1.50/US$2.25.

Kerosene is available in larger villages. There is a total ban on fires in the Annapurna Sanctuary and there's a kerosene depot in Chomrong on the route in. ACAP is setting up kerosene depots around the Annapurna Circuit.

Erosion

It's not only forest clearance that's to blame for the high incidence of erosion in the Himalaya. The world's youngest chain of mountains is still being formed, rising several millimetres per year as the Asian continental plate pushes up against the Tibetan Plateau. Monsoonal rain on the southern slopes causes further erosion as swollen rivers rush down to the lowlands.

This natural erosion makes the erosion caused by forest clearance all the more serious. Approximately 400,000 hectares of forest are cleared in Nepal each year, resulting in the loss of an additional twenty million tons of soil each year.

● **Stay on the main trail** Avoid steep shortcuts since their continued use may erode the hillside. Don't damage crops or the edges of rice fields: these surrounding ledges are designed to keep in the water when the fields are flooded.

● **Don't damage plants** The age of the Victorian plant-hunter is past and you're unlikely to get your rare rhododendron specimen through customs in Heathrow or Newark, so don't try.

Pollution

Litter is a modern problem. Before the 1960s there was virtually nothing available in the mountain villages that was non-biodegradable, apart from glass bottles. The few items that might be sold in the village shop were wrapped in paper or cloth not plastic. In the lowlands, take-away snacks and meals were and still are served on sal leaves, sewn together and pressed into the shape of a bowl.

In many villages, particularly those on the trekking routes, litter is now a significant problem. Trekkers are certainly to blame for the lavatory paper that may occasionally be seen along the trail and for the piles of plastic mineral water bottles since local people would not use either. A growing cash-based economy has led to greater local use of shops and some Nepalis are still unaware of the cumulative effect of discarding biscuit wrappers, cans or plastic fertiliser bags.

Faecal contamination of water supplies by humans and animals is, however, not a new problem although in many areas drinking water is now piped into the village from a relatively clean source. You should, nevertheless, purify all water for drinking.

● **Don't leave litter** Never drop litter on the trail but take it on with you and dispose of it at the next lodge. Even better is to bring a strong plastic bag for all your litter and dispose of it at the end of your trek in Pokhara. Picking up other people's litter would be helpful and set a good example to Nepalis and other trekkers.

If you're on an organised trek burnables should be thrown on the fire and, ideally, non-burnables should be carried out and disposed of outside the trekking area. More usually, non-burnables are buried in a pit dug at the camp-site. Stress that this must be efficiently done; although this may be difficult since you will probably leave the site before the kitchen staff.

● **Avoid bottled mineral water** Soft drink bottles and some beer bottles are returnable and therefore environmentally-friendly. Mineral water is, however, sold in plastic bottles that are not only non-returnable but also non-biodegradable. Since, furthermore, you cannot be sure that the bottle hasn't been refilled from a tap (the seals are not 100% tamper-proof) it's far better to get water from lodges and purify it yourself.

● **Dispose of used batteries outside Nepal** In her useful booklet, *Trekking Gently in the Himalaya*, Wendy Brewer Lama has calculated that if every one of the 70,000 trekkers who come to Nepal each year disposes of four flashlight batteries during their stay more than a quarter of a million batteries would be left behind annually. Since the country does not have the facilities for their proper disposal many of these batteries land up polluting the environment or even as children's playthings. Small batteries for cameras could be even more dangerous as toys. Take all used batteries out of Nepal and dispose of them in the West.

● **Don't pollute water sources** If there's a latrine available, use it, otherwise ensure you're at least 20m from a water source and bury your faeces. If you're on an organised trek, a hole is dug and a latrine tent erected over it. Sprinkle some earth into the hole after each use and ensure that it is properly filled when you break camp.

Don't pollute hot springs with soap and shampoo, whatever local people are doing. Borrow a bowl or bucket from a lodge (or you could even use your mug) and wash away from the spring. Collapsible plastic buckets are available from camping shops in the West. These are particularly useful for clothes' washing by streams. Dispose of dirty water away from the stream.

● **Burn used lavatory paper** Few Westerners can adapt to the Nepali water-and-left-hand method. They should, however, ensure that the yards of

pink Chinese loo paper that they require as an alternative are entirely inciner-ated or put in the bins provided for the purpose. Keep your roll of paper in a plastic bag with a lighter. Don't drop paper down a latrine as this may clog it.

ECONOMIC IMPACT

The economic importance of tourism for Nepal is undeniable. Until recently the people of Lo Manthang and Upper Mustang (closed to foreigners until 1992) must have looked with envy at their rich neighbours to the south in busy tourist villages like Marpha and Jomsom. Given the choice most Nepali village committees would opt to climb aboard the trekking bandwagon. The distribution of these tourist dollars is far from equal, though. Book an organ-ised trek through a foreign operator and a proportion of what you pay stays in the West to pay the company's administrative costs. Book an organised trek in Kathmandu and a large proportion remains in the city. The trek per-sonnel may not be from the Annapurna region and since virtually everything on an organised trek is brought into the area few local services are used and there may be little financial benefit to the region.

If you trek independently you will contribute more to the local economy but perhaps not as much as you might think, since the few services you use (lodges and shops) are operated by only the more wealthy villagers. They do, however, provide a certain amount of work for local people as porters for provisions and as helpers in lodge kitchens.

● **Use local services** The price of a Coke may be close to what you would pay in the West once you're several days' walk into your trek but it's large-ly composed of the porter's wages required to get it up here. Buying drinks and other things from shops not only helps local business but also helps pro-vide employment for porters. When buying things in the mountains try to buy goods from several shops rather than just from one. Patronise those shops that look as if they need your business.

❏ **Choosing a lodge**
Most trekkers tend to head either for the biggest and best-looking lodge or for the one where other trekkers are staying. Lodge-owners are well aware of this and will sometimes try very hard to attract the first trekkers arriving in the village, occasionally even trying to seat them outside in order to attract more. Overcrowding can be a problem in the most popular lodges. At dinner there may be 15 trekkers ordering eight different dishes, all to be cooked on two fires, although most lodges do seem to cope remarkably well.

Look around at a few places before deciding where to stay. Except at the height of the season, you may find an empty lodge that is equally good as the one the other trekkers are crowding into. It's also worth trying out some of the small-er lodges and teashops, at least occasionally. This can be a rewarding cultural experience that gives you a better chance to see how the family lives. Expansion and competition with the big lodges is beyond the means of many of these small lodge owners, their money going to support relatives and pay school fees.
Jamie McGuinness

Using lodges rather than camping is an obvious way to patronise the local economy. When arranging a trek with an organised group you could request to spend some nights in lodges rather than under canvas.

If you're trekking independently employ a **local porter** to carry your pack, if only over part of the trek. Unfortunately, most independent trekkers feel that being weighed down by a heavy pack is all part of the trekking experience. Perhaps colonial guilt (a British trait) also has something to do with it. Arranged once you're on your trek, the services of a porter can cost little more than £4/US$6.50 per day. It's safest to ask your lodge to suggest someone, rather than to go off with a total stranger. Ensure your porter is clear about your route and the number of days involved, make certain all porters have adequate clothing and shoes if you're trekking at altitude and be sure everyone is clear about what the pay includes. If you are going to be paying for food as well as a daily wage stipulate exactly what this includes. It's probably better to pay a slightly higher wage and not also pay for food and lodging except in remote places (Thorung Phedi and the Annapurna Sanctuary, for example) where everything is expensive.

Take care of your porter on the trail. As yet, it's not easy for independent trekkers to take out insurance against the death of a porter in their employ.

● **Observe standard charges** To ensure a fair return for certain services lodge management committees have set prices for food and lodging that are listed on menus throughout each area. You should not attempt to bargain these down. Don't, however, believe the curio sellers who tell you that all their goods are 'fixed price'!

CULTURAL IMPACT

The people of the Annapurna region probably have a longer history of contact with the world outside Nepal than does any other group in the country. Pilgrims from as far away as South India have been visiting the shrines at Muktinath for hundreds of years. Thakali lodge owners have been providing food and shelter for Indian, Nepali and Tibetan traders on the great salt route along the Kali Gandaki for almost as long. The Manangba from the Marsyandi valley have been visiting distant Asian trading centres since the early 19th century when the king granted them special travel dispensations. Many of the men in the Gurkha regiments of the British and Indian armies come from villages in the south of the Annapurna region.

In the light of this history of contact with other cultures, the cultural impact of Western trekkers here is difficult to assess. Travelling in 1956, David Snellgrove visited many of the monasteries in the region and found most with almost as few monks as today's trekker will see. None had the large flourishing Tibetan-style communities that one might have imagined in the days before the trekkers arrived here.

Whilst for the older members of the villages on the main trekking routes, foreigners are probably nothing more than passing curiosities it is undeniable that we make a far deeper impression on younger Nepalis. Many now view

West as best: Westerners are all rich, they can travel whenever and wherever they like and have girlfriends or boyfriends for casual relationships. It is unfortunate that Nepalis see us only when we are on holiday, intent on enjoying ourselves.

● **Encourage local pride** Try to give Nepalis a balanced picture of life in the West. If they ask you what you earn, try to put this into perspective by telling them how much it costs to rent a flat or buy a car, an air ticket or a week's supply of groceries. Let them know what you think is good about their way of life – the incomparable scenery, the low incidence of robbery and murder, the clean air. If you've enjoyed your stay in a lodge or had a particularly good meal, let the lodge owner know.

● **Discourage begging** Requests for 'one rupee', 'bon-bon' or 'school pen' from children or adults should all be ignored. Giving to beggars fosters an attitude of dependency. As ACAP's Minimum Impact Code (see p85) states, 'Begging is a negative interaction that was started by well-meaning tourists'. Giving sweets to children in a country with few dentists is not an act of charity. You may be approached by older children and asked to make a donation to their school. Whilst these requests may well be genuine, it's probably better to send a cheque, once you get home, to one of the aid agencies that operates in Nepal.

● **Respect holy places** Always pass to the left of Buddhist monuments (chortens, prayer-wheels and mani-walls) and turn prayer-wheels clockwise. Don't prop your pack (or yourself) up against a chorten or mani wall. Take your boots off before entering a temple and always make a donation. There's usually a donation box. It's also customary to give a small sum of money, or food, to sadhus, Hindu holy men whom you may meet on their way to Muktinath.

● **Dress and behave modestly** Too many trekkers disregard local dress standards believing that Nepalis obviously don't mind what foreigners wear because there are never any complaints. Nepalis are far too polite to complain.

Women should wear loose trousers or calf-length skirts, not shorts or sleeveless blouses. Men should always wear a shirt and preferably long trousers; if you want to wear shorts these should be long shorts not jogging shorts. Avoid body-hugging lycra clothing and bright colours. Never bathe in the nude.

● **Don't flaunt your wealth** Your wealth, however poor you may be by Western standards, is way above the wildest dreams of most Nepalis so don't flaunt it. Don't leave valuable items like cameras lying around.

● **Respect people's privacy when taking photos** Before taking someone's photograph you should try to imagine how you would feel in their position. Always ask permission before taking a photo. Don't pay people for posing, rather you should suggest sending them a copy of the photo and get someone to write down their address. If you do do this, however, it is most important to follow through your promise. A British anthropologist working in a small Nepali village was visited by a friend who took photos of a number of the villagers promising to send copies. Each day one villager would trek down to the post office to see if the eagerly-awaited package had arrived but it never did. To allay the tremendous disappointment the anthropologist had to take a set of photos herself.

● **Respect local etiquette** Many of the do's and don't's concern parts of the body. The feet are considered the least clean or holy part of the body, the head the most. You should never touch someone on the head, not even children. Avoid sitting with your feet pointing towards another person but tuck them under you or point them towards a wall. Don't step over someone or put yourself in a position so that they are forced to step over you.

Eating is done only with the right hand. The left hand is used for washing after defaecating so is considered unclean. When being given something, however, you should receive it with both hands. When greeting people don't shake hands but bring both palms together as if praying and say 'Namaste' ('I greet the god within you'). Don't point at things or people but extend your right hand instead. Don't share eating utensils or take food from someone else's plate. When drinking from a container that is shared you must not let your lips touch it. High caste Hindus (Brahmins) have a particularly strict concept of food cleanliness (*jutho*) and as an untouchable (if you're from the West and not also a Brahmin) you will be served outside the house if you're eating there. You're unlikely to be invited to sleep inside the house.

● **Don't play doctor** Some local people along the trail may ask you for medicines or to treat wounds. Except in the case of cleaning up a small cut and applying a plaster you should direct them to the nearest health post. In the Annapurna region there's one in most larger villages. If you try to administer to anything more complicated than a small cut and your efforts are not ultimately successful you won't help to build up faith in Western medicine. Locals may continue to patronise the local shaman rather than the health post

● **Always keep your sense of humour** Nepalis very rarely lose their tempers and you should try hard to control yours when things aren't working out as you would wish. A smile costs nothing.

FURTHER INFORMATION

For more information on how to minimise your impact while trekking contact the **Kathmandu Environmental Education Project** (KEEP, see p112). Also in Kathmandu, **Himalayan Guides for Responsible Tourism** runs an eco-trekking workshop to teach conservation practices to trekking staff. They publish a bi-annual newsletter, *Ecotrek*, obtainable from Wendy Brewer Lama, GPO Box 1913, Kathmandu (☎ 414195; 🖹 1-418890) or Frances Klatzel, Box 1041, Canmore, Alberta T0L 0M0, Canada.

PART 4: KATHMANDU

Kathmandu

Nepal's capital city is a fascinating mélange of mediaeval and modern that combines astounding beauty with appalling squalor and poverty.

Time has stood still in parts of Kathmandu. In the narrow alleys, around the numerous temples and shrines and along the banks of the Bagmati River people go about their daily lives in much the same way as their ancestors did hundreds of years ago. Yet the contrasts between old and new become ever more bizarre. A porter struggles under the weight of two colour-television sets, carrying them in the traditional fashion – supported only by a *namlo*, the strap around his forehead. A couple of sacred cows doze on the warm asphalt in the middle of busy Durbar Marg. They block part of the road and slow the traffic but will not be moved on. A young Tibetan monk in ochre robes passes on his way to the great stupa at Baudha, his shaven head in the grip of the head-phones of his walkman.

For first-time Asian visitors, Kathmandu is a visual feast but for longterm travellers who've journeyed up from India it's also a feast of a more basic nature. The city has some of the best budget restaurants on the subcontinent dishing up everything from pepper steaks to enchiladas, chocolate cake to apfelstrudel. Accommodation, too, is excellent and can be better value than in India. Communications are good and you can make international phone calls and send emails with the minimum of delay.

It's well worth setting aside at least a few days to see something of the city. On the bus route from India to Pokhara and back it is, however, possible to bypass Kathmandu entirely since trekking permits for the Annapurna region are easily available in Pokhara.

HISTORY

Origins

The name Kathmandu is believed to be a corruption of Kasthamandap ('square house of wood'), the 1000-year-old *dharamsala* (rest-house) that still stands in Durbar Square.

The first identifiable civilisation in the Kathmandu Valley was that of the Kirats, who occupied a number of sites in the region in the second half of the first millennium BC. They were succeeded by the Lichhavi in the ninth century AD and the Malla in the 13th century. The settlements were centred around religious sites known as piths or power places, usually on the tops of hills.

Early urban planning

Kathmandu was a town of almost 2000 houses by the beginning of the Malla period (13th century), centred on Pashupatinath. Like the other two large towns in the Valley, Patan and Bhaktapur, it was an independent kingdom. Religion controlled not only the lives of the people but also the layout of these towns. Wandering through the chaotic maze of streets and temples in modern Kathmandu, it's difficult to believe that there has ever been any town planning here; but, in fact, centuries ago Hindu philosophy determined the design of whole towns based on the Vastupurusa Mandala, a complex layout in the shape of a square. This was composed of many smaller squares assigned to different deities and their temples. The main temple and palace, the centres of spiritual and temporal power, were symbolically placed at the very centre. Agricultural land surrounded each town.

Newar architectural heritage

The dominant culture in the Kathmandu Valley, until the unification of Nepal by the king of Gorkha in 1768, was that of the Newars. They are best known for their spectacular architectural legacy – the temples and palaces that surround the Durbar Squares in Kathmandu, Patan and Bhaktapur. They built with brick, wood and tiles and are said to have invented the pagoda. Until the introduction of reinforced concrete in Nepal just 50 years ago, Kathmandu was truly the Florence of the East. Visiting in 1959, Michel Peissel described the city as 'simply one vast work of art, from the humblest of the peasant's rectangular brick homes to the most impressive of the two-thousand-odd pagodas whose gilt roofs rise above the neat rows of houses. Each house, each temple, each shrine is decorated with delicately carved beams representing gods and goddesses, or animals drawn from reality and from fantasy, carved in dark wood that stands out against the background of pale pink bricks.' (*Tiger for Breakfast*, see p50).

Rigid town planning did not allow for the enormous growth that has taken place in the area. Satellite towns were developed to house the growing population and these often became associated with a particular industry. (Thimi, for example, is still a pottery centre). Most of the towns in the Kathmandu Valley did, however, manage to conform to their original plans at least until the time of the Ranas. Jung Bahadur, the first of this line of prime ministers, visited Europe in 1850 and introduced the bizarre neo-classical style of architecture exemplified in the vast whitewashed edifices that can be seen in various stages of dilapidation in the city. Large areas of agricultural land were taken over for their construction.

Modern Kathmandu

The real attack on the strongly inter-related cultural, social and religious framework of the Valley's urban centres did not, however, really begin until

(Opposite) Keeping watch with the gods and goddesses in Durbar Square (see p114), Kathmandu (photo: Henry Stedman).

the 1950s after the restoration of the monarchy and the opening up of the country. The effects have been dramatic, though, and many parts of Kathmandu have degenerated into an urban sprawl of unsightly concrete block buildings. The district of Thamel, that today looks no different from tourist ghettos in the other Asian capitals on the backpackers' route, was largely fields 30 years ago. The Kathmandu Guest House, opened in 1968 to house Peace Corps volunteers, was the first hotel here.

Kathmandu today is plagued with the problems that beset all rapidly expanding Third World cities: overcrowding, severe pollution and traffic congestion to name but a few. The population of the Kathmandu Valley now stands at 1.4 million, with a very high growth rate of almost five per cent. None of these problems seems to tarnish the allure of the city as far as the tourist is concerned. Kathmandu draws more than a quarter of a million tourists each year, most of whom, you'll no doubt be glad to know, venture no further than the capital.

ARRIVAL AND DEPARTURE

By air
● **Arrival** Tribhuvan International Airport is a 20-minute drive from the centre of Kathmandu. The domestic terminal is next door.

In the arrival hall there's a **duty-free shop** (sample prices: 200 Marlboro cigarettes US$10; Teacher's whisky US$12) and two **foreign exchange counters**. If you'll be getting your visa in Immigration here, you can get the US$ bills required from this counter. There's also a bank in the departure hall. Across the hall at **Immigration** 30-day visas (US$25 cash) are issued to those who don't have them. Downstairs are the luggage carousels, staffed by predatory porters who expect at least Rs20 if you use their services. Passing through **customs** you may be required to put all your luggage through an X-ray machine. Don't let your films go through this.

Reaching the main hall, pick up a free city map at the **tourist office** here and a copy of *Nepal Traveller* magazine. There's also a **post office, communications agency** (for telephone calls and faxes), **bank** and **hotel reservations** counter.

To get out of the airport you need to push your way through an enthusiastic mob of hotel touts and taxi drivers crowding round the entrance. Some hotels (and even some of the budget places) offer free transport from the airport. Taxis to the city centre and Thamel should cost Rs 180 if you get your own, or Rs200 with the pre-paid taxi desk just outside to the left of the arrivals entrance. If you're really counting the pennies you can reach the bus stop for the crowded local bus (Rs 5) by walking to the end of the airport drive and turning left.

(Opposite) Saddhu (see p68). These Hindu ascetics will bless you with a tika on your forehead – for a small donation. (Photo: Jamie McGuinness).

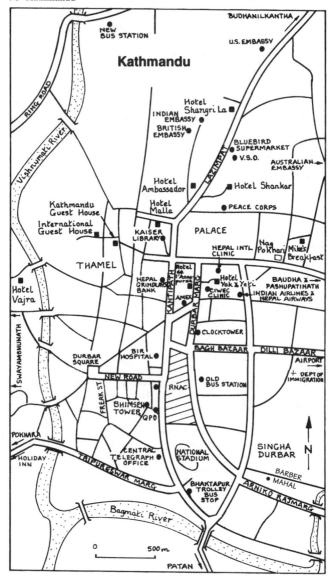

● **Departure** A hefty airport departure tax of Rs1000 (Rs600 for SAARC countries, and Rs100 for flights within Nepal) in local currency only, before you check in. At the bank here you can convert into hard currency (usually US$) only up to 15% of the rupees for which you have encashment certificates. Alternatively you can dispose of surplus rupees at the shop in the corner of the departure hall, that sells gift packs of tea and Coronation Khukri rum in exotic khukri knife shaped bottles.

By land
Some of the tourist buses will take you all the way to Thamel. Most go no further than the new bus station about 3km north of the city. Buses from the Everest region still use the old bus station by the clock tower in the town centre. Frequent shuttle buses link the two, passing by the northern end of Thamel. Sajha buses usually stop at the GPO, which is closer to Thamel.

ORIENTATION

Greater Kathmandu, which includes Patan as well as Kathmandu itself, lies at about 1400m/4593ft. The Bagmati River runs between these two cities. The airport is 6km to the east, near the Hindu temple complex of Pashupatinath, with the Buddhist stupa at Baudha 2km north of Pashupatinath. The other major Buddhist shrine, Swayambhunath, is visible on a hill in west Kathmandu. The third city in the Valley, Bhaktapur, is 14km to the east.

Within Kathmandu, most hotels and guest houses are to be found in Thamel, north of Durbar Square, the historic centre of the city. Freak Street, the hippie centre in the '60s and '70s which still offers some cheap accommodation, is just off Durbar Square. Some of the top hotels and the international airline offices are along Durbar Marg which runs south from the modern royal palace.

WHERE TO STAY

Hotel areas
● **Thamel** Most travellers find Thamel the most convenient area to stay in, although it's now largely a tourist ghetto. Everything you could want is available here, with over 100 guesthouses and hotels (from £0.65/US$1 to £60/US$90 per night), good restaurants, souvenir shops, book shops, communication centres and travel agencies.
● **Freak St** In the halcyon days of the '60s and '70s when Kathmandu was a major stopover on the hippie trail, Freak St, just off Durbar Square, was the place to hang out. Although the hash dens are now all closed it still retains a quaint, almost timeless charm. Its 15 or so hotels and restaurants are all in the rock bottom to cheap bracket.
● **Other areas** Away from the intense tourist scene are other small hotels scattered throughout Kathmandu. In Patan, there are two budget hotels off Durbar Sq and also a few good up-market hotels. Baudha and Swayambhunath have some simple hotels favoured by Buddhists and travellers.

Accommodation in Thamel

01 Chitwan Tulasi
02 Tibet Peace Guest House
03 Ktm Peace Guest House
04 Hotel Moonlight
05 Green Peace Ktm GH
06 Pumori Guest House
07 Hotel Manang
08 Hotel Impala
09 Hotel Tenki
10 Hotel Marshyangdi
11 Hotel Blue Ocean
12 Hotel Mt Fuji
13 Hotel Florid
14 Holyland Guest House
15 Hotel Lily
16 Hotel Mandap
17 Hotel Iceland View
18 Hotel Shree Tibet
19 World Wide
20 Hotel Buddha
21 Lonely Planet GH
22 Hotel Namche Nepal
23 Hotel Gauri Shankar
24 Hotel Greeting Palace
25 Pilgrims Hotel
26 Hotel Thamel
27 Shakya Guest House
28 Hotel Norbu Linka
29 Hotel Malla
30 Villa Everest
31 Hotel Shakti
32 Souvenir Guest House
33 Hotel Yeti
34 Fishtail Home
35 Mirage Guest House
36 Namaskar Guest House
37 Hotel Karma
38 Hotel Vaishali
39 Hotel Crown
40 Hotel Panda
41 Hotel Tashi Dhargey
42 Hokkaido Guest House
43 Yeti Guest Home
44 Hotel Bikram
45 Mustang Guest House
46 International GH
47 Hotel Shree Anita

48 Holy Lodge
49 Hotel Mona
50 Hotel Garuda
51 Acme Guest House
52 Hotel 7 Corner
53 Prince Guest House
54 Pooja Guest House
55 Hotel Nana
56 Red Planet
57 Blue Sky Guest House
58 Deutsch Home
59 New Orleans
60 Kathmandu GH
61 King's Land GH
62 Tourist Guest House
63 Hotel Earth House
64 Hotel Tilicho
65 Potala Tourist Home
66 Tibet Holiday Inn
67 Hotel MM International
68 Hotel Tridevi
69 Newa Guest House
70 Kunal's
71 Sagarmatha GH
72 Hotel Star
73 Pheasant Lodge
74 Cosy Corner
75 Hotel Potala
76 Gurkha Soldier GH
77 Mini Om Guest House
78 Fortune Guest House
79 Hotel Excelsior
80 Hotel Pacifist
81 4 Seasons Palace GH
82 Hotel Visit Nepal
83 Down Town GH
84 Everest Guest House
85 Student Guest House
86 Marco Polo
87 Hotel Ying Yang
88 Hotel The Earth
89 My Mom's House
90 Sherpa Guest House
91 Hotel Tashi Dhele
92 Plover Nest
93 Hotel Puska
94 Damaru Guest House

95 Buddhist Guest House
96 Mustang Holiday Inn
97 Hotel White Lotus
98 Shangri-La Guest House
99 Imperial Guest House
100 Shree Guest House
101 A-One Guest House
102 Thorong Peak GH
103 Hotel Swoniga
104 Universal Guest House
105 My Home
106 Gorkha
107 Hotel Pisang
108 Fuji Guest House
109 Mt Blanc Guest House
110 Hotel Pyramid
111 Hotel Horizon
112 Nirvana Garden Hotel
113 Hotel Hama
114 Base Camp Hotel
115 Tara Guest House
116 Tibet Cottage
117 Hotel Norling
118 Hotel Utse
119 Hotel Blue Diamond
120 Tibet Guest House
121 Hotel Poon Hill
122 Kathmandu View GH
123 Khangsar Guest House
124 Polo Guest House
125 Hotel Tayoma
126 Potala Guest House
127 Hotel Ktm Holiday
128 White Lotus GH
129 Yak Lodge
130 Tibet Home
131 Hotel Heera
132 Tibet Rest House
133 Lhasa Guest House
134 Shiddartha GH
135 Mt Annapurna GH
136 Hotel New Gajur
137 Hotel Elite
138 Hotel Jagat
139 Norling Guest House
140 Lucky Guest House

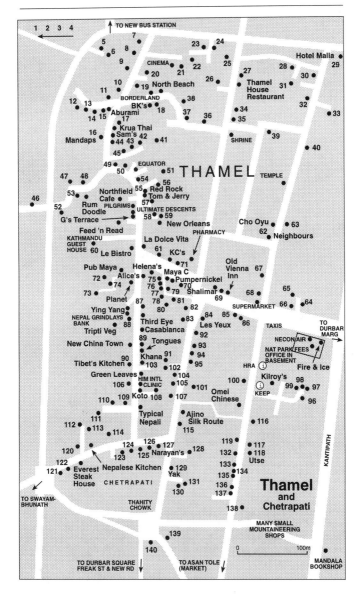

1 2 3 4

TO NEW BUS STATION

5
7
8
6
9
CINEMA
20 21
22
23 24
25
26
27
Hotel Malla
28
30
31
32
33
29
Thamel
House
Restaurant
10
11
19 North Beach
BORDERLAND
BK's
38
37
36
34
35
SHRINE
39
40
12
13
Aburami
14 15
17
18
16
Krua Thai
Sam's
44 43 42
45
41
Mandaps
TEMPLE
49
50
EQUATOR
51
54
55
56
52
53
Northfield
Cafe
Rum
Doodle
PILGRIMS
Red Rock
Tom & Jerry
57
58 59
ULTIMATE DESCENTS
Cho Oyu
63
62
Neighbours
47 48
46
G's Terrace
Feed 'n Read
New Orleans
PHARMACY
KATHMANDU
GUEST
HOUSE 60
Le Bistro
La Dolce Vita
61
KC's
Pub Maya
Helena's
Maya C
Old
Vienna
Inn
67
72
Alice's
74
73
Planet
75
76
77
78
79
80
81
82
Pumpernickel
70
Shalimar
69
68
65
66
64
SUPERMARKET
87
Ying Yang
NEPAL GRINDLAYS
BANK 88
Tripti Veg
New China Town
Third Eye
Casablanca
89
Tongues
83
84
85
86
Les Yeux
92
93
94
95
TAXIS
TO
DURBAR
MARG
NECON AIR
NAT PARK FEES
OFFICE IN
BASEMENT
HRA
Fire & Ice
Tibet's Kitchen
Green Leaves
106
110
109
Khana
91
103
102
104
105
101
107
Koto 108
HIM INTL
CLINIC
100
Omei
Chinese
Kilroy's
98
99
97
96
KEEP
Typical
Nepali
111
112
113
114
Ajino
Silk Route
115
116
120
122
121
123
124
125
126
127
128
Narayan's
132
119
117
118
Utse
133
134
135
136
137
138
Everest
Steak
House
Nepalese Kitchen
CHETRAPATI
129
Yak
130
131
THAHITY
CHOWK
Thamel
and
Chetrapati
MANY SMALL
MOUNTAINEERING
SHOPS
TO SWAYAM-
BHUNATH
139
140
TO DURBAR SQUARE
FREAK ST & NEW RD
TO ASAN TOLE
(MARKET)
0   100m
MANDALA
BOOKSHOP
KANTIPATH
THAMEL

Prices

Prices given in this section are for the high season (Oct-Nov/Mar-Apr) for single/double rooms, with **common (c)** or **attached (a)** bathrooms as indicated. You may be able to get a discount of anything up to 50% on the prices below outside the high season, depending on the length of your stay. Many hotel owners quote their prices in US dollars; you pay in rupees, though. Given the changing rate of inflation in the country, this is a sensible idea so US dollars are also used here. The dollar/pound exchange rate hovers around US$1.60=£1.

Budget guest houses (US$5/£3 or less)

In Thamel there are around 50 places to choose from in this price bracket, and in some you'll even get an attached bathroom for this price. A few hotels have triple or quad bed rooms. Check that the hot water works and try to get a room that faces away from the roads – Kathmandu is plagued by noisy dogs and honking taxis. The cheapest hotels tend to be in Narsingh Camp (behind Pumpernickel Bakery), in Chetrapati, a suburb adjoining Thamel, or on the outskirts of Thamel. The following are **keyed to the map on p101**:

01 Chitwan Tulasi (416120) $3/4 (c)
03 Ktm Peace GH (415239) $4/5 (c), $12/16 (a)
05 Green Peace Ktm GH (426817) $3 (c), $5 (a)
15 Hotel Lily (414692) $5/8 (a)
19 World Wide (425051) $4/6 (c), $8 dbl (a)
34 Fishtail Home $3 dbl (c), $4 dbl (a)
35 Mirage GH (424704) $2 (c), $4/6 (a)
36 Namaskar GH (421060) $4/5 (a)
40 Hotel Panda (42683) $4/6 (c), $8/10 (a)
42 Hokkaido GH (426051) $4/6 (c)
48 Holy Lodge (416265) $3/5 (c), $7/10 (a)
54 Pooja GH (416657) $2/3 (c), $3/5 (a)
56 Red Planet (432879) $5/7 (a)
57 Blue Sky GH (426550) $3/5 (c)
58 Deutsch Home (415010) $4/5 (c), $7/10 (a)
59 New Orleans (425736) $3/5 (c)
61 King's Land GH (417129) $3/4 (c)
62 Tourist GH (418305) $4/6 (a)
63 Hotel Earth House (418197) $4/6 (c), $6/12 (a)
70 Kunal's (411050) $3/4 (c), $5 dbl (a)
73 Pheasant Lodge (417415) $2/2.50 (c)
74 Cosy Corner (426467) $2/2.50(c) $5 (a)
75 Hotel Potala (419159) $2/3 (c)
76 Gurkha Soldier GH (221279) $2/4 (c), $6 (a)
77 Mini Om GH (229288) $2/3 (c)
78 Fortune GH (411874) $2/3 (c & a)
80 Hotel Pacifist (258320) $2/4 (c), $3/5 (a)

81 4 Seasons Palace GH (254420) $2/3c, $5 a
82 Hotel Visit Nepal (251465) $3/4 (a)
83 Down Town GH (431100) $5/10(a)
84 Everest GH (222231) $2/3 (c), $3/4 (a)
87 Hotel Ying Yang (414944) $5/8 (a)
88 Hotel The Earth (260312) $3/5 (c), $7/8 (a)
89 My Mom's House $2/3 (c), $4/5 (a)
92 Plover Nest (220541) $2/4
93 Htl Puska (262956) $3/5(c),$4/6(a)
94 Damaru GH (264489) $4/6 (c), $6/12 (a)
95 Buddhist GH (255755) $2/3 (c), $5 (a)
98 Shangri-La GH (250118) dbl: $5 (c) $10 (a)
101 A-One GH (229302) $4 (c), $6 (a)
105 My Home(256238) $5/8 (c) $7/10 (a)
106 Gorkha (214243) $3/5 (c), $4/6 (a)
109 Mt Blanc GH (222447) $2/3 (c), $4/5 (a)
115 Tara GH (220634) $3/4 (c), $5/8 (a)
122 Kathmandu View GH (260624) $3/5 (c), $4/6
124 Polo GH (242356) $3/4c, $4/5a
127 Hotel Ktm Holiday (230293) $3 (c), $5/6 (a)
128 White Lotus GH (258996) $3/4 (c)$4/5 (a)
129 Yak Lodge (259318) $2/3 (c) $4 (a)
130 Tibet Home (259019) $3 (c) $4/5 (a)
134 Shiddartha GH (227119) $3(c),$5/8 (a)
135 Mt Annapurna GH (255462) $4/6 (a)
139 Norling GH (221534) $1.80/2.50 (a), $2/3 (a)
140 Lucky GH (221446) $2/3 (a)

Freak Street, near Durbar Square, is one of the few places in the world where it is still possible to find a room, admittedly small, for around one US dollar a night. A slightly larger budget widens the choice considerably. The majority of hotels are on the main street but looking down alleys nearby yields more.

Cheap hotels in Thamel (US$6-15/£3.50-9)

Most Thamel hotels offer a range of rooms, the majority falling in this price bracket. The hotel should provide clean sheets, blankets and a desk while the better will supply towels and toilet paper and perhaps be carpeted. Little features to check are: is there a vent or window in the bathroom, a clothes line and a rooftop garden? Features aside, when choosing a hotel, go by the reception staff – are they friendly and helpful or lackadaisical? Most people new to Kathmandu begin looking at hotels in the heart of Thamel. However, there are plenty of hotels in every direction, none of which are more than a few minutes' walk from the centre.

The best known of the hotels in Kathmandu must be the long-running ***Kathmandu Guest House*** [60] (☎ 413632, 🖹 417133, email: kgh@thamel.mos.com.np), a Thamel landmark. Popular with groups, it's bursting in the high season. They have a few rooms from US$6-8/$8-10 (c) but most accommodation here is US$17/20 or more in the new wing.

02 Tibet Peace GH (415026) $4/5 (c), $10/15 (a)
04 Hotel Moonlight (413528) $15/20 (a)
06 Pumori GH (426879) $4/5 (c) $8/12 (a)
08 Hotel Impala (415549) $10/15 (a)
12 Hotel Mt Fuji (422684) $8/12 (a)
13 Hotel Florid (416155) $5 (c), $10/15 (a)
14 Holyland GH (411588) $6/10 (a)
17 Hotel Iceland View (416686) $10/16 (a)
18 Hotel Shree Tibet (419902) $10/15 (a)
21 Lonely Planet GH (412715) $6/7 (c), $8/10 (a)
22 Htl Namche Nepal (417067) $5 (c), $5-20 d (a)
23 Hotel Gauri Shankar (417181) $15/20 (a)
24 Htl Greeting Palace (417212) $10/15 (a)
25 Pilgrims Htl (416910) $8/10 (c), $15 (a)
27 Shakya GH (410266) $7/10 (c), $10/12 (a)
30 Villa Everest (413471) $7/16 (c), $30 (a)
31 Hotel Shakti (410121) $7/9 (c), $12/18 (a)
32 Souvenir GH (410277) $4/6 (c), $8/15 (a)
33 Hotel Yeti (414858) $5/6 (c) $12/14 (a)
37 Hotel Karma (417897) $10/15 (a)
41 Hotel Tashi Dhargey (415378) $15/20 (a)
43 Yeti Guest Home (419789) $4/6 (c), $8/12 (a)
44 Hotel Bikram (417111) $6/10 (a)
45 Mustang GH (426053) $5/8 (c), $10/15 (a)
47 Hotel Shree Anita (414150) $4/5 (c) $7/8 (a)
49 Hotel Mona (422151) $15/20 (a)
50 Hotel Garuda (416340) $9-20/13-25 (a)
51 Acme GH (414811) $4-10 (c), $6-20 (a)
52 Hotel 7 Corner (415588) $9/12 (a)
53 Prince GH (414456) $7/10 (a)
55 Hotel Nana (418633) $8/10 (a)
60 Kathmandu Guest House (413632) $6/8 (c), $17/20 (a)
65 Potala Tourist Home (410303) $6/10 (c) $12/15 (a)

68 Hotel Tridevi (416742) $15/20 (a)
69 Newa GH (415781) $12/16 (a)
71 Sagarmatha GH (410214) $4-8 (c), $10/20 (a)
72 Hotel Star (411004) $8/10 (a)
85 Student GH (251448) $7/10 (a)
86 Marco Polo (251914) dbl: $5-12 (c,a)
90 Sherpa GH (221546) $9 (c) $12/17 (a)
91 Hotel Tashi Dhele (251720) $12/18 (a)
96 Mustang Holiday Inn (249041) $8-20/10-30 (a)
97 Hotel White Lotus (249842) $4/8 (c), $10/14 (a)
99 Imperial GH (249339) $12/15 (a)
100 Shree GH (250048) $6/10 (a)
102 Thorong Peak GH (250013) $14/18 (a)
104 Universal GH (240930) $8 (c), $8/10 (a)
107 Hotel Pisang (252540) $12/15 (a)
108 Fuji GH (229234) $4/5 (c) $10/20 (a)
110 Hotel Pyramid (246949) $10/12 (a)
111 Hotel Horizon (220904) $6 (c) $20 (a)
113 Hotel Hama (251009) $3/5 (c), $8/12 (a)
114 Base Camp Hotel (258105) $8/10(c), $12/15 (a)
116 Tibet Cottage (226577) $4/6 (c), $8/12 (a)
117 Hotel Norling (240734) $15/20 (a)
118 Hotel Utse (226946) $13/20 (a)
119 Hotel Blue Diamond (226320) $12/15 (a)
120 Tibet GH (251763) $9/10 (c), $15/17 (a)
121 Hotel Poon Hill (257666) $12/18
123 Khangsar GH (260788) $8/10 (a)
126 Potala GH (220467) $8-10/15-20 (a)
131 Hotel Heera (259542) $7/10 (a)
132 Tibet Rest GH (225319) $6/9 (c), $8/12 (a)
133 Lhasa GH (226147) $5/8 (c), $8/12 (a)
136 Hotel New Gajur (226623) $14/18 (a)
137 Hotel Elite (227916) $4/8 (c), $8/12 (a)
138 Hotel Jagat (250732) $8/12 (a)

❑ The Kathmandu **area code** is 01. If phoning from outside Nepal dial ☎ +977-1

Moderately-priced hotels

There are numerous reasonable hotels in the US$15-30/£9-18 price range. Most have attached restaurants. All rooms have attached bathrooms with hot water, and in the more expensive rooms a TV and perhaps an air-conditioner and heater. Some hotels have a few de luxe rooms in this price range too.

09 Hotel Tenki (425694) $20/28 (a)
11 Hotel Blue Ocean (412577) $15/25 (a)
16 Hotel Mandap (413321) $21/27 (a)
20 Hotel Buddha (413366) $30/40 (a)
26 Hotel Thamel (417643) $18/25 (a)
39 Hotel Crown (416285) $20/25 (a)
46 International GH (410533) $20/25

64 Hotel Tilicho (410132) $15/25 (a)
66 Tibet Holiday Inn (411453) $20/25 (a)
67 Hotel MM International (411847) $20/25 (a)
79 Hotel Excelsior (411566) $20/25 (a)
103 Hotel Swoniga (253253) $25/35 (a)
112 Nirvana Garden Hotel (256200) $30/40 (a)
125 Hotel Tayoma (211149) $15/30 (a)

Three-star standard hotels

Around the three-star standard are two well-managed traditionally built hotels. *Hotel Vajra* [see map on p98] (☎ 272719, 📠 271695, email: vajra @mos.com.np) was conceived and paid for by a Texas billionaire, and built by Newar craftsmen, with wall-paintings by Tibetan and Tamang artists. Rooms are US$41/44 with attached bathroom and there are cheaper rooms for under US$20 with wash-basins and shared bathrooms. It is located near Swayambhunath. The traditionally decorated *Summit Hotel* (☎ 521894, 📠 523737, email: summit@summit.wlink.com.np) in Patan is popular with expeditions wanting a peacefully-located hotel. Prices range from US$25 to US$95. Both have a pleasant atmosphere, attractive gardens, restaurants and appropriate amenities.

Close to each other in north Thamel are the *Hotel Marsyandi* [10] (414105) and *Hotel Manang* [07] (☎ 410993), both popular with trekking groups. There are rooms here from US$30/40. The *Hotel Norbu Linka* [28] (☎ 414799) is similarly priced.

Four- and five-star hotels

Until its unfortunate demise in 1970, the top place to stay was the Royal Hotel. Its success was largely due to its proprietor, the legendary White Russian émigré, Boris Lissanevitch. It was the country's first Western hotel, opened in 1954 in a wing of the palace that is now the Bahadur Bhavan. Virtually everything for it had to be imported from Europe, shipped to India and then carried in by porters. Staying here you'd be guaranteed to meet interesting people and many of the mountaineering expeditions made it their Kathmandu base.

Most of the city's top hotels are now much like expensive hotels any-where in the world. The *Hotel Yak & Yeti* (☎ 248999, 📠 227781, www.ya kandyeti.com), with rooms from US$1165/175 to US$600 for a suite. Centrally located, it has everything you'd expect from a five-star hotel, although the modern wings don't exactly blend with the old Rana palace which forms part of it. The Yak & Yeti Bar with its excellent Chimney Restaurant was moved here from the Royal Hotel when it closed. Rich

Nepalis, however, consider the *Soaltee Holiday Inn Crowne Plaza* (☎ 272550, 🖹 272205, email: office@shicp.com.np) as the best of the big hotels, although it's not so well located, being in the west of the city, in Kalimati. Rooms range from US$170/180 to US$675. It's said to have the best casino on the sub-continent.

Back on Durbar Marg is the *Hotel de l'Annapurna* (☎ 221711, 🖹 225236) with rather ordinary rooms from US$120/130-325, a large pool and seedy casino. Similarly priced but inconveniently located is the *Everest Hotel* (☎ 488100, 🖹 490288) on the road to the airport.

The *Hotel Malla* [29] (☎ 418383, 🖹 418382, email: malla@htlgrp.m os.com.np), just north of Thamel, is pleasant with rooms from US$140/170. It has a fitness centre and swimming pool. The best value in this group is the *Hotel Shangri La* (☎ 412999, 🖹 414184, email: hosang@mos.com.np), in Lazimpat, with rooms from US$120/130 and a peaceful garden. Also in Lazimpat, the *Hotel Radisson* (☎ 411818, 🖹 411720, email: radkat@mos.com.np) has just opened, with rooms from US$175/185. Opening in late 1999 is a 400-room branch of the *Hyatt* chain, near Baudha.

The Indian-owned *Hotel Vaishali* [38] (☎ 413968, 🖹 414510) is Thamel's first four-star hotel. Rooms are from US$90/110 although travel agents can offer substantial discounts.

Probably the best hotel in Kathmandu is *Hotel Dwarika's* (☎ 470770, 🖹 471379, email: dwarika@mos.com.np), which has opted out of a star classification. If Kathmandu is a living museum, this is the ultimate place to experience it. The red brick buildings are decorated, inside and out, with ornate panels lovingly restored from old Kathmandu houses. Every room (US$135/155) is an individual work of art, and the restaurant's offerings are similarly exotic. Golfers may be interested in the new branch of *Le Meridien* which should now be open beside the Gokarna Forest Golf Club – a new, eco-friendly course designed by Gleneagles.

Note that all star-class hotels add a 10-14% government tax to the bill.

WHERE TO EAT

Kathmandu's restaurants have long been renowned amongst travellers throughout South Asia for their ability to serve passable approximations of Western dishes. Until recently, however, you'd probably have been more appreciative of Kathmandu's apple-pie and enchilada cuisine after a trek rather than on arrival direct from the West. It's surprising how quickly you forget how things are really supposed to taste! Standards have risen quite considerably over the last few years with restaurants competing for more authentic dishes, some even importing chefs from abroad.

The cost of meals in restaurants doesn't vary as greatly as hotel prices. Most main courses cost less than US$3/£2 in the smaller places but in the best restaurants expect to pay US$5-10/£3-6.

Be especially careful about what you eat before you set out on your trek; you're more likely to pick up a stomach bug in a Kathmandu restaurant than in the hills. A test on the quality of the tap water in Thamel showed it to contain more than ten times the WHO-recommended safe maximum level of faecal matter. The better restaurants are serious about hygiene but don't believe all restaurants that tell you their salads are washed in iodine. Similarly filtered water is not reliably clean; stick to bottled or hot drinks. Unless otherwise indicated the restaurants described are in Thamel (see map p101).

Breakfast
Even the smallest guest houses now offer breakfast and snacks either as room service or in their own snack bars. Most of the Thamel restaurants have set breakfasts that can be good value but there are a few places worthy of special mention. There are also numerous bakeries in Thamel.

The *Pumpernickel Bakery* does a roaring trade in cinnamon rolls, bagels and other pastries and cakes. There's a pleasant garden behind it and the notice-board here is a good place to track down trekking partners.

The *Northfield Café*, by the Ultimate Descents' office, is another favourite place to start the day. You get fairly authentic American breakfasts (hash browns, pancakes and syrup, fresh coffee with free refills etc). It was originally a branch of *Mike's Breakfast*, a restaurant in Naxal (north-east of Thamel), where the fare is similar, and you can sit in the garden serenaded by items from the ex-Peace-Corps owner's classical record collection.

Lunch and dinner
● **Western** The cheapest restaurants in Kathmandu serving 'Western' fare are in and around Freak St. The *Jasmine Restaurant*, just off Freak St, still has a mellow atmosphere. The *New Mandarin* (in reality almost as old as the hills) is as popular as ever. The *Oasis Garden* is more expensive but does, as the name suggests, have a pleasant garden. Opposite, the *Paradise Vegetarian Restaurant* is probably the best place to eat in Freak St. Their crêpes with garlic cheese are recommended.

Back in Thamel, restaurant prices can be much higher, but there are still places where you'll get a cheap meal that's reasonably filling. *Helena's* is a popular place, main dishes are Rs120-250, there's good cappuccino and a wide range of cakes and pies. Chocolate cake is Rs60. *Narayan's*, in Chetrapati, is also popular, especially for puddings.

For a refreshingly different menu and good music *New Orleans* is recommended. Try their chicken burrito with chips and salad and a Mississippi mud cocktail with real Bailey's in it. You can sit by the fire or in the quiet garden at the new *North Beach*, by Hotel Vaishali, and enjoy real burgers and an original American menu .

Many places have steaks on the menu, usually (but not always) buffalo steak. It's often served as a 'sizzler' and arrives in front of you on a heated cast-iron plate doing just that. The enduring *Everest Steak House's* speciality is a wide range of real beef fillet steaks from around Rs170. If you have the appetite of a yeti try the Rs650 chateaubriand (better split between two to three people). *The Third Eye* is not so good, and also quite expensive; but in the back room you can recline on the cushions while you eat. *KC's Restaurant & Bambooze Bar* is as much a Thamel institution as the Kathmandu Guest House. The food's good but prices are distinctly up-market. A sizzling steak from the people who introduced the 'sizzler' to Kathmandu now costs Rs195; and if that doesn't fill you up you can round off your meal with their cheeseboard (yak, mozzarella and cottage cheese with wholewheat bread and pickles). Another Kathmandu institution recommended for its food is the *Rum Doodle*. Enjoy a real fire without guilt: the logs are made from crushed rice husks.

G's Terrace is a Western-Nepali joint venture and authentic Bavarian cuisine is served in this pleasant roof-top restaurant. There's Bavarian home-made potato soup with sausage and specialities like French pepper steak in cognac and cream. Most main dishes are over Rs200. *Old Vienna Inn* serves Austrian cuisine for similar prices. In their attached deli the salami rolls are delicious and can be eaten there or on the run. The *Delicatessen Center* on Kantipath is distinctly up-market, stocking a surprisingly wide range of imported cheeses and other delicacies, at unsurprisingly high prices. Several new bakeries have opened in Thamel and their pastries make a perfect quick lunch.

Probably the best restaurant in Thamel is *Kilroy's* (☎ 250440). On the eastern edge of Thamel you can dine indoors or outside by the waterfall (!). The Irish chef oversees the creation of such delicacies as 'seared breast of chicken stuffed with nak's cheese, served with mushroom sauce' (Rs295) and, of course, Irish stew (Rs280). Draught Guinness is Rs380. There's also a *café*.

Many of Kathmandu's top restaurants are in the Durbar Marg area and in the five-star hotels there are some excellent Western-style restaurants, some run by Western chefs. The buffet lunch or dinner at the *Yak & Yeti* costs Rs575.

Nepal isn't the place to suffer a Mac Attack; McDonald's hasn't arrived. The alternative is *Wimpy*, on Durbar Marg. Beefburgers are out of the question, mutton burgers being the less tasty alternative. For the best French fries

---

❏ **Baber Mahal Revisted**
This place has to be seen to be believed! The crumbling stables of a Rana palace between Kathmandu and Patan have been converted into a chic shopping centre that wouldn't look out of place in California. As well as some distinctly exclusive boutiques there are also several excellent restaurants. *Simply Shutters* (☎ 253337) offers French-influenced Western cuisine: honey roasted quail is Rs400. *Chez Caroline Patisserie* serves the sub-continent's best crème caramel and mousse au chocolat (Rs95) to die for. *Rodeo* is a branch of the Delhi Tex-Mex bar-restaurant. The waiters look somewhat self-conscious in their cowboy outfits. Not to be missed for a celebratory dinner is *Baithak* (☎ 248747). In the grand long gallery, past Ranas stare down from their portraits as you feast on 'delicacies from the Rana court'. Main dishes are Rs500 and the set dinner, the Maharaja's Feast (Rs945) is recommended.

the place to go is **BK's Frituurs** , a take-away opposite North Beach. They're served with a range of sauces served in eco-friendly leaf dishes.

● **Nepali, Newari & Thakali** There are many cheap local Nepali places out of Thamel that serve dal bhaat or momos, usually for less than Rs50. In Thamel the **Nepalese Kitchen** has a range of superior dal bhaat specials (Rs80-180) and live music several times a week. More up-market, **Thamel House Restaurant** (☎ 410388) set in a renovated 100-year-old Newar house. Main dishes range from Rs80-130 and the nine-course set meal costs Rs450.

For the best in Nepali cuisine **Bhojan Griha** (☎ 416423) is located in Dilli Bazaar and features a cultural show accompanied by an excellent dinner. The top Newari restaurant is **Krishnarpan** at Hotel Dwarika's (☎ 470770).

For a taste of the Annapurna region **Tukche Thakali Kitchen** (☎ 225890), near Wimpy on Durbar Marg, is a delight. Prices are very reasonable: Rs125 for noodle soup with chicken, Rs390 for an 11-item set dinner. Fiery Tuckhey Brandy is Rs90 a peg.

● **Tibetan** restaurants are amongst the cheapest places to eat in Thamel. For fried noodles, momos, chang and tumba, **Cho Oyu** is recommended. It's opposite Earth House. Below the Kingsland Guest House, **Tashi Deleg** is popular and also does Western food that's good value. The best-known Tibetan place here is **Utse**, at the hotel of the same name. The pingtsey soup (meat soup with wontons) is excellent, as are their momos (vegetable, mutton, buffalo or pork). Given a couple of hours' notice, they will prepare a complete Tibetan banquet. **Tibet's Kitchen** in the Sherpa Guest House has an open-plan kitchen and food is similarly clean and fresh. By Equator's office is **Lhasa**, run by a Tibetan family. The restaurant at the **Hotel Yak** is very popular, too.

● **Indian** Mughal/tandoori dishes appear on many menus but can be disappointing and unlike what you would expect in a good restaurant south of the border. Serving good Indian food has made **The Third Eye** popular but **Mandap's** is better, even if the menu is limited. Delicious chicken tikka masala, with a nan bread or rice is Rs170. **Feed n' Read**, behind Pilgrims book shop does decent southern Indian dosas for around Rs50, the perfect lunch. **Tripti Pure Veg Indian** is near Ying Yang and does what it says very cheaply.

The top Indian restaurant is the Hotel de l'Annapurna's **Ghar-e-kabab** (☎ 221711). It specialises in the rich cuisine of North India, main dishes are around Rs350 and there's live music in the evenings. You may need to book.

● **Mexican** **Northfield Café** is said to be the best place for a tostada. It is also one of the more hygienic Thamel restaurants. **Mike's Breakfast**, which spawned the Northfield, does excellent Mexican food.

● **Italian** Many restaurants serve pizza and pasta but one place stands way above the rest. **Fire & Ice Pizzeria & Ice Cream Parlour** has to be experienced to be believed. Run by an Italian woman who's imported her own computer-controlled Moretti Forni pizza oven, some of the best pizzas on the subcontinent are now turned out here – to the sound of Pavarotti. Prices range from Rs170-290 and there's wine by the glass for Rs160. Queues can be long, though. *Northfield Café* turns out the next best pizzas. For authentic pasta try *La Dolce Vita*.

● **Chinese** Most restaurants have spring rolls and chowmein on their menus although what appears on your plate is usually unmemorable. The *New China Town Restaurant* above the Nepal Grindlays exchange branch is quite good. Although the *Hotel Garuda* restaurant has only two chop sueys in the Chinese section of the menu, they are crispy, fresh and clean. Probably the best Chinese restaurant is the *Mountain City* at the Malla Hotel, just north of Thamel.

● **Thai** *Ying Yang*, opposite the Third Eye, is one of the best restaurants in Thamel. The speciality is Thai but there is also Western cuisine. Main dishes cost Rs210-260, and the chef is from Thailand. They take credit cards.

● **Israeli** Catering to the large number of Israeli visitors that the country is attracting, *Aburami* opened in 1992. The food is quite authentic and good value: hummus with chapattis, Israeli salad and felafels. They put on special meals for Jewish festivals.

● **Japanese** There are several Japanese restaurants, and all serve fairly authentic dishes at almost authentic prices. *Koto*, on Durbar Marg, is the best value of the up-market places. The set dinner is Rs390.

● **Vegetarian** All restaurants have some dishes for vegetarians who are sick of dal bhaat. *New Nirmala* has brown bread, garlic toast and excellent cream of spinach soup. If it's Indian vegetarian food you're after, try the *Foodsmen Maharaja Restaurant* tucked away near Hotel My Home. The owner, a Sikh, supervises the production of Punjabi cuisine. On Freak St, *Paradise Vegetarian Restaurant* is an excellent place.

NIGHTLIFE

Rum Doodle Restaurant & 40,000'½ft Bar is a Kathmandu institution, with yeti prints on its walls inscribed by the members of many mountaineering expeditions. As well as a wide range of drinks (hot rum punch is good) the food here is good.

The *Tom & Jerry Pub* is noisy and popular, an old favourite. There's a rooftop terrace, pool tables and satellite TV. *Pub Maya* and *Maya Cocktail Bar* are all similar. New bars seem to pop up every week or two, many with live music. The latest place is the distinctly up-market *Planet*, above Barnes & Noble bookshop, near Le Bistro.

Several of the best Thamel rafting companies put on slide shows with free rum n' coke to tempt you. **Chris Beall's slide presentations** offer good unbiased advice for trekkers about to head into the hills. The shows are held in the Kathmandu Guest House when he's in town. The KGH also has a large screen **video disc cinema** with seating for around 25 people. Hotel Sherpa and Hotel d'Annapurna (both in Durbar Marg) and the Shankar Hotel (off Kanti Path) put on **cultural shows**. The French Cultural Centre occasionally sponsors a play, jazz night or mime act and details are advertised.

The top hotels all operate **casinos**, many offering free food and transport to tempt you in.

SERVICES

Banks

Larger hotels can change money at reception. In Thamel there are several authorised money-changers but their rates, like the hotels, are not quite as good as the banks.

Nepal-Grindlays has an exchange office in Thamel. In Kanti Path, east of Thamel, Nabil Bank offers some of the most competitive rates in the city; the main branch of Nepal-Grindlays is also here.

The **American Express** office (☎ 226172, open Sunday to Friday 10am-1pm and 2-5pm) is by the Hotel Mayalu.

Credit card withdrawals are best made at Nepal-Grindlays, either branch. Rupees or US$ travellers' cheques are the two currency options.

Bookshops and libraries

Kathmandu has some of the best bookshops on the subcontinent, including many small second-hand shops where you can trade in your novel for another. There's even a Barnes & Noble but it's not connected with the American chain. Most international news, computer and fashion magazines are regularly available.

The Kaiser Library, Kaiser Shamsher Rana's private collection, is worth visiting as much for the building as for the 30,000 plus musty volumes. This Rana palace is now the Ministry of Education and Culture, just west of the modern royal palace. The British Council Reading Room is open to all and has the main UK newspapers and plenty of magazines, although they're all a week or more old. The British Council should now have relocated from Kanti Path to the grounds of the British Embassy in Lainchaur/Lazimpat.

Communications

The GPO is a 20-minute walk south of Thamel, on the corner of Kanti Path and Prithvi Path. This is where to go for Poste Restante mail. When sending a letter don't put it in a postbox but ask them to frank it or the stamps may be removed and resold. Sending mail is far more easily dealt with by the numerous communication centres in Thamel which take letters to the GPO for franking each day.

The cheapest place to make an international phone-call (minimum three minutes) is at the Central Telegraph and Telephone Office, opposite the national stadium at the southern end of Kanti Path. Since this is a 30-40 minute walk from Thamel most people make their calls at one of the **communication centres** and **cyber cafés** dotted around Thamel. They provide excellent services for a modest charge above the normal rates, and don't impose a three-minute minimum on phone calls. You can make international calls, send and receive faxes and, at the better places, send and receive email cheaply, and even access the internet. The business centres in the big hotels are generally much more expensive for the same services.

Embassies
- **Australia** (☎ 371678), Maharajgunj
- **Burma/Myanmar** (☎ 524788) Chakupat, Patan
- **China** (☎ 411740) Baluwatar
- **India** (☎ 410900), Lainchaur
- **Israel** (☎ 411811), Bishramalaya House, Lazimpat
- **New Zealand** (Honorary Consul ☎ 412436), Dilli Bazaar
- **Sweden** (☎ 220939), Khichapokhari
- **Thailand** (☎ 371410), Bansbari
- **UK** (☎ 411590), Lainchaur
- **USA** (☎ 411179), Pani Pokhari

Left luggage
All hotels and guest houses are happy to store excess luggage for you free of charge while you go off on your trek, although they expect you to stay with them on your return.

Medical clinics
CIWEC (☎ 228531, open daily 9am-3.30pm for consultations, 24hrs for emergencies) is an exceptionally competent clinic which is located just off Durbar Marg, near the Hotel Yak & Yeti. Consultations cost US$40 or equivalent in any currency. Credit cards are accepted.

Nepal International Clinic (☎ 434642, open Sunday to Friday 9am-5pm, appointments only on Saturday) is also excellent. Consultations cost US$35 or equivalent. It's opposite the Royal Palace, slightly east of Durbar Marg.

Cheaper clinics in Thamel include **Everest International** (☎ 411504) on Thamel Chowk; and **Himalaya International** (☎ 225455) near Hotel Utse. Beware of **Synergy**, who are better at advertising than consultations.

Supermarkets
Best Shopping Centre near Marco Polo Guest House has lots of imported goodies. Bluebird Supermarket in Lazimpat has a wider stock.

Swimming-pools
The top hotels all have swimming-pools and will allow non-residents to use them for a price. The largest is at the Hotel de L'Annapurna but it'll cost you US$7 to swim here. The small pool at the Hotel Shangrila costs US$5 and is set in very pleasant gardens.

Trekking agencies

All the treks described in this guide can be done independently but for the side trip into the north Mustang region (see p37) you are required to use a trekking agency. There are more than 100 trekking agencies in Nepal, most based in Kathmandu. The top outfits have their offices on Durbar Marg but there are many other reputable companies based in Thamel. They can organise anything from a porter-guide to accompany one person on a tea-house trek to complete expeditions with sirdar (trek leader), sherpas (assistants), cooks and porters. For an organised trek, expect to pay anything from £12/US$20 to £60/US$100 per person per day depending on the number of members. Be sure you know exactly what will be included and that your porters will be adequately clothed for high passes like the Thorung La.

Trekking equipment rental

There are numerous trekking equipment rental shops in Thamel where you can hire sleeping-bags (check that these are clean and give them a good airing in the sun before use), boots, rucksacks, and down jackets as well as camping gear and mountaineering equipment (of variable quality). Large deposits are required: money of any sort or valid airline tickets but credit cards should not be trusted to anyone.

Trekking permits

These are obtained from the **Department of Immigration** which recently moved from Thamel to an inconvenient location halfway to the airport. It's down the side road that runs north to Baneswar from by the Everest Hotel. On the meter a taxi here will charge Rs65, and all the taxi wallahs know where it is. When you get to the office don't get taken in by a **current scam**

□ **KEEP, HEC and HRA**

The **Kathmandu Environmental Education Project** (KEEP) raises environmental awareness among trekkers and the trekking industry. Well worth visiting, they have an information centre and library in Thamel on the corner of the lane that leads to the Mustang Holiday Inn. Also here is the **Himalayan Explorers Club** (☎ 250646, www.abwam.com/himexp/), which offers members information, communication services and left luggage storage.

The **Himalayan Rescue Association** (HRA, email: hra@aidpost.mos.co m.np; www.nepalonline.net/hra) was founded in 1973 with the primary aim of saving lives in the mountains by alerting trekkers to the dangers of altitude sickness. It's largely due to their unfailing efforts (passed into guidebooks) that the death toll from altitude sickness is now very low. Their office is worth a visit for advice and for its library. They also have forms here so you can register with your embassy. Unless you're trekking with an organised group, you're advised to do this since your embassy's assistance is necessary if a helicopter rescue is required for you. In addition to the Kathmandu information centre the HRA has two medical posts, one at Manang (see p212) and the other in the Khumbu at Pheriche. They operate only during the peak trekking seasons, however, from early October to early December, and March to April.

that is operating. You'll be approached by a 'guide' who will ask you where you're going and then get you the correct form. He then helps you fill out the form and tells you what you need to pay, including the 'processing charge' (for him). He tells you what time to come back to the office and will meet you on the steps outside with your passport. This will happen but all he will have done is to hand your passport in for the immigration staff to process: something you can do just as well yourself. Strange as it may sound, many trekkers seem to be falling for this one since the office moved.

The Department of Immigration is open for applications for trekking permits and visa extensions between 10.00 and 13.00 from Sunday to Thursday, 10.00 to 12.00 on Friday. The forms for the three main trekking areas are colour-coded: you need a yellow one for the Annapurna region. Two photos are also required (available instantly in several photographers' nearby). You can pay the Rs1000 Annapurna Conservation Area Project entry fee in the National Park Office located in the basement of the shopping centre (see Thamel map p101) or at any of the ACAP offices on the trek. See p71 for visa extension and trekking permit fees.

Permits and visas are usually ready the same day in the afternoon between 14.00 and 16.00 Sunday to Thursday, 12.00 to 15.00 on Friday. At the height of the season you may have to wait until the following day so make your application as soon after the office opens as possible.

TRANSPORT

By **bicycle** is definitely the best way to get around although traffic and pollution problems get worse each year. There are lots of rental stands around Thamel. No deposit is required; you sign the book and pay the first day's rental. Be sure you check the tyres, brakes, lock and bell before you cycle off. Lock the bike whenever you leave it as you'll be held responsible for its replacement if it gets stolen. You can rent an old Indian Hero with patched tyres for Rs40 per day or a smart new Chinese Flying Pigeon for Rs60. Some places also have mountain bikes for Rs100-200. If you're renting for more than one day (a good idea as you can keep the bike overnight at your guest house) you can usually negotiate a lower rate.

A number of places in Thamel now rent out **motorbikes**, mostly 100-250cc Japanese bikes made under licence in India. They cost Rs500-700 per day, plus Rs30 for a helmet; a cash deposit is sometimes required, usually they simply want to know where you're staying. You're supposed to have either an international driving licence or a Nepali one.

There are lots of **taxis** around Kathmandu but it's difficult to get drivers to use their meters, especially if you pick one up in a tourist district like Thamel or Durbar Marg. You won't get away paying less than Rs200 for the ride in from the airport to the city centre although the metered fare would be about Rs140.

There are also **auto-rickshaws**, metered and costing about a third less than taxis. Kathmandu's **cycle-rickshaw** wallahs understand just how your delicate Western conscience ticks, so hard bargaining is required if you're going to pay anything like local prices. There are extensive **bus** routes around the city and out to the airport but this is a very slow and crowded transportation option.

WHAT TO SEE

You could easily spend a week in the Kathmandu Valley, such is the rich concentration of sights here. Several companies operate bus tours (ask in the larger hotels and travel agencies) but renting a bicycle and wandering round independently is rather more rewarding. Getting lost is all part of the fun.

Durbar Square

First stop on the Kathmandu sightseeing trail is Durbar Square, also known as Hanuman Dhoka. This complex of ornately carved temples and monuments includes the old royal palace (closed Tuesday; entry is Rs250), the Kumari Bahal (the home of the Kumari, the 'living goddess', a young girl chosen as the incarnation of the Hindu goddess, Durga), the Kasthamandap (the wooden pavilion from which the city's name is said to have been derived) and the tall Taleju temple, built in the 16th century. The best time to be here is early in the morning when people are going about their daily pujas.

Baudha (Bodhnath)

This Buddhist stupa is one of the largest in the world. Seven kms from the city centre, it's a major place of pilgrimage, especially for Tibetans. There's a large Tibetan community here and several monasteries.

From dawn to dusk the faithful make their circumambulations (always in a clockwise direction) under the fluttering prayer-flags and the all-seeing eyes of the giant white stupa. It's a fascinating place to visit, especially at the time of a new or a full moon when there are special festivities. Nourishment of a more basic nature is available at the *Oasis Restaurant* and a number of other places near the stupa. There are also a couple of *bars* serving momos and tumba (see p82) just around the corner from the Oasis. Look for a curtain across a door; there are no signboards. Order a plate of *sukuti* (dried meat) to accompany your tumba and momos. It's all ridiculously cheap but not terribly hygienic – probably best enjoyed when you come back from your trek.

Swayambhunath

Visible from many parts of the city, this ancient stupa is the second most important Buddhist shrine in Kathmandu. It's a 40-minute walk west of Thamel. There's now an entrance fee of Rs50 for foreigners. The steep climb up through the woods is certainly good practice for a trek and there's a good view from the top but Swayambhunath has little of the atmosphere of Baudha. It's also known as the 'Monkey Temple' on account of the troupes of macaques here. Don't feed them as they can get vicious when your supplies of biscuits run out.

Pashupatinath

Hindu pilgrims come from all over the subcontinent to this Nepalese Varanasi (Benares). It's a very extensive complex of temples beside the Bagmati River, six km from the city centre.

Pashupatinath derives its fame from the metre-long linga, carved with four faces of Shiva which is kept in the main temple (closed to non-Hindus). The whole complex is dedicated to Shiva and is a focus for sadhus, wandering ascetics, some of whom may have walked here from as far away as south India. As at Varanasi, people perform their early morning ablutions from the ghats here. It's also the most auspicious spot to be cremated in the country. The funeral pyres by the river have become something of a tourist sight, attracting coachloads of scantily-clad foreigners who behave with astounding insensitivity, firing off rolls of Kodachrome at the burning bodies.

Patan

Also known as Lalitpur, the second of the three main city-states in the Kathmandu Valley is now just a suburb of the capital. Patan's Durbar Square is probably the best collection of late Malla architecture in the country and rather less touristy than Kathmandu's Durbar Square. There's also a new attraction – if there's only one museum you visit in Nepal it should be **Patan Museum**, in the palace compound of Keshav Narayan Chowk on Durbar Square. It's open daily except Tuesday; entry is Rs120 for foreigners.

It's also worth visiting Kumbeshwar Square. Water in the pond here is said to flow directly from the holy lake of Gosainkund in Langtang. At the north-east corner of the square is Kumbeshwar Technical School. Visitors are welcome at this school and orphanage set up to help the lowest castes in the area. Tibetan rugs and sweaters of considerably higher quality than those on sale in Thamel can be purchased here.

Bhaktapur

The third city, Bhaktapur, is a mediaeval gem, visited only fleetingly (if at all) by tourists. Fourteen km east of Kathmandu, it's an almost entirely Newar city that is strongly independent of Kathmandu. Some of the people who live here can't even speak Nepali. Much more than in Kathmandu or Patan, an atmosphere of timelessness pervades this place. Bhaktapur's main attraction is its Durbar Square, with its Palace of Fifty-Five Windows, but here, as in the rest of the city, many buildings have been damaged by earthquakes. The major 'quake in 1934 affected more than half the buildings. Much of the reconstruction work has been done by the Bhaktapur Development Project, a German-sponsored urban renewal programme.

It's a dusty hour-long cycle-ride to Bhaktapur from Kathmandu or you can take the electric trolley-bus from Tripureshwar which will drop you across the river, a 15-minute walk from Bhaktapur's Durbar Square.

Thimi

This small Newar town is famous for its pottery and the streets and squares are lined with recently-thrown pots drying in the sun. Ten km from

Kathmandu, Thimi makes a pleasant cycle-excursion and can be combined with Pashupatinath and/or Baudha.

Nagarkot
The most popular mountain-viewing spot near Kathmandu is Nagarkot, 32km from the city on the road that passes Bhaktapur. Since the view, which includes Everest and four of the other ten highest peaks in the world, is best in the early morning, most people spend the night here. There are, however, tours that leave Kathmandu before dawn to catch the sunrise. You can also get here by bus from Bhaktapur (two hours), on foot or by mountain-bike.

MOVING ON

By air
Nepal's air transport system has expanded rapidly since the government allowed the formation of private carriers in 1991. There are now at least seven companies to choose from but all charge the same rate for the routes they share. Routes and schedules are subject to change as the new companies settle in. **Royal Nepal** (RNAC) (☎ 220757) flies from Kathmandu to Pokhara (US$61, 35 minutes) several times daily, with extra flights in the tourist season. They have connections to Jomsom and Ongre/Manang from Pokhara (see p134) and flights to many other towns in Nepal.

Buddha Air (☎ 418864) flies speedy new Beech aircraft from Kathmandu to Pokhara (US$61, 30 minutes) four times daily. **Necon Air** (☎ 480565) flies 44-seat Avros to Pokhara six times daily. **Cosmic Air** (☎ 427150), **Yeti Airways** (☎ 421215), **Lumbini Airways** (☎ 245381) and **Gorkha Airlines** (☎ 435121) each operate at least one daily flight to Pokhara.

A departure tax of Rs100 is now collected at the airport before you fly.

By bus
● **Pokhara** The easiest way to get to Pokhara is on one of the tourist buses that run from Thamel, leaving in the early morning. Tickets can be bought at most travel agents for Rs200-300. Top of the range are the air-con buses operated by Greenline Tours (☎ 253885, on the corner of Kantipath and the main road into Thamel). They have daily buses at 07.00 to Pokhara (Rs600, seven hours) and Chitwan (Rs480, five hours). Breakfast is included.

More interesting since they're also used by Nepalis are the Sajha buses (Rs 93, seven hours) which run from near the GPO at 06.00. Tickets can be bought up to two days before departure from the kiosk here. The Sajha night bus (departing at 19.00, Rs107) is not recommended.

Buses from the new bus station north of Thamel are considerably more crowded. There are ordinary buses to Pokhara (Rs113, 10 hours) from 06.30-09.00 and de luxe ('Swiss') buses (Rs180, 7 hours) at 07.00. The original 'Swiss Bus' was operated by an aid project funded by the Swiss but it no longer runs. The appellation is now indiscriminately applied by Nepalis to any 'luxury' bus service.

● **Besisahar** Direct services run from the new bus station to Besisahar (Rs135 local, Rs180 express) taking anything up to 12 hours. The express bus should be booked one day before at the fourth window from the right at the bus station. It leaves at 07.15 and should arrive at 15.30.

● **Other destinations in Nepal and India** From the new bus station there are buses to most towns in Nepal, many departing early in the morning. Avoid the night buses, not only because they don't exactly make for a restful night but also because you'll miss some spectacular views. For the Everest region, buses use the old bus station in the centre of town.

If you're going on to India watch out for 'through' tickets. Since everyone has to change into an Indian bus at the border, there's actually no such thing. Travel agents give you a bus ticket to the border and a voucher to exchange with an Indian bus company with whom they've got an arrangement. Since things don't always run as smoothly as they might it's safer, cheaper and just as easy to buy the tickets as you go along. It also gives you a choice of buses and the option to stop off where you want.

The best crossing point into India is via **Sunauli** for Gorakhpur, Varanasi or Delhi. From the main bus station for Sunauli ordinary buses (Rs125, nine hours) leave 06.00-09.00 and there are also night buses. Similarly-priced Sajha buses leave from near the GPO. For Patna and Calcutta it's better to go via **Birgunj/Raxaul** (Rs149, 11 hours). Buses leave from the main bus station. For Darjeeling you'll have to make the gruelling trip to **Karkabhitta** (Rs336, 12-14 hours) on overnight buses leaving between 15.00 and 16.30.

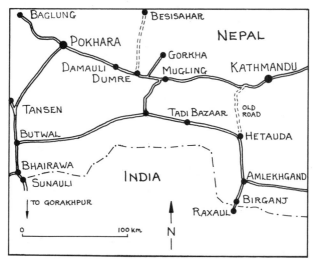

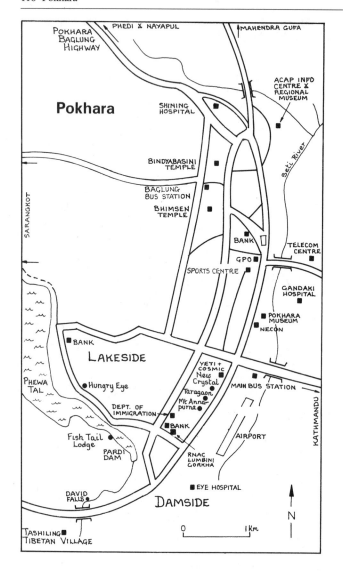

PART 5: POKHARA

Pokhara

In all my travels in the Himalaya I saw no scenery so enchanting as that which enraptured me at Pokhara. **Ekai Kawaguchi** *Three Years in Tibet*

Pokhara's superb mountain scenery has been enrapturing foreign visitors since Ekai Kawaguchi, the town's first foreign visitor, came this way in 1899. Modern travellers are no less impressed; there can be few other towns that are so close to such high mountains. Pokhara (pronounced 'POKE-rah') lies at 850m/2789ft yet peaks of over 8000m/26,267ft rise above it in a breathtaking panorama.

Two hundred kilometres (125 miles) west of Kathmandu, Pokhara is the starting and ending point for most of the treks in the Annapurna region, except the Annapurna Circuit (usually started from Dumre). It's also the perfect place to rest weary limbs after a trek and the town's relaxed atmosphere causes many travellers to stay rather longer than they'd originally planned. Along the eastern shore of Phewa Tal (Lake) a waterside version of Thamel offers accommodation to suit every budget.

The joy of Pokhara is that there really is very little to do here except laze around by the lake and over-indulge in those culinary delights you may have been pining for while away on your trek.

HISTORY

Origins
Probably at the same time that the Kathmandu Valley was a lake (about 200,000 years ago) the Pokhara Valley was also under water. Now just a few lakes (tals) remain: Phewa Tal in Pokhara, and Begnas Tal and Rupa Tal 10km to the east are the largest.

Very little is known about the early history of this area but Pokhara's location between the mountain passes and the plains has made it a focal point for peoples from both sides of the Himalaya for centuries. The area was controlled by numerous small kingdoms, usually situated on hilltops around the valley, populated by people who had migrated from Tibet. They were the ancestors of the Gurung who now live in Pokhara and the surrounding hills. In the 14th century, Moghul persecution of Hindus in India forced refugee communities north into Nepal and some settled in the Pokhara area. Rajput princes from Rajasthan brought their entire courts and armies with them to carve out their own principalities. These Indo-Aryans developed the agriculture of the Pokhara Valley and whilst the high caste Brahmins and Chhetries remained in their mountain strongholds, the lower castes were sent to work the land below.

Shah Rulers of Kaskikot

In the 17th century, Pokhara was being ruled as part of Kaskikot, one of the most powerful of the Chaubise kingdoms in Central Nepal. These Chaubise kings were cousins of the Shah kings of Gorkha (Nepal's current royal family.) Kulmandan Shah is the best known of Kaskikot's kings and also the first of the Shahs to rule a Nepalese Kingdom. He is credited with establishing a winter capital in Pokhara and he encouraged trade along the Kali Gandaki Valley through Mustang to Tibet. Mule trains brought salt and wool down from Tibet to exchange for grain from Pokhara.

By the late 18th century the Chaubise kingdoms were no longer closely united. Prithvi Narayan Shah, the king of Gorkha who had conquered the Kathmandu Valley, turned his attention west to these kingdoms, sweeping through with his powerful army to conquer Kaskikot in 1785. In the period of peace and stability that followed Pokhara quickly grew to become the major trading town in the region.

The Ranas

Although the Rana prime ministers who ruled Nepal from 1846 to 1950 could claim ancestral connections to the Kaskikot area, only Jung Bahadur, the first of the Ranas, showed any particular interest in the region, declaring himself Maharaja of Kaski and Lamjung. None of the Ranas ever visited the Pokhara area.

Under the Ranas, Pokhara became the capital of Kaski and Lamjung districts. That there are few old buildings to see in Pokhara today is the result of a devastating earthquake in 1934, and in 1948 of a fire offering being made by a priest in the Bindyabasini temple that got out of control and reduced much of the town to ashes.

Pokhara since 1950

Until the middle of this century, the only way to reach Pokhara from Kathmandu was on foot, a six- or seven-day journey. In 1951, the airfield was built but it was not until 1973 that the road linking Pokhara with the capital was finished. Another major communications project, the Pokhara-Baglung-Beni highway, is now also complete. This new highway has already sliced a day off the trekking schedules for the Annapurna region; it is hoped that the plans that it might at some time be extended up the Kali Gandaki to Jomsom will never leave the drawing board.

Improved communications brought people from the surrounding villages to swell the town's population from just 5400 in 1961 to over 120,000 in 1994. The Chinese invasion of Tibet in 1951 brought 15,000 exiles to Nepal, many to Pokhara. Dervla Murphy spent some time working with Tibetan refugees in the 1960s and *The Waiting Land: A Spell in Nepal* provides an interesting description both of her experiences and of a Pokhara before apple pie and chocolate cake were being served on the shores of Phewa Tal. Numerous international aid agencies now have their regional headquarters in Pokhara.

Pokhara is the main recruiting area in Nepal for troops for the Gurkha regiments in the British and Indian armies. Together with tourism, army wages and pensions form the mainstay of the local economy. While the Gurkha contingent in the British army decreases, tourism is booming in Pokhara, and moving up-market: in the past three years three five-star hotels have opened in Pokhara.

ORIENTATION

The lake is the main focus for travellers. It's on the western edge of town and there are two main accommodation areas here, Lakeside (Baidam) and Damside (Pardi). Lakeside is one long strip of hotels, guest houses, restaurants and shops with more places to stay up the paths among the trees. Damside is the smaller district beside Pardi Dam, to the south of the lake.

The airport and bus station are also in the southern half of the town, a long walk or a short taxi ride from the lake.

In the centre of Pokhara is the modern town; the old bazaar is to the north. Pokhara is a surprisingly spread-out town, sprawling for several kilometres down an incline that is unnoticeable until you try to ride your gearless Indian Hero from the lake to the bazaar.

WHERE TO STAY

Hotel areas

There are now over 200 hotels in Pokhara so you shouldn't have any difficulty finding a place to stay except in the high season. Most are simple guest houses with just a few rooms, many run by ex-Gurkhas.

Although there is also some accommodation near the bus station and in the centre of Pokhara, everyone heads for the lake. Lakeside has the greatest choice of places to stay and almost all the restaurants and shops. Damside is quieter and it has better views of the mountains; many of the guest houses here also have dining rooms so you don't have to go to Lakeside to eat. As Lakeside continues to develop into Thamel-by-the-Sea, peaceful Damside becomes a much more attractive alternative.

Prices

The prices given here are for single/double/triple rooms, with common (com) or attached (att) bathrooms, at the height of the season. At other times you should bargain. For the cheaper places you may get 20-40% off but for mid-range hotels you should be able to get a discount of up to 60%, depending on how many people are chasing rooms at the time. There is 12% VAT payable on accommodation: make sure you ascertain whether this is included in the price agreed upon.

KEY In ascending order by price for singles/doubles with common bathroom (c) or attached bathroom (a). In some cases, space below permits only a price range from the cheapest single with common bathroom to a double with attached bath. Telephone numbers, where available, are given in brackets after the lodge name. Prices in US$ but payable in rupees.

LAKESIDE
01 Garden Rest House (21862) $1-10 c/a
02 Garden GH $1.50/4 (c), $2/5 (a)
03 Heavens Gate GH $2-5 c/a
04 New Traveller GH (21930) $2/4 (c), $6-8 (a)
05 New Annapurna GH (25011) $2/3 (c), $6/10(a)
06 New Tourist GH (21479) $2-10 c/a
07 Kiwi GH $2/3 (c), $5-15/9-19 (a)
08 Dharma GH $2/3 (c), $15/20-35 (a)
09 Trekkers Retreat Lodge (21458) $3-4 c/a
10 Hotel Tropicana $6-10 (a)
11 Hotel Eyeball (21954) $ 3-5 c/a
12 Fewa Annex (21394) $5/8 (a)
13 Stay Well GH (22624) $3 (c), $6-8 (a)
14 Pancha Koshi GH $3 dbl (c), $6/12 (a)
15 New Friendly Home $3/5 (c), $6/10 (a)
16 Holy Lodge $3/5 (c), $10/15 (a)
17 MidnightWell dbl from $4
18 Pushpa GH $4-7 c/a
19 Santosh GH $2 dbl (c), $10 dbl (a)
20 Himalayan Country $4-6/6-8 (a)
21 The Rainbow Hotel $4/5 (c), $10/12 (a)
22 Hotel Asia $4/8 (c), $8/18 (a)
23 Hong Kong Hotel (21202) $4-30 c/a
24 Vienna Lodge dbl from $5 (a)
25 Keiko's Cottages dbl from $5 (a)
26 Pokhara Peace Home (21599) $5-15 c/a
27 Gaurishanker (25050) $5-30 c/a
28 Buddha GH $5-25 c/a
29 Tranquility Lodge (21030) $3-20 c/a
30 New Lake View GH $6/10 c/a
31 Nightingale Lodge (20338) $6-12 (a)
32 New Hotel Woodland (21970) dbl from $7
33 Chalet de Pokhara (21707) $8-10 (a)
34 Hotel Lake Side (20073) $8-10 (c), $15-20 (a)
35 Hotel Johnny Gurkha (21713) $8-25 c/a
36 Hotel Cordial $8-30 (c/a)
37 Gurkha Lodge $10-12 (a)
38 Hotel Motherland $10-15/15-20 (a)
39 Hotel Dreamland $10/15-20 (a)
40 Hotel Avocado (21183) $3-15 c/a
41 Blue Heaven GH $10-25 (a)
42 Hotel Meera (21031) $25/35 (a)
43 Fairmount Hotel (21252) $10-30 c/a
44 Hotel Shikhar (21966) $10-37 c/a
45 Hotel Sitara (21579) $12-30 (a)
46 Mountain Top (20779) $12-30 (a)
47 Mandala Rest House(21478) $13/18 (a)
48 Hotel Full Moon (21511) $15-30 (a)

49 New Pokhara Lodge (20875) $15/35 (a)
50 Hotel Barahi (21879) $15-50 (a)
51 Mountain Villa (21954) $16/20 (a)
52 Nepal GH (21963) $16-22 (a)
53 Moonlight GH $18/23-30 (a)
54 Hotel Shamrock (21027) $18-35 (a)
55 Baba Lodge (20981) $20/25 (a)
56 Hotel Fewa (20151) $19/28 (a)
57 Hotel Glacier (21722) $20-30 (a)
58 Hotel Sahana (21229) $20-25/25-30 (a)
59 Hotel Bedrock (21876) $20-48 (a)
60 Hotel Monal (21459) sgl/dbl from $25
61 Thorung La (21157) $35/55 (a)
62 Hotel Pumori (21462) $45/100 (a)
63 Base Camp Resort (21226) $72/75 (a)
64 Fishtail Lodge $99 (a)

DAMSIDE
65 Hotel Green View (21844) $2 (c), $10/15 (a)
66 Hotel Jamu (20930) $2-4 c/a
67 Hotel Nascent (21719) $2.5-5 c/a
68 Sherpa GH $2/3 (c), $8/10 (a)
69 Hotel Lake City(21431) $2/3 (c), $5/10 (a)
70 Indra Niwas (21719) $3/5 (a)
71 Super Lodge (21861) $3/5 (c), $7/12 (a)
72 Hotel Peaceful (20861) $3/4 (c), $8-15 (a)
73 Hotel Sakura (20924) $3-5 (c), $8-15 (a)
74 Purna GH $3/5 (c), $10/12 (a)
75 New Friendly GH $3-15 c/a
76 New Hotel Pagoda (21802) $3/4 (c), $10/13 (a)
77 Hotel Siddhartha (20052) $3-20 c/a
78 Hotel Himalayan (21643) $3-20 c/a
79 Hotel Mary Ward $3-25 c/a
80 Hotel Garden (20870) $3/4 (c), $5-30 (a)
81 View Pt Hotel (21787) $4-10 c/a
82 Hotel Monalisa (20863) $6/10 (c),$20-35 (a)
83 New Hotel Anzuk (21845) $7/10 (a)
84 Hotel Blue Sky (21425) $10/15 (a)
85 Hotel Try Star (20930) $10/15 (a)
86 Ashok GH (20374) $15/20 (a)
87 Hotel Annapurna (21723) $15/20 (a)
88 Hotel Holiday (21763) $15/25 (a)
89 Tibet Resort (20853) $10/14 (c), $23/34 (a)
90 Hotel Jharna (21925) $19/24 (a)
91 Hotel Mt Manaslu (20953) $20-25/25-35 (a)
92 Hotel Gurkha Haven (24527) $15/20 (a)
93 Pokhara Resort (21043) $35-45 (a)
94 Dragon Hotel (20391) $40-50 (a)
95 Hotel Tragopan (21708) $40-80 (a)

❏ The Pokhara **area code** is 061. If phoning from outside Nepal dial ☎ +977-61

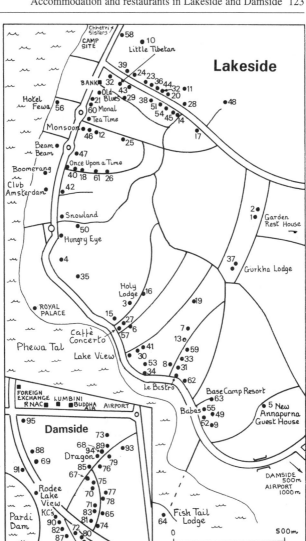

Budget guest houses and cheap hotels

● **Lakeside** Generally the further the hotel is from the main drag, the cheaper it is. There are many places to stay in this price range and most are very similar: basic, cheap and cheerful. The *New Traveller Guest House* [4] continues to be popular, as much for its garden as for its convenient location very near the lake. There are rooms from US$2 for a single with shared bathroom, to US$8 for attached doubles. Even cheaper is the *Garden Guest House* [2] and its neighbour, the *Garden Rest House* [1], on a quiet lane about five minutes from the lake. *Heaven's Gate Guest House* [3] is a little nearer the action, and nearby the trendy *Holy Lodge* [16] has a friendly atmosphere and a pleasant garden. The *Kiwi Guest House* [7] is cheap, clean and very popular. Next door the immaculate *Stay Well Guest House* [13] is well maintained and the manager very helpful.

If you're a woman travelling on your own, the *Chhetri Sisters' Guest House* (☎ 24066) is recommended. Run by Lucky, Dicky and Nicky, the guesthouse is in the north of Lakeside, along the road that runs parallel to the lake. Rooms cost from US$2-6 (c/a). They also run a trekking agency for women (see p10).

We get mixed reports about the long-running and very peacefully-located *Gurkha Lodge* [37]. It's set in a pleasant garden and there are five doubles at US$11 each in the bungalows here. An alternative that's certainly much better value is the *Tropicana Hotel* [10] in the north of Lakeside. For around US$6 you should be able to get a large sunny double room with spotless bathroom attached.

Hotel Buddha [28] is a large friendly place, and the nearby *Hong Kong Hotel* [23] has some budget accommodation amongst its pricier rooms, starting at US$4 for a single.

● **Damside** The most competently-run places here seem to be those owned and operated by ex-Gurkhas. The *New Hotel Pagoda* [76] wins the prize – it's spotless. They have rooms from US$4-7. Soccer-mad, Aldershot-supporting Captain KB Gurung rules *Hotel Anzuk* [83], a warm and friendly place to stay. Photos of the Queen and Prince Charles grace the walls. Renovations should be complete by now.

Rather different in character to these places is the *Sherpa Guest House* [68]. It's run by a friendly, helpful manager and there's also a cheap restaurant here.

Another place that often gets recommended is the *Hotel Lake City* [69], particularly for its attractive garden. The rooms are clean and good value.

Moderately-priced hotels

Several of the hotels which used to offer rooms for just a few dollars a night have spruced them up and dramatically increased their prices. Outside the high season, when many of these rooms are empty, you can get equally dramatic discounts if you bargain.

Recently taken over by Mike of Mike's Breakfast fame, *Hotel Fewa* [56] is in an enviable location: it's the only hotel right down by the water. There are rooms with attached bathroom for US$19/28, and 'for your peace of mind – no TV or telephone in room'.

The *Hotel Monal* [60] is well located on the main street in Lakeside. It's run as a German-Nepali partnership and rooms here begin at US$28 but, as with all hotels in this price range, they give generous discounts outside the height of the season. The centrally-located *Hungry Eye* (☎ 20908) is a pleasant place to stay; rooms are US$20/30 but there can be attractive discounts. There's good food in the restaurant. *Baba Lodge* [55] is similar, with rooms at US$20/25. Up the road, the *Base Camp Resort* [63] charges US$61/66.

In Damside, *Hotel Gurkha Haven* [92] is, as one would expect, run by a Gurkha. There are rooms from US$15/20 and superb views for the rooftop. Also in Damside, rooms in the *Hotel Dragon* [94] (☎ 20391) cost US$40/50 with bathtubs in the attached bathrooms. The restaurant here has been recommended.

The *Hotel Fewa Prince* (☎ 24881), on the road to Kathmandu, was recently opened in collaboration with a Japanese company. Rooms are good value at US$40/46; but for a mountain view they charge US$90/110.

Expensive hotels

Opposite the airport, *New Hotel Crystal* (☎ 20035) has rooms for US$65/75, all with attached bathrooms. The restaurant here is good.

Once the top hotel in Pokhara, the *Fish Tail Lodge* [64], operated by Kathmandu's Hotel de l'Annapurna, looks like a poor relation to the three new places below. It does, however, have a superb location on the southern side of the lake and is worth visiting just for the wonderful view of the mountain panorama reflected in the water. All rooms have attached bathrooms and cost US$82/95. It's set in well-kept gardens and reached by raft across a narrow stretch of the lake. For reservations phone Kathmandu (☎ 01-221711).

On the eastern edge of Damside is the new *Bluebird Hotel* (☎ Kathmandu 228833, email hotel@bluestar.mos.com.np) is a large marble-floored affair popular with Japanese tour groups on account of its excellent Japanese restaurant, Koto, presided over by a genuine Japanese chef. The comfortable rooms here are US$130/150.

Even more impressive is the nearby *Shangri-La Village Pokhara* (☎ 22122, email hosangp@village.mos.com.np). There are rooms with tremendous mountain views for US$150 and a garden which will get more attractive as it matures. The pool is not heated so somewhat chilly in the main trekking season.

Pokhara's top hotel is the *Fulbari Resort* (☎ 23451), attractively situated on the edge of a gorge about 5km from the centre of Pokhara. The opulent rooms cost US$200/215. There's a golf course, an excellent restaurant and Pokhara's best pool (Rs650 for non-residents, including lunch).

WHERE TO EAT

Calorie after delicious calorie line the main street of Lakeside, from the cake shops laden with waist-expanding chocolate croissants, to the larger establishments offering ever more scrumptious ways of putting the wobble back in your walk after weeks on the trail.

It's difficult to give specific recommendations for restaurants: things change so fast. Some of the old favourites are listed below.

Breakfast

Many guest houses have a limited breakfast menu including porridge, muesli, toast and eggs. There's also great competition amongst the restaurants along Lakeside to provide all-inclusive breakfast specials. These range from Rs40 for a (more than adequate) set meal of eggs, toast, hash browns, tomatoes, and coffee, up to Rs100 for an 'American' or 'Trekkers Special' – a huge feast that usually includes steak. One place that's often recommended for its breakfasts is *East Meets West*, near Club Amsterdam. *Mike's Breakfast* at the Hotel Fewa is also good.

If you want something simple like a roll and coffee there are several bakeries along the main road in Lakeside. They are not quite up to the high standards of Thamel bakeries, yet, though. Try *Hermann Helmers Bäckerie*, near the Hungry Eye.

For a post-trek celebratory breakfast binge, try one of the top hotels, since they often have all-you-can-eat breakfasts. You should phone first to check, though. The *Fishtail Lodge* sometimes does a buffet for Rs525 – with incomparable mountain views thrown in.

Lunch and supper

● **Western/Have-a-go-at-anything**   'Tourist-friendly' restaurants now proliferate on Lakeside's main street. Characterised by thatched roofs and western music, a new addition to one restaurant's menu is quickly emulated by the other restaurants here, thus most menus now look decidedly similar. That said, the food is usually of a fairly high standard, the attempts at copying different national cuisines continue to achieve higher levels of authenticity – and the beer's always cold.

One restaurant that is consistently recommended is *Once Upon A Time*, particularly favoured by Westerners living here.A number of smaller places, such as the *Tequila*, *Phewa Beach* and *Moondance*, have similar fare at cheaper prices. Many places now have pool tables to entice passers-by.

The long-established *Tea-time Bamboostan* is still going strong, and if one of the ultra-hip waiters deigns to serve you, the food isn't bad at all. They now have live bands here some evenings. Almost opposite is *Monsoon*, serving excellent breakfasts and good coffee.

Moving northwards, many restaurants now have gardens stretching down to the lake. Very pleasant in the early evening as the egrets swoop by, it is also possible to get some decent nosh, provided the mosquitoes don't devour you completely first. *Few Park*, *Boomerang* and *Beam Beam* are all good, with Beam Beam serving some delicious curries.

Nearby is the popular *Everest Steak House*, a branch of the Kathmandu restaurant, and serving the same menu: everything from the Rs100 breakfast cowboy special to the Rs650 chateaubriand.

In South Lakeside, *Baba's Restaurant* has been popular for many years. Main dishes include chicken cordon bleu and spinach mushroom lasagne.

In Damside, the *Rodee Lake View Restaurant* is the closest you can get to the water and serves excellent Tandoori food.

As you might expect, the top hotels have good restaurants. There's a buffet lunch at the Shangri-La Village for US$10.

• **Italian** The best Italian food is served at *Caffè Concerto*, in south Lakeside. Pizzas are Rs85-200, and there's fresh pasta, gnocchi and even tiramisu.

• **Nepali/Tibetan** There are several small Nepali/Tibetan places offering daal bhat or momos at give-away prices. More up-market, the *Little Tibetan Tea Garden*, serves momos and many other Tibetan dishes. *The Lhasa Tibetan Restaurant* is also recommended, and you can try gyakok here (four hours' notice required). Opposite Boomerang is *Rice Bowl Tibetan*.

• **Chinese** *Lan Hua*, in the south of Lakeside, is an authentic place with delicacies such as 'phoenix craws' and 'double cook gizzard' on the menu. A large selection of Chinese food can be found at many of the places here. Usually these are just variations on fried rice, but are nevertheless tasty and filling.

•**Austrian** At the part Austrian-owned *Little Vienna Restaurant* it's possible to dine on Weiner schnitzel, salad and French fries (Rs100), and follow that up with topfenpalatschinker (Austrian pancakes) all washed down with excellent filter coffee. It's part of Vienna Lodge.

• **Japanese** Judging from the queues of Japanese backpackers in it, the *Ajino Silk Road*, near the Hungry Eye, is good. The top Japanese restaurant, however, is *Koto*, at the Hotel Bluebird. Mixed tenpura is Rs290, tenpura udon costs Rs340 and chicken teriyaki is Rs240. It's all excellent.

• **Indian** Most of the restaurants make fair attempts at Mughal and Tandoori dishes. *The Hungry Eye*, in central Lakeside, is recommended.

• **Vegetarian** All restaurants have some vegetarian dishes.

NIGHTLIFE

The No 1 nightspot must be *Club Amsterdam* in Lakeside. There's live music some nights, beer costs Rs110 and it's open late. They do bar snacks, such as fried chicken (Rs95). It's open during the day, too, and there's a pool table (Rs50).

You might also try the Joker Dance Palace if you're not put off by the advertised 'full security by commando with metal detector'!

There are nightly cultural shows at many places on Damside - ask around. The shows at the **Hotel Dragon** and **Hotel Hungry Eye** have been recommended. Tickets are sold at the hotels or in some travel agents and bookshops.

SERVICES

Banks
Nepal Grindlays Bank (open Sunday to Thursday 10.00-16.00, Friday 10.00-15.00, closed on Saturday) now has a branch on Lakeside. They will do cash advances on Visa or MasterCard. Nearby a couple of exchange counters have opened. Double check your money here as shortchanging always seems to work in their favour. The main branch of **Nepal Rastra Bank** is in the centre of Pokhara.

Bookshops
As in Kathmandu, there's no difficulty in finding something to read here with numerous bookshops and kiosks in the Lakeside area. They stock new and second-hand titles and most operate book exchanges.

Communications
• **Post** The GPO is a long bike ride into the centre of town. If you want your postcards to reach their destinations you should, however, bring them here and watch them being franked. Poste restante letters are held here. It's open from 10.00 to 17.00 Sunday to Friday.

• **Phone and fax** In Lakeside and Damside it's easiest to use the phones in guest houses, shops and kiosks for international calls. For a three minute international call, the Telecommunications Centre is a little cheaper. It's open from 07.00 to 21.00 but is inconveniently located near the GPO.There are now many fax facilities in Pokhara, and most hotels will be willing to send faxes for a fee. You can also use the Telecommunications Centre, but they have a three-minute minimum charge.

• **Email** Several places now offer email. Try the newly-opened Pok@ra Cyber Café near Nepal Grindlays bank in Lakeside.

Left luggage
As in Kathmandu, most hotels and guest houses will store excess baggage free of charge. Keep all valuables with you, though.

Massage, haircuts and spiritual well-being
For some unknown reason, the fresh juice bars on Lakeside also do massage as a sideline. The options are confusingly varied: half-body, full-body,

(Opposite) Top: Buddha Air's Kathmandu service awaiting take off at Pokhara Airport. **Bottom:** Tibetan curio sellers set up their stalls wherever trekkers are likely to pass.

American, Japanese, German or Indian and they charge around Rs300 per hour. Next to the Tequila Restaurant is an Ayurvadic Massage Centre, which charges similar rates.

Barbers do haircuts for Rs40 and will then try to throw in a little manipulatory massage to push the price up. If this isn't what you want, say so or be prepared for a larger bill than you'd intended. If you want a shave, ensure that a new blade is used since Aids is on the increase in Asia.

Medical clinics

There are a number of clinic/pharmacies in Lakeside that do stool tests and also the Western Regional/Gandaki Hospital (☎ 20066), near the Telecommunications Centre. If you're hospitalised in Pokhara you may need a friend to bring you food and help look after you as nursing is minimal. For specialist eye treatment, the Himalaya Eye Hospital (☎ 20352) regularly treats foreigners for a nominal fee. Staffed by one Dutch and two Nepali opthalmologists it's to the south of the airport.

Shopping

Pokhara is the perfect place to browse and there are rows of kiosks and small shops in which to do it. All the goods on sale here are also available in Kathmandu.

Few travellers escape the pushy charms of the Tibetan curio-sellers who work the streets in pairs with considerable success. You can watch carpets being woven at Tashiling and Tashipalkhel Tibetan villages. Also worth visiting is the group of thangka shops just north of Lakeside, near the Hotel Sahana.

For supplies the grocery shops in Lakeside (Safeway, Saveways, Saleways, etc) stock everything a trekker could wish for: from Mars Bars (Rs40) to Mills and Boon romances (Rs150) for those cold, lonely nights in the mountains.

Some of the bakeries sell delicious wholegrain trekking bread too. It's worth pointing out, however, that for most treks you really don't need to stock up on anything.

Trekking agencies

There are a number of agencies here who will happily organise a complete trek, should you want their services. To hire a porter, it's usually cheaper to cut out the middleman and arrange things yourself. See p92 for more information. If you're a woman looking for a porter contact the Chhetri Sisters' Guest House (see p124).

Trekking equipment rental

As in Kathmandu, it's possible to rent most things from down jackets to sleeping-bags but don't expect any fancy climbing gear.

(**Opposite**) **Top:** Dishing out dal baht in Kagbeni and preparing pizzas at Annapurna Base Camp (photos: Jamie McGuinness). **Bottom:** Typical tea-house menu.

Trekking permits

The Department of Immigration has a branch in Pokhara (☎ 21167). Times vary according to how busy they are but they're usually open from Sunday to Thursday from 10.30-13.30 for visa extensions and trekking permit applications and from 16.00-17.00 the same day for collections. On Friday you must get your application in before 12.00 for collection between 14.00 and 15.00. Visa extensions and trekking permits are issued for Annapurna and Jumla for a maximum of six weeks. It's possible to turn up in Pokhara, get your permit and get at least as far as Birethanti in the same day. It's not yet possible to get visas for the north Mustang area here.

ACAP have a counter here so you can get your entry permit (Rs1000) while you get your trekking permit.

Just outside the office here are a number of photo shops that will do instant passport photos.

Working in Pokhara

There are numerous aid agencies operating here but they're unlikely to recruit foreigners locally unless you have very special skills.

TRANSPORT

Taxi

Some taxis have meters but most are meterless and you pay as much as the driver thinks you will stand. Between the airport or bus station and Lakeside you probably won't get away with paying less than Rs70.

Bus

Local buses are based at the Prithwi Chowk Bus Station in the centre of town. Buses run from here to Lakeside, to the airport, and to Besi Bus Park (for buses to Nayapul for Birethanti etc).

Bicycle and motorbike

The best way to get around Pokhara is by bike. There are lots of places to rent them from and prices are around Rs40 per day for the cheapest, to around Rs60 for the latest edition mountain bike.

In Lakeside you can rent motorbikes. An Indian Escort RX100 (licence-built Yamaha) costs around Rs500 per day. Petrol costs Rs40 per litre.

WHAT TO SEE

There really are very few 'sights' in Pokhara so you needn't feel guilty if you spend your time lazing around by the lake. There are plans for a major **International Mountaineering Museum** south of the airport.

Mountain viewing

The Pokhara panorama is undeniably impressive and dawn is the best time to view it, Fish Tail Lodge is the best place to view it from. Machhapuchhre is the most easily recognisable peak. From Pokhara it has a classic pointed shape; it looks like a fish tail only from the north.

From left to right the major peaks you can see from Pokhara are Dhaulagiri (8167m/26,795ft), Annapurna I (8091m/26,545ft), Machhapuchhre (6997m/22,942ft), Annapurna III (7555m/24,767ft) – shaped like an elephant, Annapurna IV (7525m/24,688ft) and Annapurna II (7937m/26,041ft).

Museums and exhibitions

Most interesting is the **ACAP Information Centre** which has displays about the work currently being done as part of the Annapurna Conservation Area Project. You can buy postcards, T-shirts and books here. It's part of the **Annapurna Regional Museum**, which has a small display of local flora and fauna and an impressive collection of butterflies. They're both open daily (09.00-13.00 and 14.00-17.00) except Saturday and located on the university campus in the far north of the town. The **ACAP headquarters** are east of the airport near the leprosy hospital.

The Pokhara Museum (open 10.00-17.00 daily except Tuesday) has a small dusty archaeological and ethnographic display that's probably worth the Rs5 entry charge but not the Rs10 camera fee.

Temples

The most important Hindu temple here is the **Bindyabasini Temple**, just above the old bazaar. It's dedicated to Durga, the goddess of death and manifestation of Parvati, Shiva's consort. She is appeased by the sacrificing of goats, cocks and buffaloes and, especially during festivals such as Dasain, the streets flow red around this temple. South of Bindyabasini is the smaller **Bhimsen Temple**. You can visit the **Varaha Temple**, on an island in Phewa Tal, by boat.

There are modern Buddhist temples at the two Tibetan villages and a gompa one km east of the telecommunications centre.

For the energetic, there's a monastery to the south of Lakeside on top of the hill. Its visible from Lakeside, and the views of Pokhara and the mountains from there are awesome.

Golf course

The nine-hole Himalayan Golf Course (☎ 27204) is seven km from Pokhara. It costs US$20 for green fees and a caddy and US$10 for club hire.

Bicycle excursions

Pokhara's other sights make pleasant bicycle excursions. In the south there's **David/Devi Falls**. The origins for its name get more confused with each guidebook that's published. A tourist named David, Davy, Devi or Miss Davis is said to have been swimming here when the sluice-gates on Pardi Dam, a couple of km upstream, were opened. He (or she) was drowned. The falls are quite impressive after the monsoon; much less so in the winter and spring. Nearby you can visit the **Tashiling Tibetan Village**, where there's a carpet factory. Tibetan trinket sellers will soon home in on you here and you'll also meet them in Lakeside.

To the north you could visit **Tashipakhel Tibetan Village** which has a restaurant, guest house, gompa and carpet factory. Follow the Pokhara-Baglung Highway for three km to reach it.

Also in the north but past the British Gurkha camp is **Mahendra Gufa**, a large dark cave full of bats that's not really worth the long ride up here.

The **Seti Gorge** is very impressive and so deep and narrow you may not be aware of its existence. You get a good view of it from the bridge between the GPO and the telecommunications centre.

ENTERTAINMENT

Boating and swimming
Hiring a boat to paddle yourself around the lake or out to the small temple on the island helps pass the time until the next meal. There are lots of boat hire places in Lakeside and owners will begin the bargaining at around Rs100 per hour or Rs200 'with driver'. The royal guards will wave you away if you stray too close to the King's palace, although he's hardly ever at this summer hideaway. He's said to visit in February.

You can swim in the lake (best from a boat in the middle - but wear a swimsuit) and the water can be surprisingly warm.

If there's enough wind (there usually isn't) you can rent windsurfers and a small sailing dinghy from Hotel Fewa or Hotel Monal.

Sport
Pokhara Sports And Fitness Centre is in the town centre near the GPO in Mahendrapaul. Offering a gym, sauna, tennis and aerobics, for a small fee you can hire racquets etc. It's open from 06.00 to 19.00 every day except Mondays – ring 21756 for information/bookings or contact the Boomerang Restaurant.

GETTING TO THE START OF YOUR TREK

For Birethanti it's best to get to Nayapul. The buses leave every 30 minutes from the Baglung/Besi Park Bus Station, and cost Rs35 for the two-hour trip For Baglung it's a four-hour trip (Rs45). Buses to Begnas Tal leave from behind the GPO at Mahendrapaul, costing Rs10. Buses to Dumre cost Rs35 from Prithwi Chowk, taking approximately two hours.

❑ **Holy cows**
The cow is sacred to Hinduism and Nepal's free-ranging herds take full advantage of their divine status, sunning themselves on the warm tarmac of the main thoroughfares. If your bus or taxi is held up, pray to Ganesh. He's Shiva's elephant-headed son, the god of wisdom and remover of all obstacles!

MOVING ON

By air

Get to the airport early as flight departure times are approximate. It's not unknown for a flight to leave early but you're more likely to be kept waiting. With several new airlines now offering services on these routes timings are likely to change.

Royal Nepal (RNAC) (☎ 21021) has several daily flights to Kathmandu, (US$61, 35 minutes) with extra flights in the tourist season. There are at least two early-morning flights to Jomsom (US$50, 25 minutes) daily and flights to Manang/Ongre (US$50, 25 minutes) on Monday, Wednesday and Friday at 07.00. Note that both these routes are subject to delays or cancellations if the weather is not perfect. The Manang route is not operated during the monsoon season. The ticket office is on the road from the airport to Lakeside.

Buddha Air (☎ 21429) has four flights a day to and from Kathmandu. They also do mountain viewing trips: the Annapurna Circuit in 20 minutes! The Buddha Air booking office is near RNAC's.

Cosmic Air (☎ 21846) has flights to Kathmandu and Jomsom as do **Yeti Airways** (☎ 421215) and **Lumbini** (☎ 27233). **Gorkha Airlines** (☎ 25971) may start flying to Jomsom soon; they already have daily flights to Kathmandu.

Necon Air (☎ 25311) flies Avros to Kathmandu daily. Their ticket office is near Pokhara Museum.

By bus

• **Kathmandu** Simplest is to get a ticket from one of the agencies that operate tourist buses from Lakeside and Damside. Tickets can be bought at most travel agents for Rs200-300. The journey takes between seven and nine hours and they will pick you up from your hotel.

Top of the range are the air-con buses operated by Greenline Tours (☎ 26562, on Mustang Chowk, in front of the airport). They have daily buses at 07.00 to Kathmandu (Rs600, seven hours) and Chitwan (Rs480, five hours).

Of the public buses, Sajha day buses are the cheapest. They leave from outside the GPO, in the centre of Pokhara, four km from the lake. From the ticket office here you can make reservations up to three days in advance for Kathmandu (Rs93 for early morning, Rs107 for the night service) or Sunauli. Buses to Kathmandu leave at 06.00, 07.30 and 19.00.

From the bus station there are lots of buses for Kathmandu (Rs100 daytime; Rs113 night service, ten hours) between 05.30 and 11.00 for the day buses, 19.30 and 20.45 for the night buses.

• **Other destinations** From the main bus station there are two buses direct to Gorkha (Rs60, four hours), at 07.00 and 09.30 but most other buses will get you to the turn-off to Gorkha from where you can pick up a connection. For Dumre (Rs35, two hours), you have a wide choice of buses: most pass through this town. For Tansen (Rs70, six hours), the direct bus leaves at 07.00. To Begnas Tal (Rs12, 1 hour), there are buses at 07.00, 09.00 and every couple of hours throughout the day.

Direct buses to Tadi Bazaar (Rs70, six hours) for Chitwan, leave at 05.30, then every hour until 10.30.

To reach the border with India, the best route is through Sunauli (Rs128, nine hours). There are numerous buses between 05.00 and 10.00.

PART 6: TRAIL GUIDE AND MAPS

Using this guide

The main trekking routes in the Annapurna region are described below and detailed on the accompanying maps. For route planning see the **Annapurna regional map** (pp26-7).

These route descriptions have not been laid out on a day-to-day basis since people walk at different speeds and will have different aims for their trek. Walking times for both directions along each path are given on the maps enabling you to plan your own itinerary. Some guidance is obviously necessary: **suggested itineraries** are given on p233. For an **overview** of each of the treks see pp25-38.

ROUTE DESCRIPTIONS

The route descriptions can be followed in either direction but are set out as follows:

Pokhara to Ghorepani p137
Ghorepani to Jomsom and Muktinath p143
Tatopani to Pokhara via Baglung p166
Ghorepani to Ghandruk and Chomrong p171
Birethanti to Ghandruk and Chomrong p172
Chomrong to the Annapurna Sanctuary p180
Chomrong to Pokhara via Landruk and Dhampus p187
Dumre to the Thorung La p191
Gorkha to Besisahar p222
Pokhara to Khudi via Begnas Tal p226
The Sikles Trek p237

ROUTE MAPS

Scale and walking times

These maps are drawn to an approximate scale of 18mm to one km (about one inch to one mile) but with so many hills and valleys these measurements are actually of little use to the trekker. Time taken to cover the distance is of far greater interest, although this does vary considerably from person to person. Walking times are given along the side of each map and the arrow shows the direction to which the walking time refers. Black triangles point to the villages between which the times apply. Note that **the time given refers only to time spent actually walking,** so you will need to add 20-30% to allow for rest stops. When planning the day's trekking, count on between four and six hours actual walking. Give yourself rest days and allow days for acclimatisation.

Up or down?
The trail is shown as a dotted line. An arrow across the trail indicates a slope; two arrows show that it is steep. Note that the arrow points towards the higher part of the trail. If, for example, you were walking from A (at 900m) to B (at 1100m) and the trail between the two were short and steep, it would be shown thus: A - - - >> - - - B.

Lodges and tea houses
Lodges are marked as black squares on the maps and their names are also given. Some lodges are mentioned in the text but you should not take this to mean that if a lodge isn't mentioned it's not worth staying at. You must expect changes since new lodges are springing up every few months; older lodges change hands and are often given new names, too. The other trekkers you meet on the trail are the most up to date source of information as to which are the best places to stay or eat.

Tea houses are marked with a 'T'. It's often also possible to stay at them, although accommodation is generally much more basic than at a lodge.

Village names and other symbols
Village names may be transliterated in a number of ways. The variants are given in the text, the most common option being used on the map. Altitudes are given in metres on the maps and also in feet in the text. Places where you can get water are shown by a 'W' within a circle. Post offices are marked 'PO', in the same style.

Pokhara to Ghorepani

POKHARA TO BIRETHANTI
[MAPS 1-2, p139, p140]

● **The direct route** Take a bus or taxi from Pokhara (see p133) 41km to Naya-pul. Walk down to the river from the road and use the stepping stones to cross it unless the bridge has been repaired.

It's then a very pleasant 20-minute walk to Birethanti with a wonderful view of Machhapuchhre before you.

● **The old route** Before the Pokhara-Baglung-Beni road was built it was a long day's trek from Pokhara to Birethanti. From the Shining Hospital in the north of Pokhara you made the hot three-hour walk past the Tibetan village at Hyange and across the fields of the Yamdi Khola Valley to Phedi. A stiff climb of 1½ hours brought you up to Naudanda and from here it was a further three hours' walk through Khare and Lumle to Chandrakot, perched above Birethanti. The new road has effectively ruined this first part of the trek but it's still possible to walk it. Alternatively, you could get off at Lumle, from where it's a peaceful two-hour walk to Birethanti via Chandrakot.

Many of the lodges in the villages that lie along the road have now closed down. There's a *lodge* and *tea house* in

Phedi (1130m/3707ft) – the name means 'bottom of the hill'. The views from **Naudanda (1430m/4692ft)** above it are still good and if you want to stay here the best place is *View Top Lodge & Restaurant*, on the hill at the western edge of the village. This is an excellent place to come to watch the sun rise over the stunning mountain panorama.

The road bypasses **Lumle (1610m 5282ft)** and at the southern end of the town not far from the road is the *Lumle Guest House*. Lumle is famous for the fact that it has the country's highest annual average rainfall and, no doubt as a result of this, it is the home of the nationally famous Lumle Agricultural Centre. The project was started as part of a British aid programme and currently employs more than 300 people.

Only a few of the lodges in **Chandrakot (1580m/5183ft)** are still operating now. Trinket-sellers display their wares by the tree at the northern edge of the village. One tea shop has erected a small platform here from which its customers can admire the superb mountain views up the Modi Khola towards the Annapurna Sanctuary. A steep trail drops down to Birethanti.

● **Alternative route via Sarangkot** If you want to walk all the way from Pokhara, rather than going along the road from the Shining Hospital it's more interesting to go via Sarangkot. Follow the main road along Lakeside north until it

---

❏ **Chautara**

Constructed at convenient points along the main trails in Nepal and in every town and village, you'll find these stone resting platforms. Although paid for and maintained by a philanthropic local, chautara are much more than the Nepalese equivalent of a park bench. They are designed with ledges just the right height off the ground for porters to rest their loads.

Trees are planted in the middle of the chautara to provide shade. In the subtropical climatic zone, these are two sacred trees, the banyan (easily identifiable by the roots that trail down from its branches) and the pipal, symbolising the female and male, respectively. They stand side by side in 'wedlock'. In the village, the chautara is an open air community hall where people congregate to hear the latest gossip.

becomes a path on the north shore of the lake (see map, p118). After 20-30 minutes it leaves the lake and climbs to a small plain before continuing steeply upwards.

There's a confusing number of paths here so you should ask directions frequently although it's difficult to get lost as Sarangkot is at the top of this hill, overlooking the Pokhara Valley. It may take you anything up to three hours to reach the village since this is probably your first day trekking. If you're coming down, Sarangkot to Lakeside takes at least an hour.

In **Sarangkot** there are several lodges and superb views of Pokhara below. From Sarangkot the path follows the ridge to **Kaskikot**, 1'/₂-2 hours beyond. It was the old capital of the region. There are more lodges fifteen minutes further on at **Kaskikot Deurali**. Continue along the ridge for just over an hour to reach Naudanda.

Birethanti (1050m/3449ft)

Across a big bridge, by the confluence of the Bhurungdi Khola and the Modi Khola, lies this large bazaar village. It's a pleasant enough place but, being so close to Pokhara, it receives more than its fair share of tourists. It's now even got an 'Art Gallery' although all the paintings here are for sale.

Register with the **ACAP office** just across the bridge. This apparent bureaucracy you'll be asked to do several times on the trek but it is essential practice since, if you go missing, the search party will have some idea of where to look. You can also get your ACAP entry permit (Rs1000) here if you haven't already bought it. They also sell iodine tablets.

Although there are several good places to stay here, you should be aware that the hardest section on the Pokhara to Jomsom trek is the 1200m/4000ft climb from Tikhedunga to Ghorepani. Since it's really worthwhile spending a night at Ghorepani for the views at dawn from nearby Poon Hill, and since Birethanti to Ghorepani is either one very long or two rather short days' walking, you may pre-fer to press on to Hille or Tikhedunga where there are numerous lodges.

Accommodation The top place to stay in town is the impressive *Laxmi Lodge*, built by British poet, Dominic Sasse, who was tragically killed in the PIA air crash near Kathmandu in 1992. Efficiently presided over by Bugle Major, many of the employees here are ex-Gurkhas. As well as providing luxury accommodation for wealthy trekkers, the lodge operates a charity that helps improve local health care and develop reforestation programmes in the area.

In the tourist season Laxmi Lodge provides accommodation for Foreign Window clients but, if there is room, independent trekkers can stay here (see Rs600/800 for a single/double room) in comfortable bedrooms with sheets and blankets on the beds. The bathrooms are spotless; the loos sparkle like the set for a Harpic ad. There's a large sitting and dining room with a central fireplace, a well-stocked library and a photo of Bugle Major meeting Prince Charles.

For budget travellers the *New Gurkha Lodge* has high standards of hygiene, and good food, for a fraction of the price of the Laxmi. For Western fare the *Hotel Sunrise* is a better choice and even lists whole grilled chicken on its menu. The *Riverside Lodge* has a pleasant dining area by the river. Over the bridge, the *Fishtail Lodge* is quieter, as is the *Green View*, at the opposite end of the village. The *German Restaurant & Bakery* sells trekking snacks like cinnamon rolls (Rs25) and apple muffins (Rs40).

Other services You can cash travellers' cheques at the **bank** (open Sunday to Thursday, 10.00-14.30 and on Friday until 12.30). There's a **post office** and several well-stocked shops.

A 10-15 minute walk along the Ghorepani trail brings you to a waterfall with a **pool**, a pleasant place to swim if it's hot enough; but you should be discreet and wear a swimsuit.

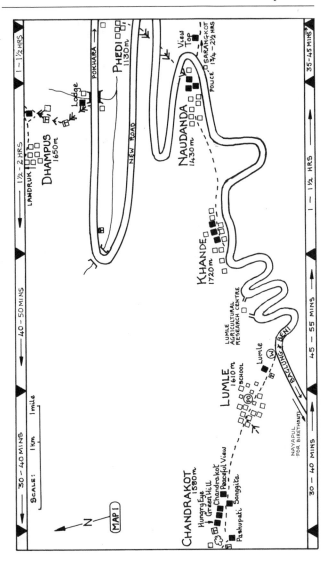

MAP 1

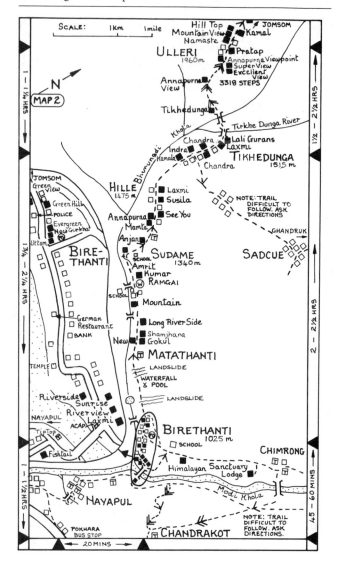

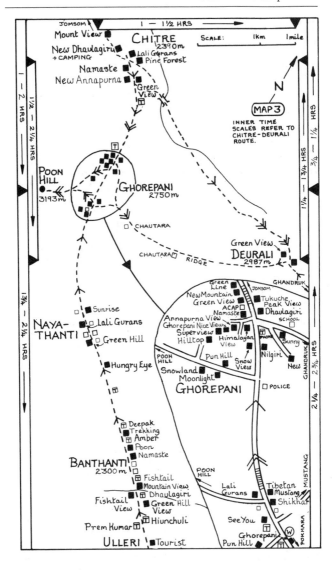

BIRETHANTI TO ULLERI
[MAP 2: p140]

The trail to Hille climbs gently and is easy to follow although landslides cause occasional detours. There are two suspension bridges across the Bhurungdi Khola which you should pass by.

Many new lodges and tea shops have opened on this stretch of the trail, particularly at the settlements of Ramgai and Sudame.

Hille (1500m/4921ft) and Tikhedunga (1540m/5052ft)

There are six lodges in Hille and about 15 minutes beyond you reach Tikhedunga with another six lodges. They're all fairly similar. Most places boast hot showers and extensive menus. In between the two bridges the *Tirke Dunga River Lodge* even boasts its own swimming pool. A short walk beyond the village brings you to the *Tikhedunga Guest House*, in a peaceful location.

The stone staircase

After the last suspension bridge in Tikhedunga, 3280 stone steps stand between you and the breathtaking views from Ulleri. It's best to pace yourself, climbing 500 steps or so at a time, then stopping to admire the view and remind yourself that trekking is not a race.

After 2000 steps you reach *Annapurna View Guest House*, and Annapurna South is indeed visible from here. It's a pleasant place to stay but most people pause only for a drink.

Ulleri (2070m/6791ft)

This pretty but not exactly spotless slate-roofed village is largely comprised of Magar people. They are Tibeto-Burman in origin and, as well as being skilled craftsmen in stone and wood, constitute the largest Nepali sub-group serving in Gurkha regiments abroad. In spite of having high earning husbands, many Magar women are financially independent through their involvement with the rug-weaving trade.

The reward for scaling the 3280 steps to reach Ulleri is good views of Annapurna South and Hiun Chuli, as well as the Bhurungdi Valley below. Many lodge owners have situated their dining areas to take advantage of the scenery.

Fifteen minutes beyond the village, on a chautara near a tea shop, is a memorial to the young son of an anthropologist who died here in 1961: 'Benjamin Jeninis Hitchcock, Benbahadur. Once sweet bright joy, like their lost children an Ulleri child'. The inscription on the stone is faded but you can still read it.

ULLERI TO GHOREPANI
[MAP 3: p141]
Banthanti (2300m/7546ft)

The trail climbs less steeply now, and you soon encounter the first few lodges of the elongated settlement of **Banthanti**. There are several places to stay here.

After the last lodge, the rhododendron forest begins. Spectacular in March and April when the whole hillside is cloaked in blossom, during the monsoon it's more renowned as a haven for millions of leeches. It's not a good idea to walk alone here as trekkers have been robbed in the forest surrounding Ghorepani.

Ghorepani (2750m/9022ft)

To watch the sun rise across a spectacular Himalayan panorama from the summit of Poon Hill, 450m/1475ft above this village is the main reason for coming up here. This famous dawn pilgrimage has brought tens of thousands of trekkers to Ghorepani, with disastrous consequences for the surrounding rhododendron forests. ACAP made the village an early focus for their conservation measures, moving the

---

❏ **Walking times on trail maps**
Note that on all the trail maps in this book the times shown alongside each map refer only to time spent actually walking. Add 20-30% to allow for rest stops.

lodges down from the hill and persuading many of the lodge-owners to install back-boilers.

Accommodation The lodges of Ghorepani are in two groups. The first group is below the ridge in the older part of the town where the water troughs that gave the village its name ('place for watering horses') are still used by the mule trains. The *Tibetan Mustang* is a pleasant place here.

Most trekkers, however, choose to climb the 200m further to Ghorepani Deurali (Pass) where the main part of the village, and most of the lodges, are situated. Many of the lodges here are fancy affairs with view towers and large dining areas. Single/double rooms are Rs60/100 but lodges charge Rs200-300 for accommodation if you choose not to eat in their restaurant.

The *Super View* and *Snowland* lodges have both been recommended. They're at the top of the village.

Moonlight attracts customers with its extensive menu that includes Royal Pun Hill Special chicken (Rs260).

A little quieter than these places is *Sunny Lodge*, which also has a bookshop.

Other services You must stop at the **police checkpost** to sign the book here. The **ACAP office** has information on current projects in the area.

Poon Hill (3193m/10,476ft) The wooden partitions in the lodges here are thin and you'll be woken long before sunrise by the sounds of trekkers preparing for the pre-dawn assault on Poon Hill. If the sky is clear you should join them; if it's heavily overcast go back to sleep.

You may meet several people with the surname 'Poon' in the area; the Poons are a large Magar family and the hill was named after them. Take great care on the path up the hill as it can be slippery in places and you could lose your footing in the half light. It takes about 45 minutes to climb to the top.

The views are literally breathtaking, a wide Himalayan panorama stretching from Dhaulagiri (8167m/26,794ft and the world's seventh highest peak) to Manaslu (8156m/26,758ft, the eighth highest) in the east, with the Annapurna range between them.

Route to Ghandruk and Chomrong see p171.

Ghorepani to Jomsom/Muktinath

GHOREPANI TO TATOPANI [MAPS 3-4: p141 & p145]
The trail out of Ghorepani drops steeply down through the rhododendron forest into the Kali Gandaki Valley, which you follow all the way to Jomsom. There are good views of the solid lump that is Dhaulagiri as you descend and no need to hurry since you will probably want to spend the night in Tatopani (about five hours from Ghorepani) and soothe your aching limbs in the hot springs there.

There are tea shops strung out along the whole of this route but **Chitre (2350m/7710ft)** is the first village you come to. There are several lodges and in the middle of the village is a junction with the path to Ghandruk via Deurali (see p171). *Mount View* is a large place that often has tour groups camping beside it. The smaller lodges can be much more welcoming.

Chitre merges into the village of **Phalate/Phalante (2270m/7448ft)** and after about 90 minutes of walking past small farm buildings and over the occasional landslide, you arrive at the more substantial settlement of **Sikha/Sauta (2000m/6562ft)**. The higher part of the village is known as Sikha Deurali, the lower simply Sikha. There are numerous lodges.

Soon after **Ghara (1700m/5577ft)** you come to a lookout point where the

Santosh Hill Top Restaurant can supply you with liquid refreshment while you admire the views up and down the valley.

A steep descent brings you down to the Kali Gandaki and the junction with the path to Jomsom to the right, and Baglung to the left. There's an **ACAP office** here.

Cross the bridge over the Ghara Khola and, shortly afterwards, a second bridge over the Kali Gandaki.

A major landslide in September 1998 has flooded the trail into Tatopani and partly dammed the river. You now need to take a steep detour up and down the hill. It takes about 40 minutes to reach Tatopani.

▲ Tatopani to Ghorepani If you're following this section in the opposite direction you should be aware that much of this stiff climb is not through forests (unlike the Ghorepani-Ulleri path) and can be very hot. It's worth making an early start from Tatopani.

Tatopani (1190m/3904ft) [Map 5: p147]

The name means 'hot springs' and these, with the sub-tropical gardens of this little riverside village, have been attracting trekkers since the 1960s. Even though it's getting touristy now, and the architectural merits of some of the new hotels leave a lot to be desired, it's still a mellow place to stay especially outside the main trekking season.

The village is a meeting-point for Magars and Gurungs from the south and Thakalis from the north. Some of the lodges here are run by Thakalis (see p155), accomplished hoteliers who have been catering to the needs of foreign travellers along this trading route to Tibet for several hundred years.

Accommodation When the owner of the *Dhaulagiri Lodge* married the French doctor from the health post this place soon became the best place to eat for miles around, although it already had an excellent reputation for its food. They're still running it and there's a beautiful garden with tables and chairs set out amongst the tangerine trees and flowering plants, and views up the valley to Nilgiri South Peak. At the *Trekkers' Lodge*, however, the food's also excellent and there's a peaceful garden, too. The *Old Kamala* has some good rooms set above it.

The modern *Hotel Himalaya* is a real eyesore but it does serve excellent Indian food and the rooms (some with bathrooms attached) can be good value compared to those in trekking lodges.

For a really cheap meal try the *Momo Restaurant* next to the phone office. Eight momos cost Rs30.

Other services There's a **police checkpost** as you enter the village from the south. You can change money at the **bank** or with the **moneychanger**. There are several shops (some of which operate a book exchange). There's also a **telephone** office.

At the northern end of the village is **Baba Multyservice**. Baba offers every-

---

❏ Tatopani souvenir

Rather than an 'I Love Tatopani' T-shirt, you could have a pair of earrings handmade for you by the gold- and silver-smiths who have their workshops in Tatopani. In Nepal gold, like hashish, is measured in tolas (one tola being about 11.5g) and there is a standard rate which corresponds to the price on the world market.

A large pair of Nepalese-style earrings weighing about half a tola would cost £45-70/US$75-110 – a lot of money, maybe but a unique and lasting souvenir. Wearing Nepalese earrings helps bridge the cultural gap between Nepali and foreign women and a gold pair will be admired by every Nepali woman you meet.

Cassie Cleeve (Australia)

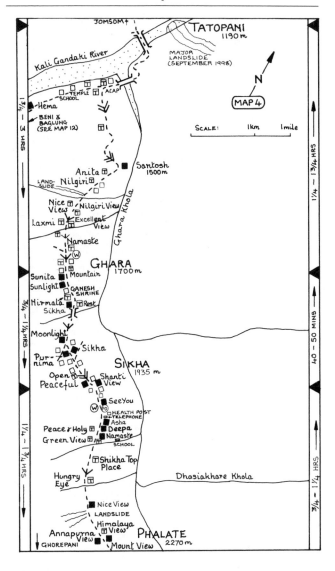

thing from a massage or a shave to a guided tour round the Annapurna Circuit.

Tatopani now has electricity from the micro-hydro scheme upriver.

Hot springs The main spring is by the river, just below the Dhaulagiri Lodge. There are a couple of pools and they can be incredibly hot. The river, on the other hand can be painfully cold. Try to borrow a bowl from the lodge if you want to have a pleasant wash and don't pollute the spring or river with soap and shampoo, even if this is what the local people are doing. During the trekking season the pools are regularly cleaned and a small charge (Rs5) is made.

If the river is low you can get to the second spring just to the north of the village but it's very small, often not much more than a trickle.

About 30 minutes downstream, along the trail to Baglung, there's another hot spring, with a pool right by the river, below Hema Guest House (see Map 12, p167).

TATOPANI TO RUPSE CHHAHARA [MAP 5: p147]

Following the Kali Gandaki north you pass **Jhatare** and just above it you go through a small tunnel, the only one on the trek. In many places along this trail you can see older paths cut high into the rock that are now disused following the landslides that frequently occur in this unstable region.

A bridge leads over the river to the Tatopani Small Hydel Project, a micro-hydroelectric scheme that was financed by Saudi Arabia.

Dana (1400m/4593ft)

In the centre of the town several impressive houses with delicately carved windows indicate that Dana was once a place of some importance. It was, in fact, the capital of Mustang District until the early 1970s, when Jomsom succeeded it. In the days when Tibetan caravans brought salt through Dana from the deserts of Western Tibet it was an important trading town

and a collection point for salt taxes. The customs post closed in 1931.

Amongst the old merchants' houses look out for a building known locally as the **Bardali Ghar**, which has a splendid carved window. It's probably the finest piece of wood-carving in the region and was moved to this house in the 1940s. It's said to have been made from over 100 pieces of teak and assembled in the traditional way without using nails. It dates from the early part of this century.

Dana is still quite a big place and there are a number of lodges here. *Dana Guest House*, to the south of the town, is a pleasant place to stay.

As recently as the 1950s the trail to the north was said to have been frequented by robbers, according to Giuseppe Tucci who passed through Dana on his way to Lo Manthang in 1952.

About an hour and a half to the north, *Rupse Lodge* is recommended. The rooms are spotlessly clean and the food good. The waterfall at **Rupse Chhahara (1600m/5249ft)** is particularly impressive during or just after the monsoon. There are several water-powered mills grinding corn beside the river.

The *Waterfall Lodge* here is highly recommended by those who don't mind the sound of roaring water all night. It's clean and friendly. A cryptic note advises 'Life is Uncertain; Eat Dessert First'! Believe it: they sell excellent home-baked cakes; 'the best chocolate cake on the trek'.

RUPSE CHHAHARA TO LETE [MAP 6: p149]

The new bridge should be completed soon. There are frequent landslides in the area so take great care if you still have to take a detour on the steep east bank trail: higher up is a memorial to a young trekker who slipped off the path here in 1994.

Passing through fields of marijuana, you reach **Kopche Pani,** a grubby village set amongst grey boulders. Climbing high above the landslide (the path is set higher each year as more of the hillside falls

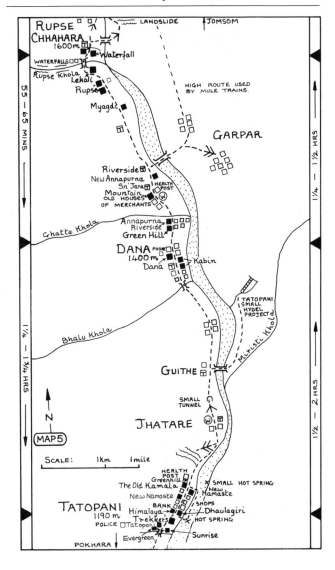

away) a welcoming signpost alerts you to the fact that you're now in the district of Mustang. Soon after there's the *Bimala Lodge* run by a very friendly family; the father speaks excellent English. It's an entertaining place to stop for lunch or to spend the night.

Ghasa/Gansa (2010m/6594ft)

Crossing the big suspension bridge and climbing up to join the west-bank trail, you come into the long village of Ghasa.

This region is both a cultural and geographical watershed. You're now in the lower reaches of Thak Khola, the area inhabited by the Thakalis (see p155). The climate is cooler than in Tatopani and there are pine trees here. Rainfall is lower and this is reflected in the Tibetan-style flat-roofed houses you begin to see in Ghasa. The Thakalis are Buddhist and just past the Solo Restaurant there are two chortens in the middle of the trail. As with all Buddhist monuments you should pass to the left of these. At the northern end of Ghasa you go through a large entrance gate that is typical of the Thakali villages to the north.

Sign the book at the **police checkpoint** in the centre of the village.

Many of the lodges sell apricot brandy which comes from the distilleries in Tukuche and Marpha. There's also pumpkin soup on the menus and some lodges sell nak cheese.

The *Eagle's Nest* is the first lodge in the south of the village and a good place to stay. The rostis here are recommended and they also have bread rolls and chocolate cake.

The *Kali Gandaki Guest House & Solo Restaurant* has a beautiful garden full of fruit trees and a well decorated dining room where they serve excellent food. *The New Florida Guest House* at the northern end of the village, is a pleasant place with views down the valley. Next door, the *National* is similar.

Climbing gently through forests of pine you reach *Green Forest Guest House*, in a peaceful location. Across the river is a massive landslide.

The trail detours around landslide to reach the bridge over the Lete Khola. The *Namaste Guest House* is craftily located to gather in those who cannot face the stiff but short climb up to Lete. It's not a bad place, though, and there are solar water heaters.

❑ Bagh Chal

Also known as Tigers and Goats (the Nepali name translates as 'Moving the Tigers'), Bagh Chal is rather like draughts. Tigers move along the lines on the board killing the goats by jumping over them. Attractive brass boards and pieces are sold in the tourist shops but the game can be played just as well with a 'board' drawn out in the dust and different sized stones to represent the four tigers and twenty goats.

The rules There are two players. The player who is the tiger places them on the four corners of the board. The other player puts one goat on the board and play commences with one tiger being moved and then one goat being placed on the board. No goat may move until all the pieces are on the board. When a tiger is beside a goat and there is a space on the other side of it the tiger may jump over it, removing it from the board. They may, however, only follow the straight lines. The art to defending the goats is obviously to try to ensure that they can never be jumped, by giving the tigers no open point on which to land.

The game is won by the tigers as soon as they have removed five of the goats; and by the goats if they can encircle all the tigers to stop them from moving.

Rosemary Higgs (Nepal)

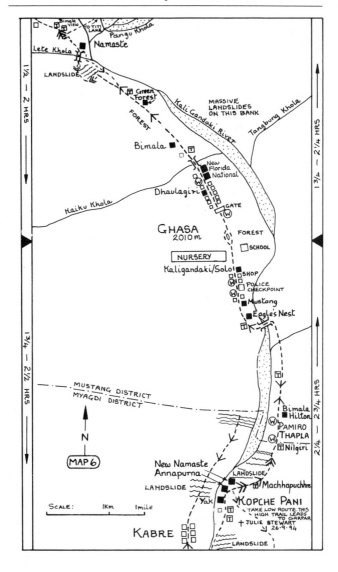

LETE TO LARJUNG [MAP 7: p151]
Lete (2480m/8136ft) and Kalopani (2530m/8300ft)

This is really just one long village with Lete at the southern end, Kalopani to the north with the houses, many more of which are now flat-roofed, strung out between the two.

The views of Annapurna I (8091m/ 26,545ft) are good from here but even better if you climb for about 30-40 minutes behind the school. If it's a cloudless evening, don't miss sunset on this magnificent peak.

If you're not short of time it would be worth spending a few nights here and making the pleasant day trip to **Titi Lake**, east of Lete. Ask for directions at your lodge.

Accommodation

The spotless *Pine Forest Lodge* is operated by polite trainee tourism workers from the Technical School opposite. In the restaurant you're served by enthusiastic waiters in uniform and the beds have *two* sheets and blankets. Fawlty Towers but fun, it's well worth the Rs125 for a double room. Beds in the dorm are Rs50. There are two rooms with attached, Western-style bathrooms. It's closed during school holidays.

The other lodges here are all good perhaps because, except during the high season, competition between them is intense. Their advertising placards line the trail. *Lete Guest House* has a table

with a charcoal-filled foot-warmer beneath it, an innovation shared by the other lodges. It's a very pleasant way to keep warm on a cold evening. At the northern end of the village, the *Kalopani Guest House* has solar heated showers and double rooms with attached bath for Rs300.

Other services There's a small **post office**, a government **health post**, a **police checkpost**, a **telephone office** and a **kerosene depot** (Rs19 per litre). Electricity should reach Kalopani in mid-1999.

From Kalopani to Larjung there are two trails: the marginally shorter but busier east bank trail which all the mule caravans take and the quieter west bank route.

On the west bank trail you pass a memorial to the five Americans and two Nepalis who died in an avalanche while climbing Dhaulagiri in 1969. Crossing the Ghatte Khola (the start of the route to the Dhaulagiri Ice-fall described below) you reach Larjung 20 minutes beyond. Note where local people walk to ford the Ghatte Khola if you don't want to get your feet wet.

It's at around this point, the bend in the river between Kalopani and Larjung, that you're at the bottom of the **world's deepest valley**. The two highest peaks in the area, Dhaulagiri (8167m/26,794ft) and Annapurna I (8091m/26,545ft) are 35 kms (22 miles) apart on either side of the

---

❏ Side trip to Dhaulagiri Ice-fall

The climb up to the ridge that faces the glacier below Dhaulagiri is very worthwhile for the tremendous views back across the Kali Gandaki towards the Annapurnas. Maurice Herzog must have followed part of this route when trying to find a way up Dhaulagiri in 1950.

The return trip from Larjung can be done in a day but you should make a very early start at around dawn. The route, shown on Map 7 (p151), can be tricky to follow at first but once you've reached the yak pasture, it's basically uphill all the way: a total altitude gain of about 1200m/4000ft.

Although you should feel nothing more than a little lightheadedness at this altitude you should read the information on AMS (p240) and don't try to spend the night up here with the yaks unless you, like them, are already acclimatised.

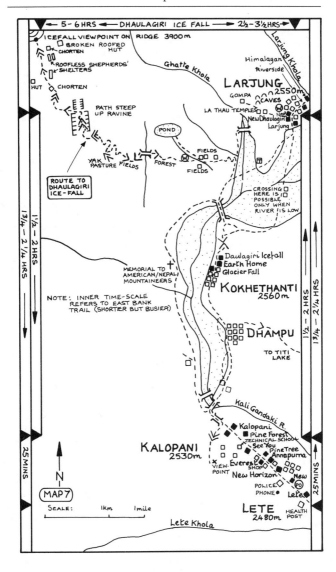

← 5-6 HRS ← DHAULAGIRI ICE FALL → 2½-3½HRS →

ICEFALL VIEWPOINT ON RIDGE 3900m
BROKEN ROOFED HUT
CHORTEN
ROOFLESS SHEPHERDS' SHELTERS
HUT   CHORTEN

Larjung Khola

Ghatte Khola

Himalayan Riverside

LARJUNG
2550m
GOMPA   CAVES
LA THAU TEMPLES
New Dhaulagiri
Larjung

PATH STEEP UP RAVINE

POND

FIELDS

YAK PASTURE   FIELDS   FOREST
FIELDS

ROUTE TO DHAULAGIRI ICE-FALL

CROSSING HERE IS POSSIBLE ONLY WHEN RIVER IS LOW

MEMORIAL TO AMERICAN/NEPALI MOUNTAINEERS

Daulagiri Icefall
Earth Home
Glacier Fall

KOKHETHANTI
2560m

NOTE: INNER TIME-SCALE REFERS TO EAST BANK TRAIL (SHORTER BUT BUSIER)

DHAMPU

TO TITI LAKE

Kali Gandaki R.

Kalopani
Pine Forest
TECHNICAL SCHOOL
See You   PineTree
Annapurna
VIEW. Everest SHOP
POINT   New Horizon   New
POLICE
PHONE   Lete
HEALTH POST

KALOPANI
2530m

LETE
2480m

N

MAP 7

SCALE: 1km   1mile

Lete Khola

1½ - 2 HRS
13/4 - 2¼ HRS
25 MINS

1½ - 2 HRS
13/4 - 2¼ HRS
25 MINS

valley. You're standing at an altitude of about 2540m/ 8333ft, which is 5¹/₂ km or 3¹/₂ miles below the summit of Dhaulagiri.

Larjung (2550m/8366ft)

Larjung and Khobang are separated by only a stream and a few fields but are, in fact, two different communities. It's well worth stopping here for two nights so that you can do the side trip to Dhaulagiri Ice-Fall (see p150).

Larjung is a place of religious and ancestral significance for Tamang Thakalis since the masks of the presiding deities of the Tulachan and Sherchan clans are kept in the Lha Thau temples just above the village. A major festival, the Lha Phewa ('the Appearance of the Gods'), takes place every 12 years in honour of the deities (next due at the end of 2005). The masks are taken out of the temple and paraded through surrounding villages in 17 days of music, dancing and hard drinking. Above Larjung are the abandoned caves once inhabited by Buddhist monks on retreat. Some are very difficult to get to and there's little to see in those you can reach.

The *New Riverside Lodge* is the cleanest place, the *Larjung Lodge* the friendliest, while also selling provisions. Their Wall Drop Salad (Rs70) has been on the menu for many years. You can also get sea buckthorn juice (Rs30) here. If there have been any changes to the route up to the Dhaulagiri ice-fall you may find some thoughtful trekker has left updated directions pinned to the wall here.

KHOBANG TO TUKUCHE
[MAP 8: p153]
Khobang (2560m/8399ft)

The trail through Khobang was once one long tunnel under the stone houses but this is rather less impressive now.

High above the village is the **Mahalaxmi Temple** where the image of the goddess receives daily ablutions of milk mixed with water from the Kali Gandaki. It's difficult to find anyone to let you in if you wish to see the temple. Down by the river, however, the temple at the **Makilakhang nunnery** is usually open and interesting to look round. The nuns live in the small house beside it and will open the door if it's locked. Be sure to leave a donation if you visit.

There are three pleasant lodges in Khobang, the *Peaceful Guest House* in particular is recommended for being just that. *Sunflower Lodge* is a friendly little place. If your boots are giving out there's a helpful **shoe-repairing** man by the trail. There's also a **health post**.

If the river is low, the trail to Tukuche is along the wide riverbed. Watch which way local people are going if you don't want to get your feet wet.

You're now in an arid region that extends far north into Tibet. Each day pressure differences above the land to the north and to the south cause a fierce wind that begins sometimes as early as 8.30 am but usually not until around 10 am and it continues for much of the day. The wind usually blows up the valley from south to north so it's not really a problem if you're walking in this direction. The locals say that if the wind first blows down the valley then up on one day, it will start later the next day.

Tukuche/Tukche (2590m/8497ft)

When Professor Tucci stopped in Tukuche (pronounced 'Tugcha') in 1952 on his way to Lo Manthang, he noted huge warehouses filled with wool, salt and turquoise from Tibet and grain, rice, cloth, cigarettes and European goods which were bartered for the Tibetan supplies. By then the trade had, in fact, begun to wane since Indian salt had become available, popular not only because it was cheaper but also because it contained iodine. The diet of most people in Nepal had until then lacked this vital mineral and consequently many suffered from goitres. When the Chinese invaded Tibet, trade declined further and some Thakalis moved out of Tukuche and the region to operate businesses in other parts of Nepal. Tourism has now brought some people back to the town.

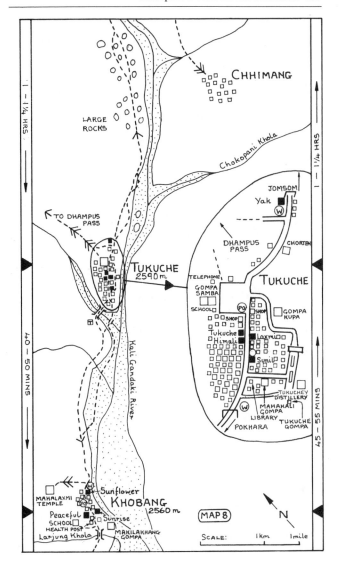

CHHIMANG

LARGE
ROCKS

Chokopani Khola

1 – 1¼ HRS

1 – 1¼ HRS

TO DHAMPUS
PASS

JOMSOM

Yak
W

DHAMPUS
PASS

CHORTEN

TUKUCHE
2590 m.

TELEPHONE

TUKUCHE

GOMPA
SAMBA

SCHOOL

PO

SHOP

SHOP

GOMPA
KUPA

Tukuche
Himali

Laxmi

40 – 50 MINS

Suni

45 – 55 MINS

Kali Gandaki River

TUKUCHEY
DISTILLERY

W

MAHAKALI
GOMPA

LIBRARY

POKHARA

TUKUCHE
GOMPA

MAHALAXMI
TEMPLE

W

Sunflower

KHOBANG
2560 m.

MAP 8

Peaceful
SCHOOL

HEALTH POST

Sunrise

N

Larjung Khola

MAKILAKHANG
GOMPA

SCALE: 1km   1mile

Today Tukuche's warehouses have crumbled away and the wind whistles through ruined buildings on the outskirts of the town. The grand façades of the houses that line the main street still give some indication of the former wealth of the inhabitants. Richest were the Sherchan clan, who held the monopoly on the salt trade. Their position was recognised by the government in the 19th century when the hereditary post of *subha* (tax collector) was granted to a member of their family. As well as having business interests in other parts of the country the family still operates the successful Tukchey Distillery from their mansion to the south of the town.

It's worth spending more than just a night in Tukuche as there are several pleasant day hikes in the area, including Yak Kharka, Shyokong Lake and Buddha Lake. Lodge owners can give directions.

Accommodation The most pleasant lodges in Tukuche are those in the centre: large houses formerly owned by rich merchants. They're built in the classic Thakali style, flat-roofed and around a courtyard to give protection from the wind.

Tukuche is excellent and has some sunny roof-top rooms, as is *Sunil* which claims to offer 'the most variation in apple deserts on the Annapurna Circuit'. But they all offer the traditional high standard of Thakali hospitality: extensive menus, hot showers, and tables with footwarmers beneath them. To the north of the town there's the *Yak Hotel* with a very pleasant solarium and an old and dusty stuffed yak in the dining room.

Other services There's a **post office** and several shops selling the powerful products of the Tuckchey Distillery. A **telephone office** opened recently.

Gompas When David Snellgrove (who wrote *Himalayan Pilgrimage* after research into Buddhism in this area) visited Tukuche in 1956 he remarked that this was the first town where he encountered hostile incomprehension to his questions. Most of these well-travelled traders wanted to have nothing to do with what they seemed to regard as a primitive religion. The lama of Gompa Samba had little interest in his calling but, like all Thakalis, was a skilled trader. 'How can I act as a lama if no one believes in me?', he complained while selling Snellgrove a toothbrush. DS would no doubt be pleased to know that one monastery, **Gompa Kupa (Kyipar)**, is flourishing today, with a lama and 12 monks. It was relocated to its more central position in 1984. The wall-paintings in the temple are by Shashi Dhoj Tulachan and worth seeing. Visitors are welcome.

The other three temples are no longer operating as monasteries and are rather run down but they can be visited if you can find someone to let you in. **Gompa Samba** contains dusty statues and the best wall-paintings (depicting the sixteen arhats, Sakyamuni's disciples). The key is kept by the people in the house next door.

Near the Tukchey Distillery, there's **Mahakali Gompa**, renamed after the Hindu goddess although it was originally dedicated to the three Buddhas of the past, present and future. Five minutes to the south of the town is the dilapidated **Rani Gompa**.

Tukchey Distillery Kalpana Sherchan runs the distillery in her 200 year old family home and explains the distillation process to visitors. It was started by her husband who studied the process overseas, had all the equipment carried into Tukuche by porters and ponies and then promptly died. Mrs Sherchan 'cried for six months' and then decided she'd have to make a go of it so left Nepal to do the same course as her husband and has now turned his idea into a thriving business. Having trained in Japan, her son is now taking over the business.

About 10,000 litres of alcohol are produced here annually, 80% of it being apple brandy. She also produces peach, orange and apricot brandy with most products in two strengths: 40% and 30%.

They're all something of an acquired taste but certainly warm you up. Market research reveals that passing Scots and French go for the higher strengths, the rest of us can manage only the weaker. They also produce apple cider (7-8% proof), rather like the rough scrumpy you can buy on Devon farms.

The house itself is interesting, being over 200 years old and even has its own private temple in a room upstairs. On his travels in 1899-1902, Ekai Kawaguchi stayed here. His servants 'having regaled themselves with the local drinks even to boisterousness, began a-quarelling', and had to be discharged, having revealed their plans to murder and rob the Japanese monk at the first opportunity.

The distillery is closed for tastings between December and February but you can still stop by to regale yourself with the local drinks.

TUKUCHE TO JOMSOM
[MAP 9: p157]

The trail north continues through a rocky area all set about with sage and juniper bushes.

Chhairo

Off the main trail and across the bridge is an old gompa and this Tibetan refugee

---

❏ The Thakalis

Wherever you're travelling in Nepal, you can almost always be sure of a warm welcome, a comfortable bed and good food at a Thakali inn. Known throughout the country as accomplished hoteliers and skilled traders, the Thakali people are of Tibetan origin but have their own language and customs. They're essentially Buddhists, although some have converted to Hinduism.

The Jomsom trek passes right through Thak Khola, the Thakali homeland which extends from just south of Jomsom down to Ghasa. Thak Khola is divided into two geographical areas: Panchagaon (the 'five villages' which comprise Marpha, Chhairo, Chhimang, Syang and Thimi) and Thakali Thasang (also known as Thak Satsae, the '700 houses', the southern region which extends from Tukuche to Ghasa).

The Thakalis who come from the southern region consider themselves to be the true Thakalis, since Tukuche, for years the dominant town in the area, lies within their borders. They refer to themselves as Tamang Thakalis and are divided into four clans, each with its own presiding animal deity and colour: Gauchan (elephant, red), Tulachan (dragon, blue/green), Sherchan (lioness, white) and Bhattachan (yak, black).

The people of Marpha (known as Mawatans) are also divided into four clans: Lalchan (meaning 'ruby'), Hirachan ('diamond'), Juharchan ('jewel') and Pannachan ('emerald') but they don't acknowledge any particular deity as their own.

The Thakalis are one of the richer groups of people in Nepal, having monopolised the trade route that follows the Kali Gandaki for several centuries. With the demise of this ancient route when the Chinese invaded Tibet, many Thakalis moved their businesses to other parts of the country.

Tourism and the development of new crops have given a significant boost to Thak Khola over the past 25 years. As well as the traditional crops of buckwheat and millet, potatoes, barley, turnips and orchards of apple, peach and apricot trees have been established with considerable success, introduced by the experimental farm near Marpha. Tourism has further boosted Thak Khola and the accommodating Thakalis have converted their *bhattis*, which used to provide food and lodging for traders, into comfortable little trekking hotels.

village. You'll probably have encountered some of the persuasive saleswomen from here already.

The **Sanga Choling Temple**, in the centre of the gompa, was built in the eighteenth century and still contains a three metre statue of Padmasambhava. In 1956, David Snellgrove reported that the temple was very well kept, tended by one lama, but was otherwise deserted. Unfortunately, in 1990 many of the smaller statues were stolen, no doubt to be sold to foreign collectors, a crime that is very much on the increase in Nepal. The gompa is kept locked most of the time now.

Marpha Horticultural Research Station

Also known as Marpha Farm, this research station was started in 1966 by Pasang Sherpa, who travelled with David Snellgrove in 1956, to introduce new strains of crops to the region. The results have been considerably successful and the apple, peach, plum, apricots and walnut trees that were first tried here now fill the orchards on both sides of the Thorung La.

You can look round the gardens and visit the distillery between 08.00 and 16.00, Sunday to Friday but they close for daal bhat between 11.00 and 12.00. The farm shop sells dried apricots and other fruit, brandy, apple juice and excellent home-made jam. Muktinath Distillery is opposite.

Continuing along the trail to Marpha another distillery, the Nilgiri, has set up in business. There are also a couple of lodges, including the up-market *Om's Home*. (There are other Om's Homes, run by the same family, in Jomsom and Pokhara bazaar). This one not only has good food and comfortable lodgings but was the first building in the valley to sport a satellite dish on its roof.

Marpha (2670m/8760ft)
[MAP 9: p157]

Trekkers, and everyone else who comes here, for that matter, eulogise over Marpha. It must be just about the cleanest, most efficiently run village in the country with excellent lodges and some of the most creative cuisine on the trek.

The long main street is paved with spotless flagstones and winds past dazzlingly white houses, each with little piles of firewood neatly stacked on its roof. No doubt the rather dictatorial town council, which is said to impose fines on villagers who do not keep the street outside their house clean or repaint their buildings annually, has something to do with the pristine state of Marpha.

Recently enlarged with along flight of steps leading down to the main street, **Solmi/Tashi Lha K'an Gompa**, in the centre of the village, supports a lama, eight monks and several trainees. Above the altar the three images are, from left to right, Amitabha ('Boundless Light'), Avalokitesvara ('Glancing Eye') and Padmasambhava (Guru Rinpoche). There are brightly coloured wall-paintings and, neatly stacked in racks, the 225 books of the Tenjur (the canonical commentary). The big prayer-wheel outside the temple is over 100 years old; it came from Tibet and was a present from the Dalai Lama.

On the cliff above the village is a small **temple** that is used for retreats.

As well as a secondary school, the town has a **library**, jointly funded by the village and a Canadian organisation. Any donations, whether in book or financial form would obviously be welcome to fill the shelves. If it's closed, enquire at Bhakti Guest House.

Marpha has electricity linked to the 260kw micro-hydro scheme on Chokopani Khola that also serves Khobang, Tukuche and Jomsom.

❏ **Walking times on trail maps**
Note that on all the trail maps in this book the times shown alongside each map refer only to time spent actually walking. Add 20-30% to allow for rest stops.

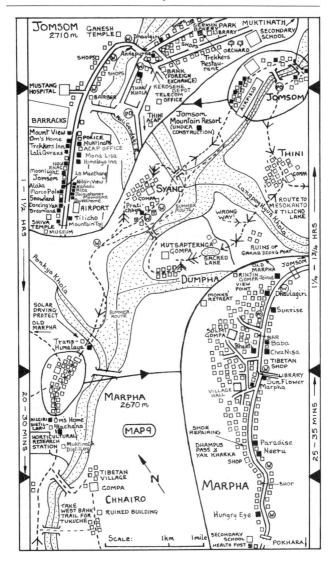

MAP 9

There are several day hikes in the area. You can walk up to **Old Marpha**, above the town in under an hour. **Yak Kharka** takes about three hours. Lodge owners can give directions.

Accommodation Marpha's lodges seem to be of a uniformly high standard and the majority have not only solar-heated showers but also electric blenders and food-mixers. Check with other trekkers to find out whose cooking is the current favourite. Recently some lodges built new rooms with attached bathrooms.

From south to north, there is the small and intimate *Hungry Eye Inn* soon after you enter the village ('hobbit-like in its cosiness, but most of all immaculate', wrote one trekker).

Further along the main street, *Neeru's*, 'the only best lodging and tasteful fooding in Marpha', has a good reputation and specialities here include brown bread, potato cheese pizza and apple momos. *Paradise*, nearby, provides stiff competition ('great apple crumble'). *Marpha Guest House* is run by a friendly family and across the street is the small but also friendly *Hotel Sun Flower*. *Chez Nisa* is similar.

Bhakti Guest House, opposite, is an interesting place to stay. It's run by Bhakti Hirachan, a local teacher and social worker who is very well informed about the area. As well as standard 'apple-pie' cuisine, there's also good local food here. *Baba Lodge* is a friendly place and they also run the massage place next door. Bob Marley rules here and it's all very laid back.

New Hotel Sunrise has nice rooms, some with excellent views across the valley. The *Dhaulagiri Guest House* is a big place that's clean and well-run. *Joinus Guest House* is a small, local lodge overlooking the apple orchards.

For more local atmosphere than the rather Westernised lodges, appealing as they are, can offer, stop by for a glass of raksi in the bar opposite Baba Lodge. Sukuti (smoked meat) makes an excellent accompaniment.

Other services Marpha has a **post office** (mail goes via Jomsom), provision shops, several Tibetan souvenir shops, a **shoe repair** centre and a **massage parlour**. A **telephone office** opened recently. There's also a **health post** (open Sun to Fri, 10.00-14.00) just south of the village.

Just north of Marpha is the posh *Trans-Himalaya Hotel*, with double rooms with attached bathrooms, TVs and Western loos. They charge Rs350 for a double but it's mainly groups that stay here. Near the hotel, a German-Nepali **solar drying project** was set up in 1994. It takes just one day to dry apples in the glass panels, and the results, of a much higher quality than the usual dried fruit available, are on sale in local shops.

Syang

Between Marpha and Jomsom, the trail passes below the village of Syang (2700m/8858ft), which has a **gompa**, founded in 1975, with a community of 35 monks and nuns. Most trekkers bypass Syang which is a very good reason for visiting it. There are tea houses and basic lodges.

Jomsom (2710m/8891ft) [MAP 9: p157]

There's no reason to stop in this modern town unless you're catching a flight or need to change some money. Since the early 1970s it's been the capital of Mustang district and it also houses the Royal Nepalese Army School of High Altitude Mountain Warfare.

The increase in the frequency of flights into Jomsom has brought more tourists to this area in the last five years or so. Hotel standards have risen dramatically and the best places now offer facilities that are more what you would expect in Pokhara than on a trek. In some you can drink shots of Johnnie Walker Black Label or sip cups of cappucino as you watch the *Oprah Winfrey Show* on Star TV. Was this what you came trekking for?

The impressive **Mustang Eco Museum**, right at the southern end of the

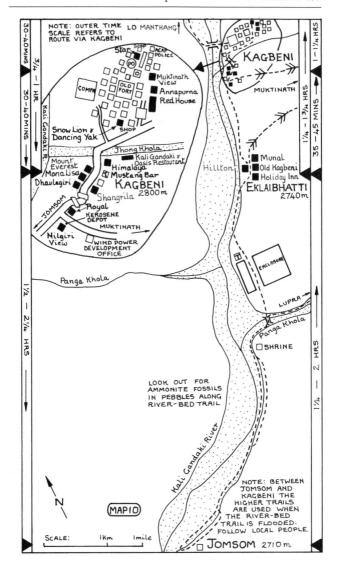

town, is well worth a visit, even though you have to climb a discouragingly long flight of steps. There's a cultural video show on Mustang, a photographic exhibition, a display of local costumes and a library. A traditional herbal medicine doctor is sometimes in residence here and uses the extensive herb garden which has been planted around the museum. The opening hours are Sunday to Friday 9am to 5pm in summer, 9am to 4pm in winter; Saturdays and holidays 9am to 1pm; entry is Rs50 for foreigners.

Beside the **police post**, where you must sign the book, is an **ACAP information office**. It has some interesting statistics and we're pleased to note, upon reading some of the captions here, that they've obviously got a copy of this guide book in their office!

Accommodation A 'five star' hotel, the *Jomsom Mountain Resort* (see p32) is being built on the ridge above the town, set to open in late 1999.

Currently the best lodges are along the street by the airport. *Om's Home* is an 'A' grade place with 'A' grade prices, Rs400/600 for a carpeted double room with attached tiled bathroom and flushing loo! With common bathroom their doubles cost Rs150. The food is good but pricey. The *Trekkers' Inn* is also impressive but then most of the lodges here are of a high standard with varied menus, tables with footwarmers beneath them and hot showers, some of which are electrically heated.

One of the nicest places in town in the new *Rita Guest House* which has a solarium restaurant on both sides of the building to catch both the morning and evening sun. Doubles cost Rs150 (com). Rather better value and run by a friendly woman, the *Moonlight Guest House* is a great place to stay. The rooms are set around a sunny courtyard at the back. The new *Xanadu Guest House* is a smart

place and one traveller called the coffee served in the *Magic Bean Coffee Shop* here 'divine'. For cheaper food visit the *momo shops* opposite the barracks.

On the south bank of the river the *Thak Khola* attracts custom through its claim that Jimi Hendrix slept here (in Room No 6, in October 1967) leaving his words: 'If I don't see you in this world, I'll see you in the next one. Don't be late', on the restaurant wall. Would-be poets following in his footsteps have added to the graffiti on the walls of Room No 6:

'What did Jimmy do in this room
With the roar of the river
The howling wind
And stinking socks?'

Mick Jagger is also reported to have dropped by.

At the north end of town there is a *German Bakery Coffee Shop* serving croissants, apple pie and superb nak cheesecake.

Flights Several airlines have early morning flights to and from Pokhara (US$50, 25 minutes) using Jomsom landing strip (which, incidentally, is owned by Marpha village). The fact that flights are dependent on perfect weather occasionally causes a backlog of stranded passengers, although more frequent flights have reduced the problem.

Most of the airlines have ticket offices opposite the landing strip, and currently include **RNAC**, **Yeti**, **Lumbini**, and **Cosmic**.

Other services Most useful is the **bank** (but no credit card advances); if it's closed there's also a **moneychanger** by the Trekkers' Inn. There's a **post office** and post restante seems to work here but allow about a month for an airmail letter from home. Nearby is a **telecom office** where international phone calls can be made, and the **district office** where trekking permits can be extended.

(Opposite) Top: The hot springs at Tatopani (see p146). **Bottom:** Dhaulagiri (8167m 26,794ft), and the Ice-Fall below it loom over Khobang and Larjung.

❏ **Side trip to Katsapternga Gompa (3000m/9840ft)**
Set on a high spur with superb views up and down the Kali Gandaki Valley this Kagyupa sect gompa is famous for its five 'Treasures of the Bodily Representation', a set of small terracotta images which came from the monastery of Samye, in central Tibet. Pilgrims come for the celebrations in the seventh month of the Tibetan calendar (August-September).

It's no longer a working gompa and it's kept locked most of the time but a lama sometimes comes up here from Thini in the early morning or evening. Even if it's closed it's a pleasant walk up past the sacred lake, beside which Padmasambhava is said to have left his footprints, and worth it just for the views.

If you can find someone to let you into the gompa you might be able to see a unique relic: one lama spent his whole life concentrating on the sound of the Tibetan letter 'a', the most basic vowel in any language and when he had died this letter was found imprinted on his skull, part of which is kept here.

If you decide to take this alternative route via Dumpha and Thini, add 1½ hours on to the timings between Marpha and Jomsom.

There's a **pool table** in the Joinushome Moondance Pub; and if you've got absolutely nothing better to do you could visit the **public youth library** and peruse their eclectic collection of books that includes *Lenin* and Barbara Cartland's *Love on the Run*.

Stool tests and X-rays are available at **Mustang Hospital**, where the clinic is open daily 09.00-13.00.

There are numerous shops for provisions in Old Jomsom, on the east bank of the river.

JOMSOM TO KAGBENI
[MAP 10: p159]
Walking this section of the trail is an other-worldly experience. The landscape is barren, the sun is often hot and the powerful wind that blows from the south can almost knock you over. Sometimes it turns and blows in the other direction. The Kali Gandaki river-bed is about a kilometre wide here but the water flows in several separate streams. Some parts of the trail are over the pebbles and rocks by the river, others high above the bank.

Take your lead from local people and, if you have to ford a stream, take off your socks and boots. Wet socks and boots are the surest way to get blisters.

Up a side canyon to the east is the village of **Lupra**, with only basic facilities for visitors. The Bon Po gompas are interesting but it's not always easy to find someone to open them for you. If you do visit you must leave some money in the donation boxes.

From Jomsom north to Muktinath is the region known as Baragaon ('the twelve villages'). The people here are not Thakalis but Towas, although some Thakalis may have moved here to operate hotels. Like the Thakalis they speak a language that is related to Tibetan.

Eklaibhatti/Eklebhatti (2740m/8989ft)
The name means 'one tea shop' but there are now four impressive lodges here. With the river relentlessly eroding away the edge of this settlement one wonders how long they will all be here. If you're not going to Kagbeni, take the direct trail

---

(Opposite) Top: Looking across the fields to Gompa Kupa, Tukuche (see p152).
Bottom: Marpha (see p156), little more than an hour's walk from Jomsom is one of the most attractive villages in the Kali Gandaki Valley and a popular place to stay.

to Muktinath up the hillside just after Eklaibhatti.

Kagbeni (2800m/9186ft)
[MAP 10: p159]

Kagbeni, a fascinating mediaeval rabbit-warren of crumbling mud-brick houses, stands in a little green oasis dominated by its red gompa, known as **Thupten Samphel Ling** (entry costs Rs100 and gives you access to the roof for excellent views of the town and into Mustang). In the centre, the ruins of the old fort bear witness to the fact that this was once an important place, strategically placed at the junction of two valleys.

If it weren't for the ugly powerlines, all that remains of a badly-planned wind-power project that failed several years ago, you would have difficulty believing you're still in the 20th century. The dusty streets are narrow and from them little doorways give into stables below each house. Above some doors are curious fetishes, wooden crosses with wool woven round them, to ward off evil. Around the north and south gates (now within the village) you can see primitive male and female figures harking back to animist beliefs practised here long before the arrival of Budddhism in the 11th or 12th centuries.

Accommodation The most interesting place to stay is the **Red House Lodge**. Run by three jolly sisters from a local noble family, part of the lodge is in one of the oldest houses in Kagbeni which even has a dusty private temple in one room. Along one wall in the dining room is some beautiful old Buddhist iconography. The cosy **Hotel Star** and friendly **Annapurna** have also been recommended. The **Kali Gandaki** has a pleasant glassed-in dining area and very clean rooms, some of which have an attached bathroom. The **Shangrila** is also recommended and has a very pleasant sun room to relax in.

All the lodges offer the local specialities which are Kagbeni bread (heavy buckwheat bread rolls) and mithi soup,

made from spinach-like Swiss chard. At the **Mustang Bar** there's said to be live music some nights.

Other services The **post office** is beside the prayer-wheel wall in the north of Kagbeni. Nearby is the police check-point and the **ACAP information centre**. This is as far up the Kali Gandaki as you can go without a special permit to the North Mustang region (see p37). Beside the Nilgiri View is ACAP's **kerosene depot**. You can rent horses from Kagbeni to Muktinath (Rs500), Jomsom (Rs500) or Marpha (Rs700). You may be able to bargain these prices down a bit.

KAGBENI TO MUKTINATH
[MAP 11: p163]

From Kagbeni the trail climbs past the remains of the wind-power project to join the more direct route from Jomsom to Muktinath. You have now left the Kali Gandaki Valley and the worst of the wind that rushes daily up it.

The route bypasses the village of **Khingar (3200m/10,497ft)**, where there are three reasonable lodges.

Jharkot (3550m/11,647ft)

Dominating a ridge on the eastern side of the valley, the mud-brick houses of Jharkot cluster round the ruins of the old fort. At the end of the ridge is Sakya Gompa. Some of the wall-paintings here have recently been restored and the temple can be visited (Rs50). Beside it is a traditional medical centre, opened in 1991 with Japanese backing.

Many trekkers prefer to stay in this peaceful village rather than in Ranipauwa. One of the most pleasant lodges in the area is the **Himali Hotel**. An American guest suggested modifications to the traditional design of the building and large windows have been incorporated to trap the heat from the sunny courtyard outside. There's a solar-heated shower. The varied menu here includes cheese fried rice, yak chowmein and excellent apple fritters. The **Hotel Sonam**, right by the trail, is also popular.

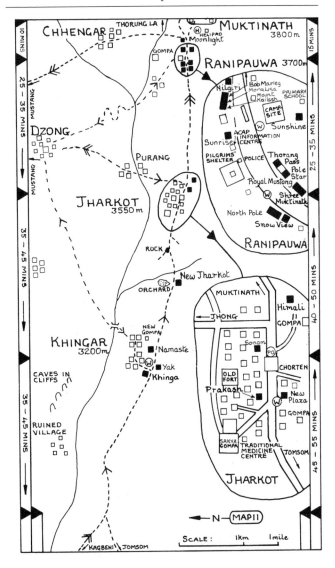

It's run by a welcoming family and offers good solar hot showers and excellent food. At the *New Plaza* there are views from some of the rooms and a pleasant roof top restaurant said to serve 'the best cheese and potato momos in the country'! *Prakash* is the newest place in town.

Ranipauwa (3700m/12,139ft)

Although most people refer to this village as Muktinath, strictly speaking that name applies just to the pilgrimage centre above Ranipauwa. Since there are no lodges within the Muktinath temple complex, everyone stays here.

The most interesting building in this small village is the old pilgrim hostel, built around a large courtyard. The wooden floors in some of the bare dormitories shine from the bodies of the thousands of pilgrims who have slept here over the years. Far fewer pilgrims walk here now; most will be rich Indians or Nepalis who occasionally fly in by helicopter.

Electricity came to Ranipauwa in 1988, in a project arranged and paid for by the people themselves, with the technical help of the Nepali group Development Consulting Services and the British charity Intermediate Technology. Initially a 9kw generator was installed but this has now been uprated to 25kw. Some of the lodges have low-wattage cookers and electric hot showers which will appeal to weary trekkers who have just staggered over the Thorung La.

If you're in the area in August or early September, it's worth trying to be up here for the **Muktinath Yartung**, a harvest festival and horse race that draws people from all over Mustang. After a dignified procession headed by the Abbot of Jharkot up to the temples, wild horsemen thunder up and down Ranipauwa picking up money put down in their path.

Accommodation The friendly *Mona Lisa* is recommended for its excellent food in its heated dining room; try the delicious veg cheese momos. The rooftop room has good views, especially at sunrise. Later, relax in the afternoon sun on the first floor terrace, watching the weary pass hoppers limp into town.

The *Sunrise* is also recommended and the *Shree Muktinath* is popular. Next door, the new *Royal Mustang* is one of the cleanest lodges in town with lovely large rooms. The long-running *North Pole* is also popular.

If you're beginning to wish you'd taken your holiday in the Caribbean rather than the Himalaya, hang out at the *Bob Marley*.

Other services Since most of the people who go missing in the Annapurna region do so on the Thorung La, it's vital to sign the book at the **police checkpoint** here.

There's also an interesting **ACAP information centre** in the village.

❑ Side trip to Dzong/Jhong

Across the valley from Jharkot you can see the crumbling ruins of the fort of Rab-rgyal-rtse ('Peak of Supreme Victory'), in the village of Dzong. From here the chief controlled the six villages in the Muktinath Valley.

Dzong, which means 'fort' in Tibetan, makes an interesting side trip from Jharkot (1-1½ hours each way). Just don't tell the police of your intentions as Dzong is officially 'off-limits'. It's also possible to walk there from Ranipauwa. Amongst the ruins of the fort there's now a school and the children will probably pester you for money.

The ancient **gompa** supports about 20 monks of the Sakya-pa sect, one of whom will open the temple if it's locked (Rs100). Inside, statues of Sakyamuni and Lama Tenzing Repa gaze out from the altar upon wall-paintings darkened by time and the flames of yak-butter lamps.

Muktinath (3800m/12,467ft)

The walled temple complex of Muktinath has been attracting pilgrims, both Hindu and Buddhist, for centuries. For Hindus it's the next most holy place in Nepal after Pashupatinath. There's even a helipad here so that the king and other rich pilgrims can visit. Muktinath's fame rests mainly on a natural phenomenon that can be seen beneath the altar in the **Jwala Mai Temple.** A nun lifts the grubby curtain to reveal, deep within the cavity, a thin blue flame of natural gas burning from a hole that also emits a trickle of water. The Hindus believe that this miracle of lighting a fire upon water was an offering made by Brahma himself. The fact that this is now very much a Buddhist temple doesn't seem to worry Nepali Hindus with their mix-and-match approach to religion; if only Indian Hindus and Moslems could learn to do the same. This temple is at the extreme right of the temple complex as you approach it from Ranipauwa.

The Newar-style **Vishnu Temple** with its courtyard of 108 brass water spouts stands in the centre of the complex. To bathe under the freezing water here (all 108 spouts) is said to bring salvation to Hindus. You can get a blessing in the temple or, for US$20 (£12), you can have a tree planted in someone's memory in the Muktinath Darshan Memorial Garden. They say they'll send you a photo each year to show how it's doing.

Beyond the Vishnu Temple is the Buddhist **Marme Lhakhang** which has recently been gaudily restored. It stands by the sacred grove of poplars said to have sprouted from the walking sticks left here by the eighty-four Great Magicians on their way to Tibet.

In the **Gompa Sarwa,** just to the left of the temple complex entrance, there are three terracotta images, from left to right: Avalokitesvara, Sakyamuni and Padmasambhava. Also known as Guru Rinpoche, Padmasambhava was a Buddhist saint who passed through Muktinath in the 8th century. He left his footprints in a stone outside the temple enclosure, near the Gompa Sarwa.

When visiting the temples of Muktinath you should be modestly dressed, take your shoes off when going inside the temples and leave donations. Please don't take photos in the Vishnu or Jwala Mai temples.

For a continuation of the route over the Thorung La, see p221.

❏ Early visitor unimpressed

Travelling this way in 1901, Japanese Zen monk, Ekai Kawaguchi, wrote:'On our way thither, we visited the famous Chumik Gyatsa. Chumik Gyatsa means a hundred fountains, and is the Muktinath of Samsrt, which Hindus as well as Buddhists regard as a place of great sanctity. The place apparently obtained the name it bears from the numberless springs abounding thereabout, and a spot of particular fame there was called Sala Mebar, Chula Mebar, Dola Mebar, which means burning in earth, burning in water, burning in rock. On seeing the spot I found this mystery to be nothing more than the fancy of ignorant natives, who saw a burning jet of natural gas escaping from a crevice in a slab of rock, that formed a lid, so to say, over and close to the surface of a beautiful crystal-like fountain, which was about one by two feet in size so that its prolonged flame looked, at the first glance, as if it were crawling over the water. I noticed, however, that the mountains round about bore ample evidences of volcanic eruptions, at one time or another, an extinct crater now changed to a pond, lava rocks, and so on, being present'. *Three Years in Tibet* **Ekai Kawaguchi**

Tatopani to Pokhara via Beni/Baglung

If you don't fancy the climb back up to Ghorepani on the return trip to Pokhara, you can continue to follow the river downstream to join the new road at Beni.

Note that because this route is at low altitude it gets uncomfortably hot here between April and October. Although the route is not as busy with trekkers as the trail via Ghorepani, many more are now going this way and standards of accommodation have risen in recent years.

Note that this part of the valley is particularly prone to landslides, however, so you may have to spend some time taking detours around them.

TATOPANI TO TIPLYANG
[MAP 12: p167]
Leaving Tatopani
From Tatopani cross the bridge to the east side of the Kali Gandaki and, shortly afterwards, the bridge over the Ghara Khola. Passing the trail up to Ghorepani, continue south along the Kali Gandaki. *Hema Guest House* is a reasonable place and there's a hot spring with a small pool by the river near here. Continuing south the trail rises and falls through small villages and in places is cut into the rock high above the river. The beautiful *Fall Base Cottage* by the waterfall makes an ideal refreshment stop on this trail.

Tiplyang (1040m/3412ft) Cross the suspension bridge to reach this small village where there are some tea houses, five basic lodges and a little shop. *Sherchan Lodge* has a fridge full of cold drinks.

From Tiplyang the trail follows the west bank of the river, through acres of marijuana. Landslides are frequent in this area. It is possible to stay in one of the several basic lodges in the village of

Baisari, but most trekkers prefer to continue on to the more comfortable lodges in Galeshor.

TIPLYANG TO BENI
[MAP 13: p168]
Galeshor/Ranipauwa (1170m/3839ft)
Although Beni is under an hour's walk away, it makes more sense to stay in this quieter and far more attractive riverside village: 'a veritable Shangri-La', one trekker called it.

There are two good lodges here, both on the southern side of the suspension bridge. The ever-expanding *Riverside Guest House* has wonderful views from its large terrace. The up-market alternative is the *Paradise Guest House* which boasts satellite TV and hot showers.

Beni (830m/2723ft)
This bustling market town and administrative centre has three good lodges. The Thakali-run *Hotel Yeti* (☎ 20142) is the smartest place, relocated to an impressive new concrete building such as you'd find in Kathmandu. It's still run by the same charming people and in the restaurant there's an extensive menu and chocolate cake on request. Roast chicken and chips is Rs 180. Double rooms are Rs150 with common bath, Rs300 for a double with bath attached.

In the centre of town is the *Hotel Dolphin* (☎ 20107), similarly priced and also with a popular restaurant. *Namaste Lodge*, down by the river, is a friendly family-run place with simple, clean rooms for Rs50 (com).

The town's other facilities include a large hospital, numerous pharmacies, police station, cinema, bank and many STD/ISD telephone offices where you can make international phonecalls.

BENI TO BAGLUNG
[MAP 14: p169]
Buses run along the east bank road to Baglung and on to Pokhara (Rs70, 4½ hours). If you can get a group of people together taxis are another option. Road building on both sides of the river has

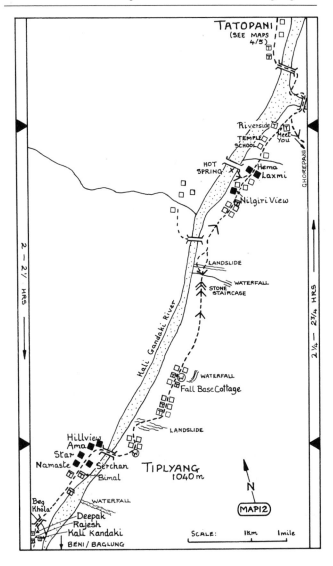

TATOPANI
(SEE MAPS 4/5)

GHOREPANI

Riverside
Meet You
TEMPLE SCHOOL
HOT SPRING
Hema Laxmi
Nilgiri View

LANDSLIDE
WATERFALL
STONE STAIRCASE

WATERFALL
Fall Base Cottage

LANDSLIDE

Hillview
Ama
Star
Namaste
Serchan
Bimal

TIPLYANG
1040 m

Beg Khola
WATERFALL
Deepak
Rajesh
Kali Kandaki

BENI / BAGLUNG

Kali Gandaki River

2 – 2½ HRS

2¼ – 2¾ HRS

N

MAP 12

SCALE: 1Km   1 mile

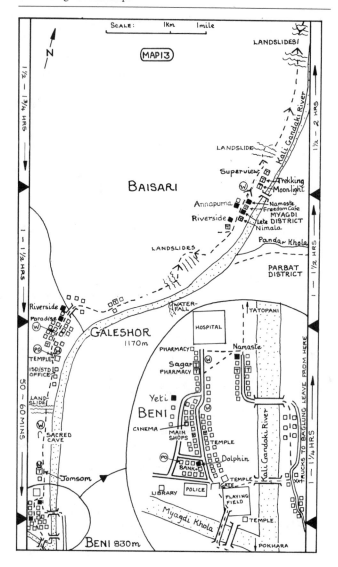

SCALE: 1Km   1mile

N

MAP 13

LANDSLIDES!

BAISARI

Kali Gandaki River

1½ — 1¾ HRS

½ — 2 HRS

LANDSLIDE

Superview

Trekking
Moonlight

Annapurna
Namaste
Freedom Cafe
MYAGDI
DISTRICT
Lete
Nimala

Riverside

Pandar Khola

1 — 1½ HRS

LANDSLIDES

PARBAT
DISTRICT

1 — 1½ HRS

Riverside

Paradise

GALESHOR
1170m

WATER-
FALL

TATOPANI

HOSPITAL

PO

TEMPLE

ISD/STD
OFFICE

PHARMACY

Namaste

Sagar
PHARMACY

Yeti

BENI

CINEMA

MAIN
SHOPS

TEMPLE

50 — 60 MINS

LAND-
SLIDE

SACRED
CAVE

PO

Dolphin

BANK

TEMPLE
GATE

Kali Gandaki River

TRUCKS TO BAGLUNG LEAVE FROM HERE

1 — 1¼ HRS

Jomsom

LIBRARY

POLICE

PLAYING
FIELD

TEMPLE

Myagdi Khola

TEMPLE

BENI 830m

POKHARA

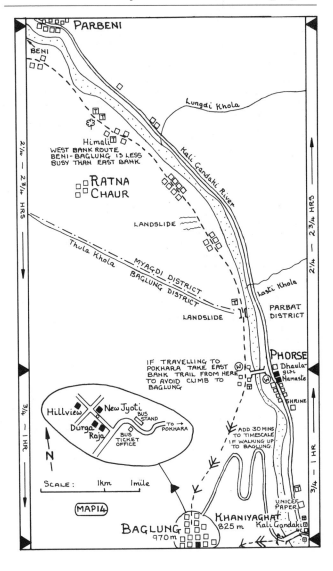

PARBENI

BENI

Lungdi Khola

Kali Gandaki River

Himali
WEST BANK ROUTE
BENI-BAGLUNG IS LESS
BUSY THAN EAST BANK

RATNA
CHAUR

LANDSLIDE

Thula Khola
MYAGDI DISTRICT
BAGLUNG DISTRICT

Lasti Khola

PARBAT
DISTRICT

LANDSLIDE

2¼ — 2¾ HRS

2¼ — 2¾ HRS

PHORSE
Dhaula-
giri
Namaste

IF TRAVELLING TO
POKHARA TAKE EAST
BANK TRAIL FROM HERE
TO AVOID CLIMB TO
BAGLUNG

SHRINE

Hillview   New Jyoti
                    BUS
                    STAND
Durga
Raja
            BUS
            TICKET
            OFFICE

TO
POKHARA

ADD 30 MINS
TO TIMESCALE
IF WALKING UP
TO BAGLUNG.

N

SCALE: 1km   1mile

MAP14

3/4 — 1 HR

3/4 — 1 HR

UNICEF
PAPER

BAGLUNG
970m

KHANIYAGHAT
825m
Kali Gandaki

❑ **Karam**

You'll see this game, a kind of 'flick snooker', played in tea houses or street corners throughout Nepal. It's played on a board with coloured counters, by two or four players. One red counter is used as a cue and one black one as the final play.

The rules Place all pieces except the red in the centre. Player one puts the red counter on the home line and flicks it into the centre to spread the other counters. Player two takes the red and tries to put his or her own coloured counters in the corner pockets. Take turns at doing this.

If your opponent's counter goes into the pocket, it must be placed back in the centre of the board together with one of your counters that has already been pocketed. When you've got all your counters into the pockets you must finish with the black counter.

Tara Winterton (UK)

made the walk to Baglung unpleasant, but the west bank trail is the quieter.

Phorse (825m/2707ft) is by the suspension bridge on the east bank and there are some basic lodges here and some tea houses in **Khaniyaghat (825m/2707ft)**. Just before Khaniyaghat is the UNICEF paper depot. Paper made locally from the bark of the daphne is collected here and sent to craft printers in Bhaktapur.

Continue through Khaniyaghat until you reach the collection of tea houses by the main **road**. There are sometimes taxis waiting here and buses coming down from Baglung will pick up passengers for Pokhara (see below). If you want to be sure of a seat, however, you'll have to climb the hill to Baglung which sits 145m/476ft above the river.

Baglung (970m/3182ft)

As well as being the administrative headquarters of Baglung district, Baglung is famous for the sacred forest that lies at the southern end of this promontory, high above the river. The tall sal trees have been protected for hundreds of years and are all that is left of a large forest that once covered the whole area. There's a temple at the centre of the forest.

Baglung is a large town with many shops and several places to stay, all in the Campus Rd area. They include *Hotel Raja* with rooms for Rs100 (common bath), the *New Jyoti Hotel* (☎ 20215) at Rs90/180 (com) and the *Hillview Hotel* (☎ 20118) with double rooms with common bath at Rs160 and with attached bath for Rs250.

The bus stand is in the south of the town. Local buses leave Baglung every half hour from 06.00 to 18.00 for the 74km-journey to Pokhara (Rs35, $3\frac{1}{2}$ hours). There are a few faster express buses throughout the day (Rs45, 2 hours). Taxi prices will depend on how keen they are to make the journey. They'll charge between Rs1000 and Rs1300.

Ghorepani to Ghandruk/Chomrong

This forest trail through the rhododendrons makes a convenient link between Ghorepani and the large Gurung town of Ghandruk, via Tadapani. From Tadapani you can descend to the Kimrong Khola and reach Chomrong, a village with excellent lodges and glorious views. Chomrong is also the starting point for the Annapurna Sanctuary trek.

You should be aware that the first part of this route can be very slippery if it has rained recently. During the monsoon the rhododendron forests are infested with leeches.

GHOREPANI TO DEURALI
[MAP 3: p141]
Leaving Ghorepani
From Lower Ghorepani a sign points to a trail that ascends steeply to a long and undulating ridge, climbing above 3000m before dropping into Deurali. It's a very pleasant walk and there are excellent views each side of the ridge. The rhododendrons here are spectacular in March and April when they are in flower.

Deurali (2987m/9800ft) is just two lodges and a Tibetan curio stall by the junction with the path down to Chitre. You can climb to a viewpoint above the settlement for sunrise if you're staying here.

DEURALI TO GHANDRUK AND CHOMRONG   [MAP 15: p173]
From Deurali the trail descends quite steeply at times into the impressive river gorge to the peaceful little village of **Banthanti** and a collection of small lodges with friendly helpful owners. You often see langur monkeys in the trees in this area. Crossing the wooden bridge, the trail climbs passing *Clean View*, a lodge with wonderful views over the valley. The

trail then descends steeply to a second bridge. From here it's an exhausting climb to Tadapani.

Tadapani (2595m/8514ft)
The name of this village means 'distant water' and Tadapani is not to be confused with Tatopani ('hot water'), in the Kali Gandaki Valley. There are superb views from here.

Most of the accommodation here is of a reasonable standard, although the area around Tadapani has been subject to much deforestation over the years. With this in mind, ACAP have requested that trekkers select lodges that have backboilers or use kerosene rather than firewood.

Route to Ghandruk
From Tadapani this easy trail heads south to **Baisi Kharka** where there are a several small lodges. There's then a choice of routes. Take the left-hand trail for the lodges at the northern end of Ghandruk and descend to the main Ghandruk-Chomrong trail where you turn right. Alternatively, take the right-hand route from Baisi Kharka which brings you into Ghandruk at the top of the town. See p174 for more information on Ghandruk.

Routes to Chomrong
The **direct route** was down into Melaje and through Kimrong Khola but this route was disrupted by a landslide and the bridge swept away. Check with lodge owners in Tadapani. You may have to follow the route below to Chiukle, and then from Chiukle head north-east down the terraces in a straight line towards Kimrong Khola. When you reach the river, follow it to a small wooden bridge which you cross. Walk along the north bank of the river which brings you into Kimrong Khola by the Hotel Peaceful.

The **alternative route** is more interesting. Leave Tadapani on the path that begins from near Grand View Guest House. After a short distance, this trail veers to the north and comes out into a small clearing before dropping steeply through the rhododendrons. After another clearing you follow a wall, cross a stile and reach the Namaste tea shop at Chisapani. The trail then drops steeply to **Chiukle**, where there are two lodges. A maze of small paths leads down through the terraced fields to the big suspension bridge, built in 1989, over the Kimrong Khola.

From the bridge, the trail climbs past the school and along the terraces to the little village of Klisigo Chiukle where the Kamala Lodge is run by a hospitable and friendly family. Ten minutes beyond is a series of waterfalls, a refreshingly cool spot. From here the trail climbs a little and contours along the terraces to join the main Ghandruk-Chomrong route (see p178).

Birethanti to Ghandruk/Chomrong

BIRETHANTI TO CHOMRONG DIRECT ROUTE   [MAP 16: p175]

The construction of a direct trail along the valley from Syauli Bazaar to Himal Qu (New Bridge) has further broadened the route options to Chomrong. Now, with some hard walking, it is possible to reach Chomrong in one long day if you're fit.

Taking a taxi to Nayapul, then walking to Birethanti should take under two hours and this leaves you with a full day's walking to Chomrong. A day and a half would be more realistic for most people, though, leaving Pokhara early in the morning and aiming to spend the night in Jhinu Danda. If you feel up to the last horribly steep hill, you may even make Chomrong that day.

The route

For Birethanti to Syauli Bazaar see p174.

Leaving Syauli Bazaar

From the two lodges of Syauli Bazaar climb through the village passing tea houses, then from the school take a flat modest trail to Beehive. Ask to make sure you are on the correct trail. The path stays relatively near the river bank and $1^1/_4$ to $2^1/_2$ hours later you arrive at the **Beehive Lodge**, a little above the bridge between Landruk and Ghandruk. This is the only place for refreshments or lunch between Syauli Bazaar and Himal Qu.

BEEHIVE TO JHINU DANDA [MAP 15: p173]

It is a further $1^1/_2$ to 2 hours mostly through pleasant forest (leech infested during the rainy months) to the lodges of **Himal Qu** (New Bridge), p187. After crossing the Kimrong Khola it is a short

---

❏ **Route times (Map 15 opposite)**
The following times refer to routes shown on the map opposite:

Deurali to Tadapani: $1^1/_2$-$2^1/_4$ hours
Tadapani to Deurali: 2-3 hours

Tadapani to Ghandruk: 2-$2^1/_2$ hours
Ghandruk to Tadapani: $2^1/_2$-$3^1/_4$ hours

Tadapani to Chomrong (or vice versa) via Chiukle: $3^1/_2$-$4^1/_2$ hours

Tadapani to Chomrong (or vice versa) via Kimrong Khola: 3-4 hours

Ghandruk to Chomrong (or vice versa) via Kimrong Khola: 3-4 hours

Chomrong to Landruk via New Bridge (Himal Qu): $2^1/_2$-3 hours
Landruk to Chomrong via New Bridge (Himal Qu): $2^1/_4$-$3^1/_4$ hours

Beehive to New Bridge (Himal Qu): $1^1/_2$ to 2 hours

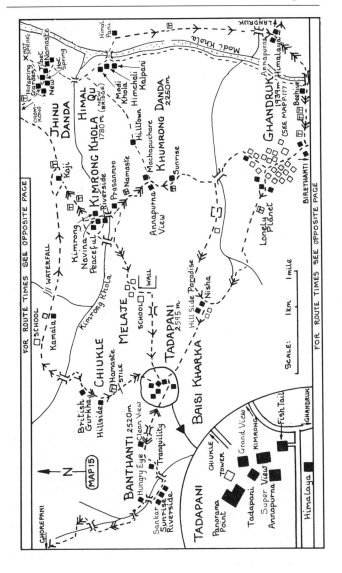

but stiff climb to **Jhinu Danda**, p187. Both these places are good overnight stops; it is a desperately long tough haul up to Chomrong from here if attempted at the end of the day.

See p178 for the continuation to Chomrong.

BIRETHANTI TO GHANDRUK (MAP 16: p175]

Leave Birethanti either by the path past the post office or along the path beside Laxmi Lodge. Both routes join after the school and follow the Modi Khola valley through fields. Twenty-five minutes beyond Birethanti you reach Ker & Downey's comfortable **Sanctuary Lodge**. It's set in a delightful tropical garden just above the river with views up the valley to Machhapuchhre. The bedrooms here even have attached bathrooms (with Western-style sit-down loos). When the lodge is not being used by their clients, rooms may be let to independent trekkers (US$20 including a dinner fit for the most pukka sahib).

Less than ten minutes beyond the Sanctuary Lodge is **Chimrong**. There used to be a bridge over the Modi Khola here, leading to Chandrakot. This has been destroyed and is unlikely to be rebuilt for some time since the main route to the road now goes via Birethanti.

For Ghandruk, the trail more or less follows the river to **Syauli Bazaar** where there are several pleasant places to stay. From here the path climbs steeply up to the village of **Kimche** where there's a basic lodge. The stone path then levels out and in **Chane** meets the trail to Tikhedunga ($3^{1}/_{2}$ to $4^{1}/_{2}$ hours from here). In Chane there are a couple of tea shops which, like most bhattis, also offer basic accommodation. Few trekkers stay in these kinds of places now which is a shame since a night in a truly local inn can be an enjoyable and enlightening experience.

On the eastern edge of Chane a large landslide during the 1995 monsoon wiped out the trail. Across the mess of rocks and boulders the path becomes a wide paved trail, well-kept here and reminiscent of remaining parts of the Inca Trail that trekkers still follow on the way to Machu Picchu in Peru.

Ghandruk (1939m/6362ft)

This picturesque town of slate-roofed houses surrounded by terraced fields is a pleasant place to spend a night. This is a largely Gurung town of about 7000 people. Traditionally, Gurungs are Buddhist but some, particularly those pursuing government positions, converted to Hinduism.

The headquarters of the Annapurna Conservation Area Project are here (in the

---

❏ **The Gurungs**

Forming the largest group in the Annapurna region, the Gurungs are a Tibeto-Burman people who were originally herders in western Tibet. Most Gurungs are now involved in agriculture, working the terraces that surround villages like Ghandruk but a large proportion of Gurung earnings comes from the few amongst them who are employed in Gurkha regiments abroad.

In the hills, Gurung men are easily recognisable by the bag they wear criss-crossed around their chest (see p32), and the *jama* (a type of kilt) held up by a large belt, sometimes with a military buckle. Women wear a sari-like *fariya* and often have a nose-ring and necklaces of turquoise and coral.

Although essentially Buddhist, some Gurungs are now Hindu but often both Hindu and Buddhist festivals are observed. 'The Gurungs are a very jolly tribe', say DB Shrestha and CB Singh in *Ethnic groups of Nepal and their Ways of Living*, 'They make merry on each and every occasion'. Certainly, their good humour and friendliness are immediately apparent to the foreign trekker.

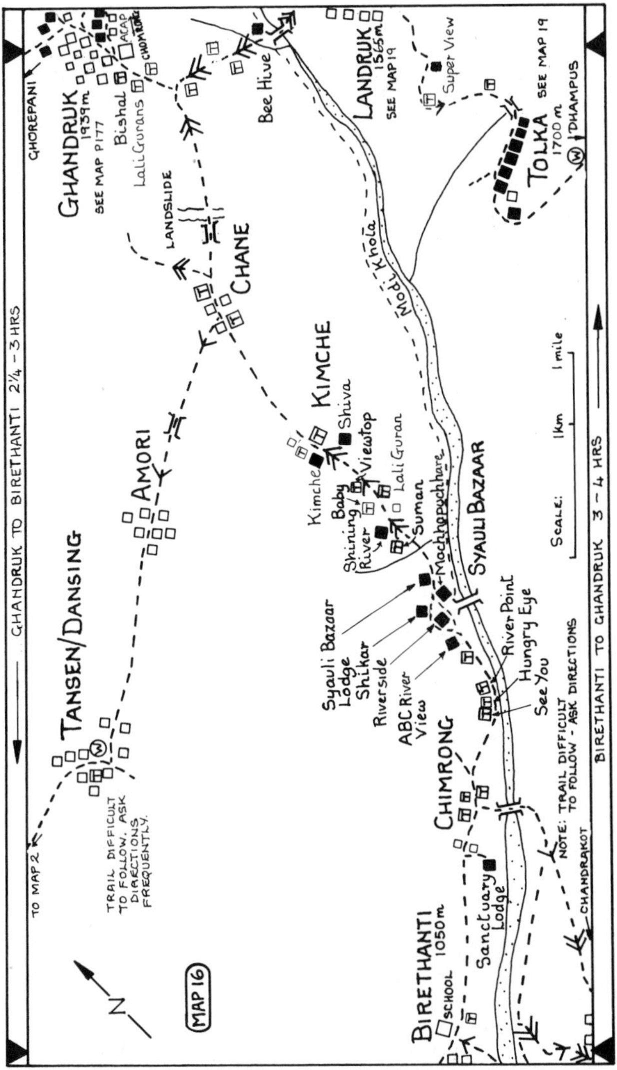

MAP 16

N

TANSEN/DANSING

TRAIL DIFFICULT TO FOLLOW. ASK DIRECTIONS FREQUENTLY.

TO MAP 2

GHANDRUK TO BIRETHANTI 2¼ – 3 HRS

GHANDRUK 1939 m.
SEE MAP P.177

Bishal
Lali Gurans
CHOPYTAREA

Bee Hive

LANDRUK 1565 m.
SEE MAP 19

Super View

TOLKA 1700 m.
SEE MAP 19

DHAMPUS

LANDSLIDE

CHANE

AMORI

KIMCHE

Kimche
Shining River
Baby
Shiva
Viewtop
Lali Guran
Suman

Machhapuchhare
SYAULI BAZAAR
Modi Khola

SCALE: 1 Km   1 mile

BIRETHANTI TO GHANDRUK   3 – 4 HRS

Syauli Bazaar Lodge
Shikar
Riverside
ABC River-View

River Point
Hungry Eye
See You

CHIMRONG

NOTE: TRAIL DIFFICULT TO FOLLOW - ASK DIRECTIONS

BIRETHANTI 1050 m.
School
Sanctuary Lodge

CHANDRAKOT

impressive white buildings at the lower end of the town). Looking at the hotel development that has been going on in the last couple of years, however, it's depressing to see that ACAP can only do so much and is obviously unable to control the architectural style of the new hotel buildings. Lodge owners here seem to think that trekkers would like to see Ghandruk transformed into a kind of Thamel-in-the-Mountains and are replacing their classic low rise buildings with multi-storey concrete monstrosities. The worst offender is the Mountain View Lodge. Vote with your feet and stay in the more traditional places here.

Accommodation Most of the lodges have the environmentally-friendly features that ACAP encourages: backboilers, solar-panels etc; but the larger lodges are no longer built using traditional materials and techniques as was originally hoped. The lodges with the best views are at the top end of town but you could hardly complain about the views from any part of Ghandruk.

The *Trekkers Inn* is ACAP's three-times winner of Lodge of the Year. As well as fulfilling ACAP's criteria for minimising environmental damage, it is also a welcoming and friendly place, run efficiently by the indefatigable Jagan Gurung. They could have done a better job at making the new building blend in a bit better, though.

The *Milan,* run by friendly people, is a popular place to stay. 'Probably the nicest place we stayed in on the trek', wrote one visitor. *Sakura* and *Sangrila* have also been recommended for good food and lodging. All are past winners of the Lodge of the Year Award.

The most comfortable place is Ker & Downey's *Himalaya Lodge* (see p32) where trekkers can stay for Rs500 if it's not being used by a group.

There are also numerous camp-sites but the *Eco-Camping Place* has ACAP's endorsement for being environmentally-friendly.

ACAP headquarters It's well worth visiting the display here, which details ACAP's work in the area and has models of back-boilers and other energy-saving water heaters and cookers. There's an interesting 20-minute video which they show at 9.30 am, 12 noon and 3pm, or at other times for groups. They also sell ACAP T-shirts, postcards, maps, stickers and posters.

For further information about ACAP see p87.

Other services Just beside the ACAP headquarters is a **health post** (open daily, 10.00-14.00). In an emergency, a message can be sent using ACAP's radio. The **post office** is in the same building as the Sakura Lodge. Telephone calls, including international calls can be made from the **telephone office**, which is part of the Everest Bar and Restaurant below the Milan (☎ 061-29322).

Not far from the Mountain Guest House are two competing **museums**. Each housed in a traditional dwelling they display furnishings, dress and tools to show the traditional Gurung way of life. Entrance is Rs30 at both. Between them is the **Local Youth Eco-Trekking Centre**

☐ **Power to the people**
Electricity recently arrived in Ghandruk, although its installation was not without problems. Again, ACAP's policy of not imposing new schemes upon the people but rather backing projects that the people wanted and were prepared to instigate themselves has proved best. When the pipe that supplied water to the generator burst, the people lobbied the Nepali company that supplied it and ensured that a replacement was quickly supplied. Each house has two 25w bulbs; lodges also have low-wattage cookers.

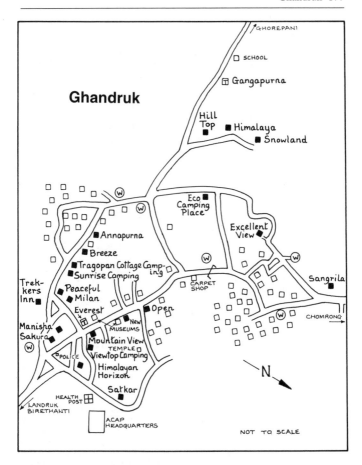

Ghandruk

GHOREPANI
□ SCHOOL
⊞ Gangapurna
Hill Top ■ Himalaya
■ Snowland
Eco Camping Place ■
Excellent View ■
■ Annapurna
■ Breeze
■ Tragopan Cottage Camping
■ Sunrise Camping
Trekkers Inn ■
Peaceful ■ Milan
Everest ■
Open ■
CARPET SHOP
Sangrila
Manisha ■
Sakura ■
New MUSEUMS
Mountain View ■
TEMPLE □
POLICE
Viewtop Camping
Himalayan Horizon ■
Satkar ■
HEALTH POST ⊞
LANDRUK BIRETHANTI
ACAP HEADQUARTERS
CHOMRONG

N

NOT TO SCALE

where guides and porters can be arranged (in advance via the operator at the telecom centre, if you wish).

GHANDRUK TO CHOMRONG
[MAP 15: p173; MAP 17: p181]

Leaving Ghandruk

The main trail to Chomrong leaves Ghandruk on the northern side of the village, past Sangrila Guest House. About

10 minutes beyond you cross a bridge over a stream. The wide path to Baisi Kharka and Tadapani leaves the main trail just north of this stream.

Khumrong Danda (2250m/7382ft)

For Chomrong, continue along the main trail which begins to climb towards the small pass you can see ahead, Khumrong Danda. You won't need any encouragement to stop for a drink here and there are two small tea houses, one of which also has basic accommodation. There are excellent views of Annapurna South, Hiun Chuli, Machhapuchhre, and the deep valley in between.

There are two small lodges here. Despite its name, the most peaceful spot to stay is *Hill Town Lodge*, half an hour north-east along the ridge on a pleasant trail. Surrounded by forest, the lodge is run by an ex-health assistant from Ghandruk. Locally he is known as The Doctor. It is possible to descend directly, ie very steeply, to close to Himal Qu (New Bridge) from here, although it is better to return to the main trail at Khumrong Danda.

Kimrong Khola (1780m/5840ft)

Dropping steeply from Khumrong Danda, you can't see the bridge across the Kimrong Khola. After crossing the stream head down following its bank to a ruined building, once a lodge. Continue down on the terraced fields and pass over a small wall where the trail leads to the suspension bridge. Swing upstream until a trail leads up on stone steps to the lodges of Kimrong. Alternatively, when the river is low instead of dropping to the ruined building continue across more rocky debris to a trail that heads to a temporary bridge and to *Riverside Lodge*. From here there is a choice of two trails, the main trail slightly upstream to the main village and *Peaceful Lodge*, where the original path for Chomrong climbs and traverses. Alternatively, from Riverside a set of newer stone steps leads to *Navina* and *Kimrong* lodges, and away from Peaceful Lodge. Altering of a trail to gain advantage over another lodge is common in this region.

For Chomrong, behind Kimrong Lodge is a stone path. To avoid going to the main village immediately turn off this to climb straight up through fields on a rough track to some stone steps where you rejoin the main path. This short set is of course designed to unfairly divert the return traffic, so if you get confused –

they've only made steps at the beginning and end of the section – you know who to blame.

Daulu/Taulung (2180m/7152ft)

From Kimrong Khola the trail climbs very sharply to Kaji, passing the turn-off for the high route to Tadapani via Chiukle. Contouring across terraced fields you reach Daulu at the end of the ridge. By the *Summit View Lodge* a set of steep stone steps drops from Daulu to New Bridge, and two possible routes to Pokhara, one via Landruk and Dhampus, the other faster although less interesting route via Syauli Bazaar and Birethanti. See p174.

Chomrong (2170m/7119ft) [MAP 17: p181]

From the upper part of Chomrong you can at last see why Machhapuchhre got its name 'Fishtail Peak'. The views from here of the other peaks that surround the Annapurna Sanctuary are so impressive that you can't spend less than a night here. This is, in fact, an excellent place for a rest day since most of the lodges have sunny terraces, ideal for relaxing and enjoying the scenery.

This is the start of the trek to the Annapurna Sanctuary, and if you're camping, fires are forbidden above Chomrong (although you shouldn't be making fires anywhere in the Annapurna region.)

Chomrong's original micro-hydro electricity supply was installed and paid for by a Japanese trekker, Katsuyuki Hayashi, in 1982. He was known locally as the Japanese Electricity Man. In an ongoing effort the villagers are establishing a better project with a generating capacity of 30kw, due to be completed by the time you read this. ACAP provided technical and managerial assistance, the locals have contributed 30% of the money, of which the Asian Development bank (ADB) loaned them 15%, and the Kadoorie Charitable Foundation, 70%. The Kadoorie, a group of wealthy Hong Kong Chinese, have also contributed to other projects and bridges in the region.

This is the sixth micro-hydel project ACAP has assisted with. After testing and commissioning the project will be (or now has been) handed over to the local community. The electricity should reach 65 households and 16 lodges. The charges are a flat fee of Rs1.50 per watt per month capacity, ie so a lodge with 300 watts worth of bulbs and a rice cooker (300w), will pay Rs900 a month, whether they use the power all the time or not. This encourages the use of low wattage fluorescent bulbs while for cooking there is only enough power for the low wattage rice cookers. No doubt some of the lodges will soon have microwaves.

Earnings go to the Village Electrification Committee for maintenance and for the salary of the manager and two operators, and when you compare this with the largely anonymous power companies back home you can begin to realise what significance projects like this have for a small community. It can only further strengthen the community's dependence on each other, indirectly a way of preserving the culture, as ACAP is well aware.

Accommodation There's an ever-expanding range of places to stay here beginning from the *Summit View Lodge*, at what is really Daulu. The competition is intense and during the monsoon everyone renovates and repaints in an attempt to outdo each other. All offer dining with a view, and many bedrooms even have a view of Machhapuchhre.

They also offer food as tasty as it gets while trekking. In the first and second editions of this guide the **pizza** at one lodge was highly recommended, so now every place advertises pizza with lettering as big as their lodge name. I tested pizza at three lodges; each had a crispy base and was excellent in its own way. As well as intense competition between pizzas the region boasts another speciality: **fried Mars, Twix or Snickers rolls**. The chocolate bar is wrapped in pastry and fried, the bar inside turning to a delicious goo. This may sound horrifyingly unhealthy, but after a week or two on the trail, you'll be checking whether they're served with custard as well!

Down in the main part of Chomrong is the *Captain's Lodge*. Both the lodge

---

❏ Bees mean honey

Sharp eyes may spot a curious log hanging from a village house in the lower country. A closer inspection will reveal a small hole cut in the log, and bees buzzily going about their business. The log is hollow and the ends are only roughly sealed but beware of getting too close since bees have been known to mistake an ear or nostril for the hive, with predictable consequences. Local honey is one of the cottage industries that has successfully taken off in the middle hills. Buying some honey is best accomplished with the help of a guide or porter-guide, and takes frequent asking until you find someone who actually has some for sale. Often the honey is unfiltered, littered with wax and dead bees, and it is considerably thicker than the runny honey found in lodges, which is diluted by 30-50% with water at the purifing stage. Lodge owners used to further dilute the honey with water or sugar, but this practice is much less common than it used to be.

On the Annapurna Sanctuary trek, even as high as Machhapuchhre Base Camp you may also see natural hives of the large *Apis Laboriosa* honey bee. They prefer to make large combs that hang under rock overhangs, or occasionally in trees. The high altitude hives, at up to 3600m, are only used for a couple of months of the year before the comb is abandoned and the bees migrate to lower, warmer altitudes where they form a cluster beneath an overhanging rock or dead log. During the migration they take as much as 80% of their body weight in honey to feed themselves over the cold months! **Jamie McGuinness** and the crusty character who presides over it (and over the village) are Chomrong institutions and it can be fun to stay here. Dinner is a sit-down affair served at 6.30pm sharp, by candlelight. The Captain can't really be bothered with pizza but he'll knock one up for you if you insist. His pumpkin soup, on the other hand, is excellent and he prides himself on his hot chocolate pudding and apple roll with chocolate centre. His daughter runs the *Garden Villa*, which boasts tiled bathrooms on both floors.

Other services In the lower part of the village the **kerosene depot** sells a range of provisions as well as fuel. Prices here for things like chocolate, beer, muesli, honey and biscuits are lower than in all the lodges.

You can rent camping gear from the Captain; his stocks include tents, stoves, sleeping-bags, down jackets, boots, gloves, hats and sunglasses. The Captain has been involved in many climbing expeditions and is probably the best person to contact in an emergency.

Chomrong to the Annapurna Sanctuary

The Annapurna Sanctuary trek
At the top of the trail that begins in Chomrong and follows the Modi Khola lies a natural amphitheatre known as the Annapurna Sanctuary. This little valley is as magical as the name suggests, with ten peaks of 6000-8000m (20,000-26,000ft) rising from it.

Annapurna Base Camp, or, more correctly, Annapurna I South Base Camp since Herzog's camp for the original conquest of the peak (see p185) lies on its north side, is, at 4130m/13,550ft, the highest place here that offers accommodation. Although the route is for the most part uninhabited, groups of lodges have been set up along the way so that it is no

longer necessary to camp. Sections of this trek are subject to avalanches particularly in the spring. Although you won't be aware of the mountain, one part of the trail passes almost directly under Hiun Chuli and there are annual avalanches and landslides in this area. Don't loiter while crossing avalanche-prone gullies.

The knowledge that avalanches can fall may be scary but the risk of one falling on top of you is actually minimal. You can check on conditions at the ACAP information booth in Khuldigar before leaving. If you're trekking outside the main seasons they can tell you which lodges are open. In January and February it is occasionally impossible to reach the Sanctuary.

CHOMRONG TO DOVAN
[MAP 17: p181]
Leaving Chomrong
From the lower part of the village, you descend to the suspension bridge over the Chomro Khola and climb, steeply at first.

Passing through Tilche, represented on the trail by the small Annapurna General Store, a stiff climb brings you to the few tea shops of **Bhanuwa**, and the large new *Sherpa Lodge*. A little further up are the scattered lodges of **Sinuwa**, a perfect place to stop and admire the view back down the Modi Khola behind you. The top two lodges afford views up the valley as well; the white building in the base of the valley at a similar level to you is Dovan, and with good eyes you may be able to pick a roof or two of Deurali, higher in the valley.

As a sign by the last of Sinuwa's lodges proclaims, this is the start of ACAP's Annapurna Sanctuary Special Management Zone. Wood fires are forbidden above Chomrong (although you shouldn't be making fires anywhere in the Annapurna region) and it is mandatory for all lodges to cook on kerosene or gas. Groups as well as their porters must cook on kerosene or eat in the lodges and if you're trekking with a group you should make sure that this happens. The Sanctuary region is one of the few in the

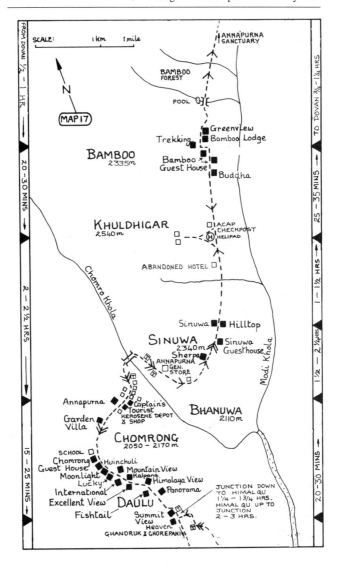

FROM DOVAN ½ – 1 HR
20 – 30 MINS
2 – 2½ HRS
15 – 25 MINS

TO DOVAN ¾ – 1¼ HRS
25 – 35 MINS
1 – 1½ HRS
1½ – 2¼ HRS
20 – 30 MINS

SCALE: 1 km   1 mile

N

MAP 17

ANNAPURNA SANCTUARY

BAMBOO FOREST

POOL

Greenview
Trekking   Bamboo Lodge
Bamboo Guest House
Buddha

BAMBOO 2335m

KHULDHIGAR 2540m

ACAP CHECKPOST
HELIPAD

ABANDONED HOTEL

Chomro Khola

Sinuwa   Hilltop

SINUWA 2340m
Sherpa
AHNAPURNA GEN. STORE

Sinuwa Guesthouse

Modi Khola

BHANUWA 2110m

Annapurna   Captain's Tourist
Garden Villa   KEROSENE DEPOT & SHOP

CHOMRONG 2050 – 2170m

SCHOOL
Chomrong Guest House   Huinchuli
Moonlight   Mountain View
Lucky   Kalpana
International   Himalaya View
Excellent View   Panorama
DAULU
Fishtail   Summit View
Heaven
GHANDRUK & GHOREPANI

JUNCTION DOWN TO HIMAL QU
1¼ – 1¾ HRS.
HIMAL QU UP TO JUNCTION
2 – 3 HRS.

country where lodge owners have pledged to not use any firewood. And they don't, so trekking companies can't use the excuse, as they do in many regions, that tea houses use wood. Also don't accept the lame excuse that the porters don't have kerosene. They can't provide it themselves: the trekking company has to.

In an effort to manage the region ACAP has placed a surprising number of other restrictions. From Sinuwa upwards they limit the size of each lodge to six or seven bedrooms, so there are no large lodges. Sign boards are black with yellow writing only and lodges have been forced to group together in designated places, deemed to be the safest locations. Approximately half the lodges from Sinuwa upwards are owned by Chomrong villagers.

The trail also changes in character from wide stone steps to a surprisingly narrow path enveloped by mixed rhododendron forest which sets the valley ablaze with colour during April. Watch your footing along the first stretch, especially when wet. Some sections are exposed and a slip could have nasty consequences. ACAP and the Chomrong Lodge Management Committee are slowly upgrading sections of the trail.

Khuldigar (2540m/8333ft) Past a long defunct hotel, is a junction, normally signposted. Up the steps is a helipad, while the flat trail leads, in a moment, to an **ACAP checkpost**, the last on the trail. There are no lodges here, and ACAP's Trekkers' Education Centre has also been closed. Visit the Ghandruk centre instead.

Bamboo (2335m17660 ft) The path from Khuldigar to Bamboo is steeply downhill and you soon enter the damp bamboo forest from which the collection of lodges takes its name.

Heaters and a heating charge become part of the menu from here on up. Heating is simply a kerosene stove under the table, and tablecloth of blankets that extend to the floor. Stick your legs under, and there's enough warmth to dry your boots. Some also have miniature clothes lines hidden underneath capable of drying almost anything in an hour or two. While they are a classic system, and render lodges a lot more comfortable, a roaring

---

❏ Altitude sickness at ABC

While very few people have died up at Annapurna Base Camp, the occasional person is forced to retreat, often in the middle of the night, suffering severe altitude sickness. Many people stay overnight at Bamboo, Himalaya, Dovan or Deurali then trek directly to Annapurna Base camp finding the walk tough, especially the last hour or two; and of them 40-50% develop a headache and may not feel like eating, while 10-20% develop a severe headache and may even vomit in the night. Usually most of these symptoms clear an hour after waking, that is if they did get some sleep. Perhaps two or three out of ten won't sleep too well.

What you should do, however, is to stay the night at Himalaya or Deurali, then MBC, then ABC, and you will be very unlucky to get any symptoms. The trek becomes pleasant, as it should be. It is telling that the two trekkers I met who were trekking this trail a second time with friends chose to stay at MBC then ABC. Trekking companies and guides, you would think would also promote this as a way of extending the trek a day in the name of comfort, but have yet to cotton on. Instead most seem happy to let some of their members suffer.

Especially when the weather is clear the sneaky way to beat the altitude is to stay no higher than at MBC, and bright and early hike up to ABC for the sunrise. You will be back at MBC in time for lunch, and down in Deurali or Himalaya in time for an celebratory afternoon pint.   **Jamie McGuinness**

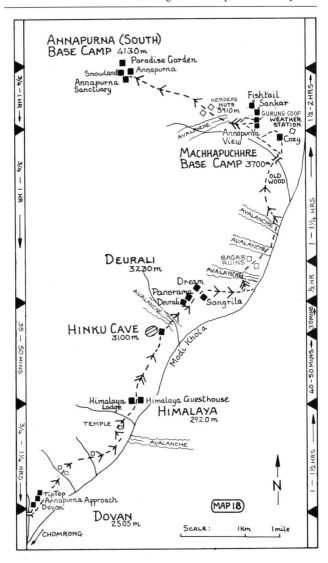

ANNAPURNA (SOUTH)
BASE CAMP 4130m
Paradise Garden
Snowland Annapurna
Annapurna
Sanctuary
HERDERS
HUTS
3910m
Fishtail
Sankar
GURUNG COOP
WEATHER
STATION
Annapurna
View
Cozy
MACHHAPUCHHRE
BASE CAMP 3700m
OLD
WOOD
AVALANCHE
AVALANCHE
BAGAR
RUINS
DEURALI
3230m
Dream
Panorama
Deurali
AVALANCHE
Sangrila
AVALANCHE
Modi Khola
HINKU CAVE
3100m
Himalaya ∎∎ Himalaya Guesthouse
Lodge
HIMALAYA
2920m
TEMPLE
AVALANCHE
N
TipTop
Annapurna Approach
Doyan
DOVAN
2505m
CHOMRONG
SCALE: 1Km 1mile

MAP 18

¾ – 1 HR
¾ – 1 HR
35 – 50 MINS
¾ – 1¼ HRS

1½ – 2 HRS
1 – 1¼ HRS
½ HR
30 MINS
40 – 50 MINS
1 – 1½ HRS

stove in an enclosed space generates dangerous carbon monoxide gas unless well ventilated. Carbon monoxide is lethal; you can't taste or smell it. CO permanently attaches itself to your red blood cells rendering them ineffective – and at altitude you need them more than ever! Always ensure there is plenty of fresh air coming into the dining room.

Dovan (2505m/821 8ft) From Bamboo the trail climbs steadily, crossing first the Bamboo Khola and then several small streams, until eventually it reaches three lodges in a forest clearing at Dovan. If you choose lodges by the smile of the lodge owner, Mrs Gurung of *Tiptop Lodge* wins the prize and serves very good food, too.

DOVAN TO ABC   [MAP 18: p183]

The next stretch of forest from Dovan to Himalaya is the sacred home of the deity Paunchhi Baraha Than. About half an hour from Dovan a **shrine** stands in his honour, and it is traditional to leave flowers or strips of coloured cloth here. In times gone by it was said that any eggs, meat or women taken north of here would anger the deities and bring bad luck.

Next door to the shrine is a view of an impressive waterfall. Legend has it that there are 108 falls (a holy number for Buddhists) during the monsoon. Perhaps one of the reasons for prayers here is that in winter or after a heavy snowfall it is from here on up that avalanches are a concern. Between Dovan and Himalaya are two minor avalanche gullies, and one more major gully. The other side of the valley, especially opposite the shrine, is raked by avalanches too. Your chances of getting hit by one, however, are extremely low; more people have died from altitude sickness, which is entirely preventable. If there is no snow, other than the glaciers on the highest parts of the peaks, there in no avalanche danger, and no need to worry.

A few minutes up is the first view of the thundering Modi Khola. Across a stream, landslides have taken their toll,

and, at least in September 1998, the detour involved ascending several crude ladders made by rhododendron branches. Now, although the trail mostly remains above the Modi Khola, it climbs at the same rate as the tumbling stream descends – steeply!

Himalaya (2920m/9580ft) The small lodges here stand beside a little stream. It is around here that you may find the hills getting tougher; it's not increasing old age, it's the altitude. The thinner air means you have to breathe more and stop 'to admire the view' more frequently.

Hinku Cave (3170m/10,400ft) Forty minutes or so from Himalaya stands the huge rock that forms Hinku Cave. A favourite camping shelter and landmark for mountaineering expeditions, the tea house here is, alas, no more. The site is still sometimes used by porters and trekking groups so don't use it as a lavatory. This is still a pleasant place to rest weary limbs and in the distance one can see the lodges of Deurali about 30 minutes' away.

Between Hinku Cave and Deurali is an area of boulders and low scrub (no trees), an unmistakable sign of an avalanche area. The gully is also prone to avalanches, which thunder through the deep gash in the mountainside. It is rare that there isn't avalanche debris here.

Deurali (3230m/10,597 ft) The lodges here huddle together. If the weather takes a turn for the worse, many people find themselves under equipped so Dream Lodge and Sangrila rent or sell such items as gloves, gaiters, hats and sunglasses. Stocks run low during a snowfall.

To MBC Older maps mark Bagar, between Deurali and MBC. The lodges here were closed by ACAP because of avalanche risk.

Just before and just after Bagar the trail crosses several streams, all of which experience avalanches. Every so often the route makes a detour to avoid clambering over avalanche debris. If in doubt follow locals or guides. Don't make the mistake of following the main stream coming from Annapurna III. Amongst the rocks you may see marmots, which live in large underground colonies around here.

Machchapuchhre Base Camp
Khili Dung (3700m/12,139ft)
You now enter the sanctuary itself and it was at this eastern end of the valley that the base camp for the 1957 attempt on Machhapuchhre was established. You cross a stream on a small wooden bridge

---

❑ CLIMBING ANNAPURNA I
The two most famous climbs on this 8091m/26,545ft peak (the world's tenth highest) are Maurice Herzog's original conquest with the French expedition in 1950 and Chris Bonington's South Face expedition in 1970.

The Conquest of Annapurna – 1950
When most modern mountaineering expeditions set out, their objectives are usually well defined, sometimes down to the exact route to be followed up a peak. In the light of this Maurice Herzog's 1950 expedition seems delightfully amateurish and their success all the more heroic. Their single objective was to be the first expedition to conquer a peak over 8000m yet not only were they unsure as to which 8000m peak it should be, Dhaulagiri or Annapurna, but the maps of the area were so inaccurate the first problem was simply to reach the mountains themselves. Only one team member had ever set eyes on the Himalaya before and not in this area since Nepal had only just opened its borders to climbing expeditions.

Being unable to find a viable route up Dhaulagiri they crossed the Kali Gandaki and pioneered a route up the north face of Annapurna I. On 3rd June 1950, Herzog and Louis Lachenal reached the summit and could look across the Annapurna Sanctuary to Machhapuchhre. They paid heavily for their victory with severe frostbite in the terrible conditions on the descent. Herzog was never to climb again, losing most of his fingers and toes. He returned to a career in politics in France where he was eventually made Minister of Sport.

Even if you're not particularly interested in climbing Herzog's account of the expedition, *The Conquest of Annapurna 1950*, is a gripping read and gives good descriptions of some of the villages in the region.

Annapurna, South Face – 1970
Looking up at the solid wall of rock and ice that forms the south face of Annapurna from the Sanctuary, it seems inconceivable (certainly as far as a non-climber is concerned) that anyone could find a way up it. Indeed, before 1970, nothing so steep and demanding had ever been attempted in the Himalaya.

A series of camps was established up the slope, the highest, Camp 6, at 7300m and pairs of climbers installed in each. With a copy of Chris Bonington's account of the expedition, *Annapurna South Face*, you can make out the exact route that was followed. As with the first attempt on Annapurna, the expedition became a race against the fast-approaching monsoon. On 27th May Don Whillans and Dougal Haston, having set out to establish a seventh camp, continued up to reach the summit and the point where, twenty years before, Herzog and Lachenal had first looked down into the Sanctuary. Although it was planned that most team members would have a chance to reach the summit, only these first two did. The expedition was not without its share of tragedy. On the descent one of the climbers, Ian Clough, was killed in an avalanche below Camp 2. He was buried just above Annapurna Base Camp.

to a junction. The **Machhapuchhre Cozy Guest House** is at the top of the steps, along with a helipad and a weather station. Following instead the left-hand path you arrive at the other four lodges, including the **Gurung Cooperative**. All seem to have snug warm kitchen/dining areas and good food. Prices are the same as at ABC. If you're being badly affected by the altitude you should not press on to Annapurna Base Camp since it's 430m/1410ft higher and 1½-2 hours further on.

If you stay here take a look over the moraine behind the lodges; it includes the route to Annapurna III Base Camp. You can only find out what's up that valley with a lot of rope and a guide. Unfortunately, three hours towards Annapurna III is a rock so steep that it requires fixing a rope. ACAP would like to keep this 'inner sanctuary' pristine so don't count on them blasting a path or fixing steel cable for trekkers.

Annapurna Base Camp/Chelo Gya (4130m/13,550ft)

The path up here is not particularly steep but if you're tired and unacclimatised the trek can seem relentless. If you've just spent the night at Machhapuchhre Base Camp and are well rested you'll probably find this stretch very pleasant, a gentle uphill stroll along the river, through tranquil meadows with many boulders to rest upon and gaze in awe at the surrounding peaks. If you begin to suffer altitude sickness soon after arriving consider carefully whether you should descend to MBC while it is still light. Descent is always the best medicine for AMS.

The four lodges stand on a level area that was the base camp for the 1970 Annapurna South Face expedition (see p185). It's a chilly spot but if you're acclimatised it's worth spending the night here since you can be up to watch the sunrise over the peaks. You'll also be able to climb up one of the sides of the valley on hard snow (ie before it turns mushy and becomes difficult to walk on) for even better views.

Porter have their own shelter built by ACAP, and it is even more sparsely furnished than the lodges. Although there is no official helipad helicopters are able to land here. Calling one is another matter, and may take several days. If you are suffering serious altitude sickness descend immediately; don't even think of trying to call a helicopter.

Even viewed from the terrace of one of the lodges, with a warming cup of tea in your hand, the panorama is breath-taking. Annapurna I rears above a rubble covered glacier (best seen on the edge of the moraine) while to the south Hiun Chuli and Annapurna South loom behind. Machhapuchhre is magnificent and even Annapurna III can be seen. For a view of Gangapurna climb the moraine with a few rock cairns to the south.

Apart from admiring the view and taking a short hike up behind the lodges there is little else easily achievable, probably much to the relief of trekkers suffering the altitude. The trek to **Tharpu Chuli (Tent Peak) Base Camp** is too dangerous to be recommended but you can gauge this for yourself. The route begins with a modest memorial to two Japanese climbers about 150m below the lodges, where it drops down onto the glacier. Directly opposite the lodges on the other side of the rubble-covered glacier you must climb the steep moraine via the small stream. Rock fall is a real danger. Then up on the grass, traverse perhaps half a kilometre towards Annapurna I before climbing steepish grass slopes. High camp is situated up on what looks like a rocky knob, and the tents, if there is anyone up there, are visible from the ABC lodges.

Since trekkers have taken over ABC the occasional expedition crazy enough to attempt Annapurna I from this side now makes base camp on the rubble-covered glacier or in one of the ablation valleys closer to the mountain. To summit in the autumn mountaineers usually arrive late in August to acclimatise, and aim to summit at the very end of September or into the first half of October. Spring expeditions arrive in March with the intention of summiting at the beginning of May. The walk to Advanced Base Camp, as it is often called, is a tough and relatively unrewarding walk, made more difficult by the fact that there is no established point where expeditions put their camp. If you venture onto the rubble-covered glacier be aware that there's no path, only a line of flags that are easy to miss. If cloud rolls it would be dangerous as you could easily get lost.

Heading down
The porters who supply the lodges take only a day from Chomrong up to here, sometimes with 35-40kg, and head down the next day all the way back to Chomrong. As a trekker you can try this but it is a tough day! Most people break the descent to Chomrong into two relatively easy days. From Chomrong the fastest route to Pokhara is via Himal Qu (New Bridge) then the direct route to Birethanti via Syauli Bazaar. The more scenic routes are: via Landruk, perhaps 2-2¹⁄₂ days to Pokhara; via Tadapani and Ghorepani, 2¹⁄₂-3¹⁄₂ days to Poldiara, and via either Tadapani or Ghorepani to Tatopani to the north, and all the way to Jomsom for a flight out to Pokhara: allow six to eight days.

Chomrong to Pokhara
(via Landruk or Syauli Bazaar)

CHOMRONG TO NEW BRIDGE [MAP 17: p181]
Leaving Chomrong Follow the main trail out of Upper Chomrong to Summit View at **Daulu/Taulung**. A signpost there points the way to Jhinu Danda, 45 minutes away down a steeply descending path dotted with tea houses.

Jhinu Danda The hot spring near here makes this a popular place to stop,

although it's a 20-minute walk down to the river to reach the two small pools. In Jhinu Danda there are five lodges including *Namaste Lodge*, the largest place and the only lodge here with a generator.

The main path dog-legs back down to a concrete bridge over the Khumrong Khola. Passing terraced fields and the occasional house, there is a signposted junction; contour for New Bridge, or climb the stone steps to Hill Town Lodge (see p178) and one (steep) route to Tadapani.

New Bridge/Nayapul/Himalpani
Drop briefly to a set of four lodges and the large suspension bridge over the Modi Khola. Here, or Jhinu Danda. are not bad places to spend the night, particularly if you're travelling in the opposite direction, as the climb up to Daulu and Chomrong is best done in the early part of the day, before it gets too hot. If coming from Landruk, after crossing the bridge two sets of equally wide steps beckon, both lead to tea houses.

HIMAL QU (NEW BRIDGE) TO SYAULI BAZAAR [MAPS p175 & 174]
This new trail is the quickest route to Pokhara. The lodge owners of Landruk, Dhampus and Ghandruk would rather you didn't know about it! From the Kalapani Lodge, the last in Himal Qu, a small path heads south, without crossing the Modi Khola. It winds through forest, staying fairly close to the river. The first lodge is Bee Hive, above the bridge from Landruk to Ghandruk, perhaps 1¹⁄₄-1¹⁄₄ hours down. There are no tea shops yet in between. It is a further 1¹⁄₂-2 hours to Syauli Bazaar, and the main trail to Birethanti. While Chomrong locals can get to Pokhara in a long day, staying at Birethanti makes the day more comfortable for trekkers.

NEW BRIDGE/HIMAL QU TO LANDRUK [MAP15: p173]
Across the Modi Khola is the pleasant *Himalpani Lodge*. As with many lodges away from the main overnight stops, they

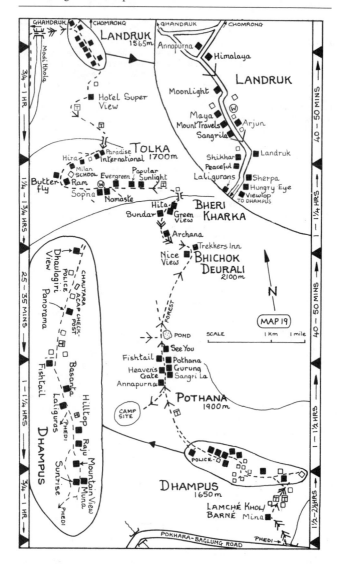

offer a friendly smile and hope that passing trekkers might stay. Mostly trekkers don't, which is a pity, since some of the more out of the way lodges are much more of a rewarding experience.

The trail to Landruk continues through the trees along the river before gaining height, passing through terraced rice fields. After crossing a small suspension bridge take the stone steps that climb to the first few lodges of Landruk. From Himalaya Lodge one path leads steeply down to the river and the other gently climbs to the main part of the village.

Landruk (1565m/5135ft)
This large Gurung village, directly across the valley from Ghandruk, stretches 500m up the hillside. There are good views up the Modi Khola to the Annapurnas from here. The many lodges all offer showers – allegedly hot – and dining with a view.

LANDRUK TO DHAMPUS
[MAP 9: p188]
Leaving Landruk Between Landruk and the pass, Bhichok Deurali, the trail winds around two side valleys and climbs 550m/1804ft.

Tolka/Medigara (1700m/5577ft) This
is another set of friendly lodges and some good views. The path meanders through the village past the school (where you may be asked for a donation, a genuine cause but you should ask for a receipt if you give anything). The route continues on the level until it reaches the remains of the old suspension bridge at Bheri Kharka, after which there's a stiff climb through the trees to the pass. There are numerous small lodges, many little more than tea houses; *Green View Guest House* and *Hita Guest House* are reasonable places to stay.

Bhichok Deurali (2100m/6890ft) The
tea houses at this pass are the perfect excuse for a stop. There are views through the rhododendrons in several directions, and Dhaulagiri is visible from

here. *Nice View Lodge* is appropriately named and it has a glassed-in dining area, as does the *Trekkers' Lodge*.

The path, now partly paved, descends gently from Bichok Deurali to Pothana and Dhampus. This amble through the forest is probably most welcome after your recent exertions. **Pothana (1900m/6236ft)** has more lodges for trekkers than houses for local people. Just past it is a small trail west leading up to a popular camping site known as Australia Field with a superb Annapurna vista.

Dhampus (1650m/5413ft)
Tourists come up to Dhampus from Pokhara for the night to watch the sunrise over the mountains since there are several places to stay, mostly surprisingly basic. The **Dhaulgiri View Hotel** is, however, a very comfortable place to stay, more like a Pokhara hotel than a trekking lodge. **Basanta Lodge** is the top place to stay and part of the Ker & Downey group (see p32). When it's not being used by trekking groups independent trekkers can also stay here for Rs500.

There are several routes to Pokhara and one can't help noticing that the road is, rather disconcertingly, on another ridge, dropping into the deep valley. The first option is to turn off at the Fishtail Lodge and descend via Gharte Khola to the road, which can be seen in the distance. Ask a local to point out where you are supposed to end up, and ask again at any confusing junction on the way there. The more normal route is to continue along the ridge past the string of lodges, and descend steeply off the ridge towards the road.

At the bottom by the road is Phedi; there are taxis or buses to Pokhara. Only local buses will stop for you, not the long distance buses from Baglung heading for Kathmandu. Taxi-drivers know that in your relief at the thought of not having to use your legs for a change, you'll probably pay almost anything for the privilege of squeezing into their battered Corollas. Bargain hard.

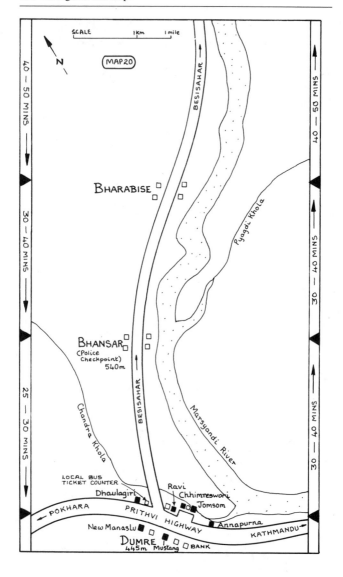

Dumre to the Thorung La

Dumre (445m/1460ft)

Populated mainly by Newars, dirty dusty Dumre is nothing more than a junction town on the Prithvi Highway. Avoid staying here unless you arrive late. Trucks and buses (see below) can make the trip from here to Besisahar in around four hours without breakdowns but since these are common it's likely to take much longer, often up to eight hours. Direct buses are now available from Kathmandu and although these are no more reliable than the services which start in Dumre, at least you won't have to fight for a seat. If you're walking, the first place with basic accommodation available is around 2¹/₂hrs along the road at Turture.

Accommodation There are quite a few places to choose from, though they're all very basic. The ***Chhimkeswori Hotel*** seems to be the place that's most popular with travellers. You'll get a reasonably clean double with fan for around Rs100. On the other side of the main road the ***Hotel Mustang*** is good value at Rs80 for a double with fan. The ***Hotel New Manaslu*** is run by very friendly people but rooms lack fans.

Other services The **bank** (signboard in Nepali only) is four doors east of the Hotel Mustang. Note that the only other banks this side of the Thorung La (ie until Jomsom) are in Besisahar and Chame. There's also a **post office**.

Getting away Buses, trucks and jeeps for Besisahar run from the centre of Dumre. The local buses (Rs100) have no schedule, they go when there's absolutely no possibility of cramming in another body. This is long after they're actually full so don't go for an empty vehicle or you're likely to have a long wait. Tourist buses (Rs200) also operate along this route. Tickets are available from Chhimkeswori Hotel, as all the touts will inevitably tell you. You're guaranteed a seat on one of these, but be prepared for long waits with your fellow passengers as you queue at the two police checkpoints up the road. If you're coming from Kathmandu it's best to get a direct bus for Besisahar to avoid waiting around in Dumre.

It's sometimes possible to get together with other travellers and rent a whole jeep, rather than just a place in it. However you go, the ride is dusty so ensure your belongings, especially cameras, are packed in plastic bags and within sight as there have been some thefts.

There are frequent buses throughout the day to Pokhara (Rs35, 2¹/₄ hours; Rs50, 2¹/₂ hours express) and Kathmandu (Rs65, 5 hours) as well as to many other places in Nepal.

DUMRE TO BESISAHAR [MAPS 20-24]

First stop on the road north is at the police checkpoint in the Gurung settlement of **Bhansar (540m/1772ft)**, 15 mins by truck from Dumre. All foreigners are required to fill in their names and passport and trekking visa/permit numbers. If the police aren't about truck drivers don't bother to stop.

Turture (540m/1772ft) This village has some very basic accommodation but, as with the other 'hotels' in villages between Dumre and Besisahar, they're not representative of the kind of lodgings you can look forward to further up the valley. The

---

❑ **Walking times on trail maps**
Note that on all the trail maps in this book the times shown alongside each map refer only to time spent actually walking. Add 20-30% to allow for rest stops.

Buddha and *Gorkha* are on the main road; the *Marsyangdi*, *Muktinath* and *Shakti* are on the side road down to the bridge.

Paundi (520m/1706ft) This settlement is situated where the Paundi Khola joins the Marsyandi River. There are a number of tea houses here including the *Hotel Shuraj & Lodge*, *Hotel Paundi & Lodge*, *Hotel Himalaya & Lodge* and *Ashok Hotel* but as you will now have realised, 'hotel' is something of a misnomer. As in many parts of the Indian subcontinent, it's come to mean a place to eat rather than sleep but you can unroll your sleeping bag at most of these places.

There are several little shops, including one selling face masks against the dust. It might be worth buying some fruit here as you won't see much, other than apples in season, when you get up into the hills. There's a good swimming place under the bridge.

Bhoti Odar (550m/1804ft), or 'Botty Odour' as local VSO workers call it, is not as bad as the name would suggest. The accommodation is quite reasonable and the best available between Dumre and Besisahar.

The best places to stay in Bhote Odar are probably the *Ravindra Hotel & Lodge* and the *Thakali Hotel & Lodge* which boasts a 'love room'. This turns out to be nothing more than a double bed, although it's something of a novelty in the hills. There's another **police checkpoint** here and a **pharmacy** south of the town.

Philiya Sangu/Phalesangu/ Phalenksanku (660m/2165ft)
The name that no one knows how to spell is said to be derived from the English 'plank' and the Nepali *saaghu* meaning bridge. A substantial suspension bridge now crosses the Marsyandi here. There is basic accommodation in Philiya Sangu.

An **alternative route** crosses the river to follow a higher trail and you can rejoin the main route either at Besisahar or Bhulebhule (see p197). It's not an easy path to follow, however, so ask directions frequently.

On the main route following the road, you're now only 2-2¹⁄₂ hrs from Besisahar on foot.

Besisahar (820m/2690ft) [MAP 24: p196]
The booming capital of Lamjung District lies at the end of the road. It has been expanding rapidly since the road reached it and much of the new business is funded by Gurkhas retiring here on their British or Indian Army pensions.

Accommodation The best lodges are near the road-head in the southern part of town. The *Hotel Tukuche Peak* is a modern place, much like anything you'd find in Pokhara, with hot showers and a fridge full of cold beer. It's currently the top place in town and the best place to eat.

The *Hotel Himalayan* and the *Hotel Mountain View* are other places that get good reports. The hotels in the north of the town are rather more basic but this may change as the area is developing fast.

Services There's the second last **bank** up the valley (the last being in Chame), a **post office**, and a **hospital**. International phone-calls may be made at the **telecommunications centre** or at one of the many STD/ISD booths. There's also a cinema, and if you haven't seen a Hindi/Nepali movie yet this may be as good a place as any.

Getting away Several buses a day make the bumpy journey to Dumre. They leave from the other side of the river. If you miss the last one, usually at about 1.30pm, you might be able to get a ride on a truck.

(Opposite) **Top:** Machhapuchhre (6997m/22,942ft), the Fish Tail Peak, from Chomrong. **Bottom:** The lodges of Annapurna Base Camp (4130m/13,550ft).

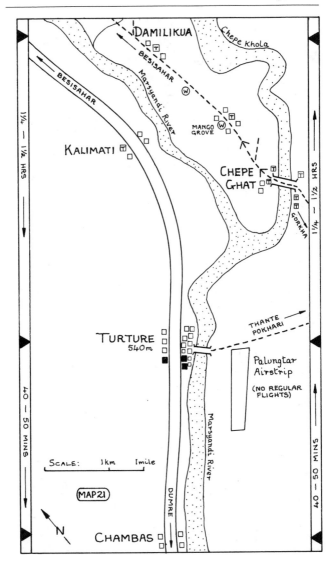

(**Opposite**) Clearing snow; Manang (see p212; photo: Charlie Loram)

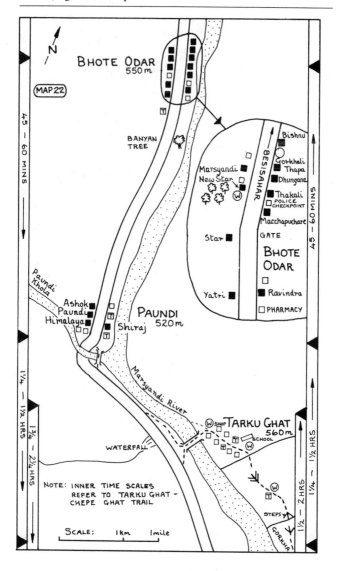

N

BHOTE ODAR
550 m

MAP 22

45 – 60 MINS

BANYAN
TREE

Bishnu

BESISAHAR

Marsyandi
New Star

Gorkhali
Thapa

Dhungana

Thakali
POLICE
CHECKPOINT

Macchapuchare

Star

GATE

BHOTE
ODAR

45 – 60 MINS

Yatri

Ravindra

PHARMACY

Paundi
Khola

Ashok
Paundi
Himalaya

Shiraj

PAUNDI
520 m

Marsyandi River

1¼ – 1½ HRS

1¾ – 2¼ HRS

SHOP TARKU GHAT
560 m

SCHOOL

WATERFALL

1¼ – 1½ HRS

2 – 2½ HRS

NOTE: INNER TIME SCALES
REFER TO TARKU GHAT –
CHEPE GHAT TRAIL

STEPS

GORKHA

½ – 1 HR

SCALE: 1 km   1 mile

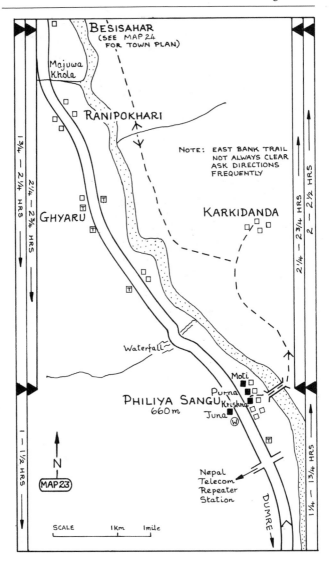

BESISAHAR
(SEE MAP 24
FOR TOWN PLAN)

Majuwa
Khola

RANIPOKHARI

NOTE: EAST BANK TRAIL
NOT ALWAYS CLEAR
ASK DIRECTIONS
FREQUENTLY

GHYARU

KARKIDANDA

Waterfall

Moti
Purna
PHILIYA SANGU Krishna
660m Juna

1¾ — 2¼ HRS

2¼ — 2¾ HRS

2¼ — 2¾ HRS

2 — 2½ HRS

1 — 1½ HRS

1¼ — 1¾ HRS

Nepal
Telecom
Repeater
Station

DUMRE

N

MAP 23

SCALE   1 Km   1 mile

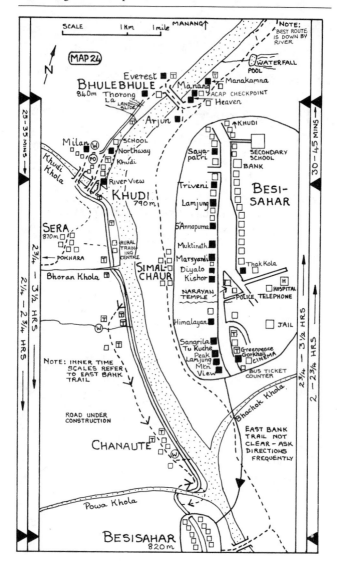

BESISAHAR TO BHULEBHULE
[MAP 24: p196]

The road north through Besisahar is being pushed through to Ngadi, for transport vehicles for the hydroelectric project in the area. So far only a rough track has been made as far as Khudi but since there are no bridges there are no vehicles.

Ten minutes' north of Besisahar the trail drops down to cross the Powa Khola. Across the river you can either follow the new road which is easier, or make a short but stiff climb to join the old trail.

Khudi (790m/2592ft)

This Gurung village, with its large government seed nursery, stands above the Khudi Khola. The new bridge was completed several years ago in anticipation of the collapse of the more convenient but dilapidated eastern bridge which is not a great advertisement for the workmanship of John M Henderson & Co Ltd of Aberdeen.

The owners of the *River View Lodge* have cunningly constructed a third footbridge to lure trekkers to their establishment. If you are in need of sustenance or a peaceful place to stay then this is as good a place as any. There's a **post office** and just north of the secondary school is a small Hindu temple dedicated to Shiva.

Route to Begnas Tal and Pokhara
See p230.

Bhulebhule (840m/2756ft)

The trail crosses to the east bank of the river here. The name of this village is said to be onomatopoeic, referring to the sound of the water in the spring nearby. You should stop for a break here to admire the first good mountain views on this trek. You can see Himalchuli (7893m/25,896ft) and, to the left of it, Ngadi Chuli (7835m/25,705ft), also known as Peak 29 or Manaslu II.

ACAP has opened a **checkpoint** in Bhulebhule so you'll be asked to sign in as you pass. There's now a **telephone office** in the village.

Accommodation is better here than in Khudi but varies considerably between the lodges. The relocated *Thorong La Guest House* is the first place you get to and boasts not only the most comfortable rooms in town but also an almost bottomless reserve of cold beer (Rs100) in their kerosene-powered fridge. Over the bridge is the *Arjun Lodge* with its pleasant garden. The *Manang Lodge* ('You can observe the well behaviour of Tibetan') is also a good place to stay. It's run by a charming family from Bagarchap. There's a rudimentary shower in the garden and they even have some rooms with double beds. The dining area overlooks the river and specialities include tuna pizza (Rs120) as well as Tibetan food.

Five minutes north of the village is a fine waterfall and two **pools** for cooling off or washing. As this is also the village water supply you should take care not to pollute it.

BHULEBHULE TO GHERMU
[MAP 25: p198]

Just south of **Taranche** you come to a stream. For the last few years, the villagers have been doing a good trade in helping trekkers across the sometimes slippery single plank on the bridge. When the water is above the stepping stones, the alternative is to wade across if the bridge hasn't been repaired.

Ngadi (930m/3051ft) is about 15 minutes beyond. Now they've paved over the drain that runs through the centre of the village this place is a lot cleaner and more pleasant to stay in. The homely *Hiker's Lodge* has a quiet garden restaurant with good views. It is run by a friendly local school teacher and his wife who are only too happy to help you with your Nepali. The *Kamal* and *Himalaya* have also been recommended. Massages are available for aching limbs.

Cross the big suspension bridge over the Ngadi Khola (also known as the Musi Khola) and skirt around the conical hill to begin the hot ascent to Bahundanda pass-

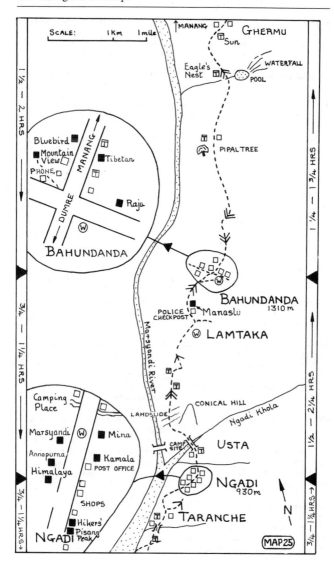

SCALE: 1 Km   1 mile

↑MANANG GHERMU
Sun

Eagle's
Nest   WATERFALL
POOL

Bluebird
Mountain
View   Tibetan
PHONE
PIPAL TREE
Raju

BAHUNDANDA

BAHUNDANDA
1310 m

POLICE
CHECKPOST Manaslu

LAMTAKA

Marsyandi River

CONICAL HILL
LANDSLIDE   Ngadi Khola

Camping
Place

Marsyandi   Mina   CAMP
SITE   USTA
Annapurna
Kamala
Himalaya   POST OFFICE   NGADI
930m
SHOPS
Hikers'   TARANCHE
Pisang
NGADI Peak

N

MAP25

½ — 2 HRS
¼ — 1 ¾ HRS
¾ — 1 ¼ HRS
½ — 2 ¼ HRS
¾ — 1 ¼ HRS →
¾ — 1 ¼ HRS →

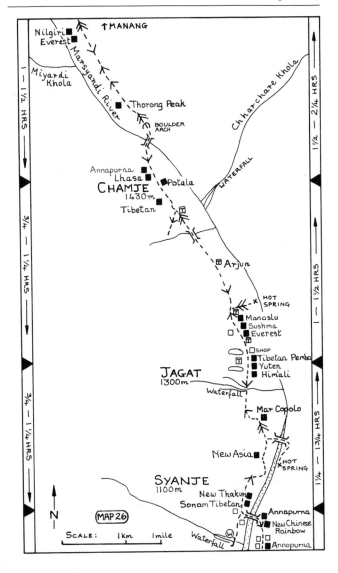

↑ MANANG

Nilgiri ■
Everest ■

Miyardi
Khola

Thorong Peak ■

BOULDER
ARCH

Chharchate Khola

Annapurna ■
Lhasa ■
CHAMJE
1430m

■ Potala

WATERFALL

Tibetan ■

⊞ Arjun

HOT
SPRING ✕

■ Manaslu
□ ■ Sushma
⊞ ■ Everest

□ SHOP
□ ■ Tibetan Pemba
⊞ ■ Yuten
JAGAT   ■ Himali
1300m

Waterfall

■ Mar Copolo

New Asia ■

HOT
✕ SPRING

SYANJE
1100m
New Thakuri ■
Sonam Tibetan ■
□   ■ Annapurna
□   New Chinese
Rainbow
ⓦ
Waterfall   □ ■ Annapurna

1 ½ HRS →

¾ — 1¼ HRS →

¾ — 1¼ HRS →

2¼ HRS →

1½ HRS →

1¾ HRS →

N

MAP 26

SCALE: 1km   1mile

ing through terraced fields and the small settlement of **Lamtaka/Lampata (1150m 3773 ft)**. The *Hotel Manaslu* is a reasonable place, 10-15 minutes below Bahundanda. Beside it is the **police checkpoint**.

Bahundanda (1310m/4298ft)

Whichever direction you're going, the tea shops of Bahundanda are a welcome stop after the sweaty slog up to this ridge-top village. Bahundanda means 'Brahmin Hill'. The best place to stay here is the very pleasant *Hotel Mountain View*, up the 'Stair Way to Heaven'. It has an enthusiastic young owner and a good view. The restaurant is pure vegetarian but has a slick menu including exotic specialities like French fries with cheese and ketchup.

International calls are possible from the **phone office**. It's in the shop by the steps to the Hotel Mountain View.

Dropping steeply, the trail continues through terraced rice fields. In about 1¼ hours you reach **Ghermu**. Buy some of the delicious guava and green oranges to refresh you. There are several lodges on this stretch of the trek.

SYANJE TO CHAMJE
[MAP 26: p199]
Syanje (1100m/3609ft)

Two lodges in Syanje ('Sigh-ang-ee') have superb views of the waterfall; the *New Chinese Rainbow Lodge* and the *Annapurna Lodge* just before the big suspension bridge. On the other side, the *New Thakuri Guest House* has an attractive sitting area right above the river.

Following the river and climbing gently you pass healthy marijuana plants to reach the Tibetan-run *Hotel New Asia* in about 20 minutes. There's a kerosene depot here. Across the river are some **hot springs**, just some of the many that can be found along this valley. Since most hot springs are close to the river they're often submerged during the monsoon season.

As the climb gets steeper you can see Jagat on the ridge above.

Jagat (1300m/4265ft)

The heavy boulders strewn about the lower part of this little settlement give it a somewhat claustrophobic air. There's a good range of accommodation, however. The *Tibetan Pemba Lodge* is very pleasant, as are the *Sushma Guest House* and the *Manaslu Lodge* at the northern end of Jagat. There are some more hot springs about 20 minutes away, down by the river.

Chamje (1430m/4692ft)

Just south of Chamje is the popular *Tibetan Lodge*, decorated with prayer flags. Although busy in the season, it seems to be resting on its laurels. Try the other lodges in Chamje where the owners are more welcoming.

Cross the long suspension bridge and climb through more fields of marijuana past the *Thorong Peak Hotel*, a quiet and attractive place to stay with excellent views. The wide valley has now become a narrow gorge with the river thundering through it. There are steep drops beside the path in some places.

It's a long hot climb up to the wide valley of Tal, a welcome sight just around the corner from the little tea house at the top. This is the district border with Manang and it's not just an administrative boundary. From the point of view of culture, architecture and climate, the differences across from Lamjung district are striking: the people are Buddhists of Tibetan ancestry; mud and thatch houses give way to stone buildings with flat roofs; the rainfall is considerably lower in these northern regions and subtropical vegetation starts to give way to the firs and pine trees of the highlands.

TAL TO BAGARCHAP
[MAP 27: p201]
Tal (1700m/5577ft)

It's been said that this small town is reminiscent of the American Wild West and I guess you could imagine horses being tied up outside the shops and hotels along the wide dusty main drag. The name Tal

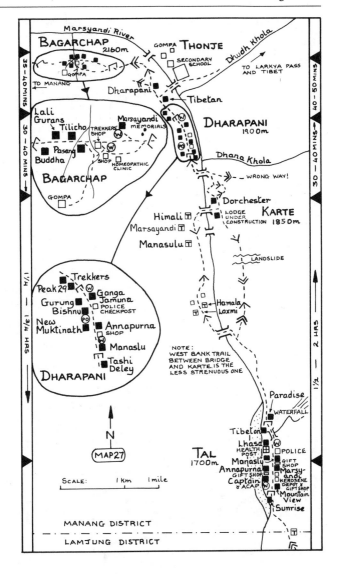

MAP 27

means 'lake', since the whole of this wide valley was once a lake. Just north of the village is a spectacular waterfall that makes a refreshing but powerful shower.

It's well worth spending a night in Tal. There are several lodges including the atmospheric *Manaslu Guest House* run by a jolly Gurung woman. For years she's been dishing up her excellent and nutritious 'Potatoes, Beans, Veg, Pumpkin Special' with corn bread. There's also Tibetan bread with cheese, and apple pie. The accurately-named *Paradise Guest House* and **bakery** is well located near the waterfall at the northern end of Tal, in a garden full of flowers.

There's an **ACAP checkpost and information centre**, a **kerosene depot**, and a surprisingly well-stocked **health post** (iodine, tiniba for giardia, paracetamol and penicillin). According to the health officer here the most common health problems in the area are worms, scabies and skin problems, toothache and conjunctivitis (caused by smoky houses).

There are several **gift shops** in Tal whose owners will probably find you soon enough.

Leaving Tal you reach a **mani wall** in the middle of the path. You should always walk to the left of Buddhist shrines and monuments. Pass the fields of maize, barley and potatoes and the valley soon narrows again. Before the bridge check with local people whether it's better to take the west bank trail, or the more strenuous but quieter east bank route.

Karte (1850m/6070ft) Both trails meet again at Karte, little more than a couple of

lodges. These include the *Dorchester* which, while lacking the luxury of its London namesake, improves greatly on its location.

Heading north, take the short high route to avoid a rock-fall by the river.

Dharapani (1900m/6234ft) The village is approached through stone gateways, characteristic of all villages in Manang. Across the narrow gorge loom high cliffs. The Manaslu Circuit follows the valley opposite, across the bridge to Thonje and up the Dhudh Khola to the Larkya La (5210m/17,093ft). Tibet is beyond (about 50km from Thonje) over the Gya La, which is still used as a trading route although not as busy now as in 1950, when Tilman was here. He noted 'long strings' of dzos (cross-bred yaks) ferrying grain and rice up the valley and Tibetan salt down it.

There are several good guest houses here, including the smart *Tashi Deley* to the south, the *Annapurna* in the middle of the village, and the *Trekkers' Hotel*, just beyond the northern gateway. International phone calls are possible from the *New Muktinath Hotel*. You'll need to sign the register at the **police checkpoint** as you pass through.

The route to Manang continues ahead. Up till now you've been travelling roughly north but the trail now swings due west.

Bagarchap (2160m/7087ft)
This once delightful village was the scene of a tragic natural disaster in November 1995. A devastating landslide swept without warning through its heart, flattening

---

❏ Gyasumdo
Although you're now in Manang District, this southern region, Gyasumdo, is culturally distinct from the area around Manang town. Manang District is an administrative unit, comprising three cultural groupings: Gyasumdo, Nyeshang (Manang Valley) and Nar-phu (in the east).

Gyasumdo means 'meeting-place of the three roads', since it is centred on Thonje. Three routes converge on Thonje: the route to Manang Valley, the route from Tal and the route to Tibet over the Gya La.

17 houses and killing several people, some trekkers among them. Standing by the memorials at the eastern gateway, you can clearly see the path of destruction which obliterated some buildings, while others, just metres away, stand unscathed.

Some of the lodges are currently still here although they may close and relocate to Danagyu. There's the *Marsayandi Lodge*, which still offers excellent food, and the friendly *Pasang Guest House*, both of which have excellent views of Annapurna II and Lamjung. The large *Buddha Hotel* on the western edge of the village also looks good.

Tibetan influences in the area are obvious: there are stone houses with firewood stacked on their flat roofs and above the village is the first *gompa* (Buddhist monastery and temple) you see on this trail. Known as **Diki Kalsang Gompa**, it was accidentally burnt down in December 1994, but having just been rebuilt, it luckily escaped further damage in 1995.

DANAGYU TO CHAME
[MAP 28: p204]
The route continues through forests of pine and fir to **Danagyu (2300m/7546ft)**. This village has grown in size since the Bagarchap disaster, as some of the destroyed lodges have relocated here. The *New Tibetan* has been recommended. A considerable amount of building work has also gone into this part of the trail. Previously, the only way into the Manang Valley from the south was over the 5785m/18,980ft Namun La along a now rarely-used route that runs from Khuldi to Danagyu.

Crossing a concrete bridge you pass a powerful waterfall, inhabited, according to local legend, by a water demon. Just after the steep stairway that follows the narrow gorge there's a junction for the alternative high route to Koto Qupar. It's probably now better to take the higher route because there have been many landslides in this area recently. Check with local people. Hung with lichen, the trees here include maple, oak and rhodo-

dendron. The most impressive rhododendron forests in the Annapurna region, however, are north of Pokhara around Ghorepani.

Latamrang (2400m/7874ft) There are
a few small lodges here. The *Tatopani Lodge* is run by an ex-Gurkha. If the bridge across the river is not down you can reach the small hot spring on the other side.

The apple orchards of **Tanchok** (just a small tea house) give way to impressive forests of pine, with some yew and larches dotted around. The *Marsyandi*, alone in these quiet woods by the river, is a peaceful place to stay.

Koto Qupar (2600m/8530ft) The
lodges are in two groups, some by the entrance gate and the others just before the **police checkpost** which guards two routes. The side trail across the bridge leads through the narrow Nar Valley to the two high altitude villages of Nar and Phu. This trail connects with a route that crosses into Tibet over the 6260m 20,538ft Lugu La Bhanjyang. The people of Nar-Phu are of Tibetan descent and although their remote region is administered as part of Manang district, their culture and language are unique. Sign the book at the checkpost and continue ahead for Manang.

CHAME TO PISANG
[MAPS 29 & 30: p205, p208]
Chame (2670m/8760ft)
A large white gate with a corrugated iron roof marks the entrance to Chame ('Charmay'). It's the district headquarters of Manang and has all the trappings of an administrative centre, including electricity, a phone office and well-stocked shops.

'Keep Chame Clean' says a notice but the place isn't exactly spotless; Tilman commented on its filthiness, passing through in 1950. For trekkers, Chame has just two attractions: the bank and the hot springs.

The most popular places here are the *New Tibetan Hotel* and the *Tibetan*

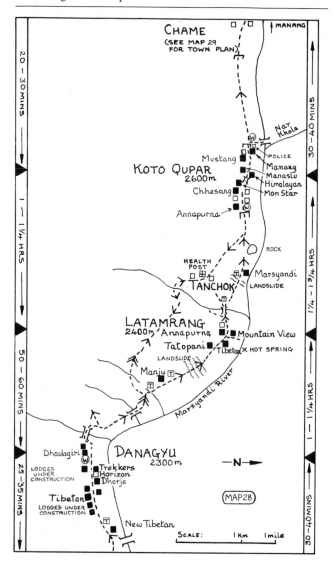

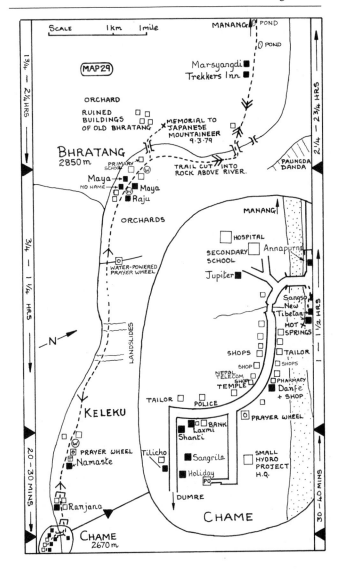

SCALE 1km 1mile

MAP 29

MANANG⌀ POND

⌀ POND

Marsyangdi ■
Trekkers Inn ■

1¾ — 2¼ HRS

ORCHARD
RUINED
BUILDINGS
OF OLD BHRATANG □ □
□ □ □

BHRATANG
2850 m

✕ MEMORIAL TO
JAPANESE
MOUNTAINEER
9.3.79

2¼ — 2¾ HRS

PAUNGDA
DANDA

PRIMARY
SCHOOL □ Ⓦ

Maya ■■
NO NAME →□ □ Ⓦ ■ Maya
□ ■ Raju

TRAIL CUT INTO
ROCK ABOVE RIVER.

2¼

ORCHARDS

MANANG

3/4 — 1 1/4 HRS

WATER-POWERED
PRAYER WHEEL

□ HOSPITAL

SECONDARY
SCHOOL

□ Annapurna ■

Jupiter ■

MANANG

LANDSLIDES

N →

□
□ Sangso
New
Tibetan ■
HOT ✕
□ SPRINGS

1 — 1/2 HRS

□ TAILOR
SHOPS □ SHOPS
SHOP □
NEPAL
TELECOM □ SHOP □ PHARMACY
TEMPLE ■ Danfe
+ SHOP

KELEKU

Ⓦ PRAYER WHEEL
↑ Namaste

TAILOR □ □
□ POLICE

■ ■ □ BANK
Laxmi
Shanti

⊙ PRAYER WHEEL

2.0 — 30 MINS

Tilicho □

■ Sangrila
■

SMALL
HYDRO
PROJECT
H.Q.

30 — 40 MINS

□ □ Ranjana

DUMRE

■ Holiday
PO

CHAME

↑ CHAME
2670 m

Lodge one behind the other with the whole place beginning to look like a tourist complex. Away from the main part of the town in a wonderful riverside location, right by the hot springs, the lodges can get very crowded at the height of the season. The food is quite good in both though also quite expensive but the sunny terrace, with flowerbeds of pink and white cosmos, is a wonderful place for breakfast.

At the other end of town the clean, well-run *Trekkers' Holiday Hotel* is recommended.

Hot springs After a hard day's trekking there's nothing better than to soak your aching limbs in near boiling mineral water. A small pool has been built by the springs just accommodating two people in the shallow water. Take care not to pollute either the hot spring or the river with soap or shampoo; virtually impossible unless you borrow a bowl from your lodge. Don't skinny dip (wear a swimming costume) and don't soak your feet too long as it softens the skin and you'll be more susceptible to blisters.

Other services The bank is not the fastest of the subcontinent's financial institutions so allow up to an hour for a transaction. It's open Sunday to Thursday from 10.00 to 14.00 and on Friday from 10.00 to 12.00. When things are busy they may stay open a little longer. For

---

❑ Nyeshang

The area in Manang District that is known as Nyeshang extends up the Manang Valley from Pisang to Khangsar.

The main villages in Nyeshang are Manang, Braga and Ngawal, known as Manang-tsok-sum ('three communities'). In recent history, however, they don't appear to have had very close links, in spite of speaking the same language. David Snellgrove noted when he visited the area in 1956 that the people of Manang and Braga had only just made peace with each other after five years of war. Tilman remarked that Ngawal had close relations with Nar village, over a 5322m/17460ft pass in the culturally different Nar-phu region.

The people are of Tibetan origin but their language, Nyeshang, is not a Tibetan dialect. Whilst some can afford to travel, trade and run lodges for trekkers, most eke out a meagre living from buckwheat and potatoes, subsisting on a diet of buckwheat tsampa and Tibetan tea.

Tilman, among the first Western travellers in Nyeshang, was amazed when 'a man whom we attempted to photograph retorted by whipping out a camera himself' (*Nepal Himalaya*). Even in the 1950s, however, some of the men here were almost as well-travelled as the great mountaineer himself. From 1790, throughout the time when Nepal was operating a policy of isolationism, the people of Nyeshang were given special permission to travel abroad by the king. Snellgrove reported that some of the temples in the area were hung with Chinese silks from Singapore.

Contact with the world beyond Nyeshang seems to have had only negative effects upon the people. Snellgrove noted that they had lost their zeal for religion, the important gompa at Bodzo having been deserted and others very run down. The writings of Tilman, Snellgrove and Maurice Herzog are unanimous in branding the people as the least friendly, most parsimonious and amongst the dirtiest they met in their travels in this part of the Himalaya. Forty years on things seem to have greatly improved; lodge-owners are friendly and their kitchens, although unlikely to win any awards for cleanliness, are no worse than others this side of the Kali Gandaki.

travellers' cheques there's a service charge of Rs 30 and a commission of 0.5%. For cash there's a commission of 1% but no service charge. If you haven't brought your passport with you a trekking permit will suffice as ID.

There's also an efficiently-run **post office** and a **phone office**. There's a good **health post** staffed by a doctor (most health posts are run by a health assistant) and basic medicines can be bought here. There are also a couple of **tailors'** where you can have trekking trousers made up, and several other well-stocked **shops**. You can even buy suncream and film here. The town has a 45kW micro hydro-electric system, built in 1980, which operates between 18.00 and 23.00.

The trail to Manang continues along the river through **Keleku** to **Bhratang** (2850m/9350ft) which is surrounded by apple orchards and has a number of lodges, the two on the north side of the trail being the best. Here, as in other villages in the area, pine needles are strewn across the trail so that they are broken down into compost by the boots and hooves of passing traffic.

Across the river is **old Bhratang** which was a Tibetan refugee village. The people were mainly Khampas, notorious for being warriors, but they were resettled in the mid 1970s. Carved on a rock near the ruins of their village is a memorial to Japanese mountaineer, Akira Ochiai, who died near the Thorung La in 1979.

Between Bhratang and the bridge over the Marsyandi is an impressive section of the trail, blasted out of solid rock. As you approach this bridge **Paungda Danda**, a magnificent cliff of granite, looms up ahead like a gigantic wave. Across the suspension bridge you climb through the peaceful forest and in under an hour you emerge in the wide Manang Valley, another world indeed. There's been a lot of hotel building in recent years. You'll pass the excellent *Trekkers' Inn* and *Marsyangdi Guest House* in a peaceful spot near a pool.

Pisang (3200-3300m/10,500-10,827ft)
The altitude in Pisang is enough to set off the first symptoms of altitude sickness (see p240) in some trekkers. If you have any signs of AMS spend at least one night acclimatising here before moving on up the valley.

There are numerous lodges strung out along the trail in **Lower Pisang (Dong Gang)**. One of the first you come to is the smart and comfortable *Peace Guest House* where you can warm yourself in the heated dining room while enjoying freshly baked apple pie. The *Hotel Maya* has had a good reputation for many years for producing excellent meals. Potatoes feature prominently on all menus in the Manang Valley. They're tasty local varieties that are delicious boiled in their skins.

Although the lodges in **Upper Pisang** are rather more basic than the ones below

---

❏ **Low route or high route to Manang?**
The quickest and easiest way to reach Manang is along the low route via Ongre. Walking fairly fast you could make the journey in under three hours along a trail that, apart from the climb to the viewpoint, is fairly level.

The extra effort and time involved in taking the high route is more than worthwhile; the views from this route are some of the best on the whole trek and combine with the altitude (you climb about 500m/1640ft above lower Pisang) to really take your breath away. 'Climb high, sleep low' is part of the advice given to guard against altitude sickness (see p240) so taking the high route will help you acclimatise better than following the low one. The high route is also far more interesting, passing through the ancient villages of Ghyaru and Ngawal and past the ruins of an old fort.

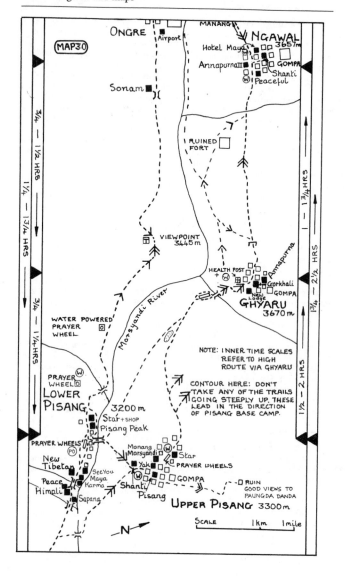

MAP30

ONGRE   Airport

MANANG

NGAWAL 3657m

Hotel Maya
Annapurna III
Peaceful   Shanti   GOMPA

Sonam

RUINED FORT

VIEWPOINT 3445m

Marsyandi River

HEALTH POST
+   New Lodge   Gorkhali   Annapurna
GOMPA

GHYARU 3670m

WATER POWERED PRAYER WHEEL

NOTE: INNER TIME SCALES REFER TO HIGH ROUTE VIA GHYARU

CONTOUR HERE: DON'T TAKE ANY OF THE TRAILS GOING STEEPLY UP. THESE LEAD IN THE DIRECTION OF PISANG BASE CAMP.

PRAYER WHEEL

LOWER PISANG   3200 m

Star + SHOP
Pisang Peak

PRAYER WHEELS

New Tibetan
Peace
Himali   SeeYou Maya Karma   Sapana

Monang Marsyandi   Star
Yak   PRAYER WHEELS
GOMPA

Shanti Pisang

UPPER PISANG 3300m

RUIN
GOOD VIEWS TO PAUNGDA DANDA

— N →

SCALE   1 km   1 mile

Time scales (left margin): 3/4 — 1½ HRS · 1/4 — 1¾ HRS · 3/4 — 1¼ HRS

Time scales (right margin): 1 — 1¾ HRS · 1¾ — 2½ HRS · 1½ — 2 HRS it's well worth spending the night up here and the climb is not as bad as it looks, taking about half an hour. The lodges are small, just a room or two in someone's house. Little appears to have changed here in centuries and the place has a positively mediaeval atmosphere to it. Living quarters are upstairs in the houses, reached from the stables below by a ladder carved from a single tree trunk.

The mountain scenery is superb. Across the valley Annapurna II looks close enough to touch. Pisang Peak rises behind you.

Watch out for flying arrows in the middle of the village. The area near the prayer wheel wall is used for archery practice, still a popular sport in many of these high villages. The **temple** above the village, contains a terracotta statue of Maitreya (the future Buddha).

PISANG TO MANANG
THE HIGH ROUTE   [MAPS 30-31]
From Upper Pisang the route roughly follows the contours of the land until you reach a wall of prayer wheels and mani stones.

The trail is not clear up to here and there may be more obvious goat tracks leading steeply upwards along the way, which you should avoid (it's the route to Pisang Base Camp). There's an alternative path from just over the bridge from Lower Pisang which passes a small green lake and takes you through thin forest.

Ghyaru (3670m/12,041ft) From the mani wall you descend to cross the tributary and then take the wide trail leading steeply uphill. After the hard climb of about 350m/1 148ft to Ghyaru you won't have any difficulty in stopping to admire the tremendous views from here. The tallest mountain, with the small pointed peak, is Annapurna II (7937m/26,040ft); you're looking at the impressive north face. To the left is Lamjung Himal (6931m/22,740ft) and to the right, above Manang, are Annapurna III (7555m 24,787ft) and Gangapurna (7455m

24,459ft). There's accommodation in Ghyaru (including a new stone and concrete lodge which should now be open). This is lucky since you may well be tempted to spend the rest of the day staring at the awe-inspiring scenery.

The temple is usually locked but the wall paintings are worth seeing if you can find someone to let you in. It was the only temple in the valley that the usually indefatigable Snellgrove was unable to gain access to during his Buddhist survey of the Manang Valley in 1956.

You're now above the tree-line and it can sometimes be windy and dusty up here. Five minutes outside Ghyaru you pass a white chorten containing a water-powered prayer wheel. There are also many mani walls on this route.

The trail passes above the ruins of a fort and in 30 to 40 minutes after these you reach Ngawal.

Ngawal/Bangpa (3657m/11,998ft)
This is another mediaeval village like Ghyaru, with flat-roofed stone buildings and ladders to reach the living quarters above the stables. The views across the valley to the Annapurnas are as impressive as from Ghyaru. The trekking peaks, Chulu West (6419m/21,060ft), Chulu East (6200m/20,336ft) and Chulu Far East (6060m/19,877ft), rise to the north.

Snellgrove spent a few nights here in 1955. He was disappointed by the temple ('nothing but a few rough clay images') and not warmly disposed towards the locals, one of whom stole his torch, the first theft in several months of travel. There's now a flourishing **new gompa** just outside Ngawal with many young trainee monks.

This is a wonderful place to stay and there are four basic *lodges* run by welcoming owners.

From Ngawal the trail drops steeply, sometimes following the electricity wires and bypassing Paugba to join the lower Pisang-Manang route at **Mungji**.

PISANG TO MANANG
THE LOW ROUTE   [MAPS 30-31]

Follow the trail through Lower Pisang for the low route to Manang. It's a pleasant walk through the forest, climbing gently at first, with one steep section to reach the **viewpoint** on top of the spur. There are tall prayer flags and a small shrine here. Continue down to the wide level valley passing a number of tea houses. The *Sonam Hotel* has good vegetarian food and even a curio shop. The manager also dabbles in patent medicines prescribing dubious-looking powders as a cure-all.

Ongre/Humde (3330m/10,925ft)

This consists of Manang airstrip and a few houses and lodges in a small but spread-out settlement. One of the longest prayer wheel walls in the region, consisting of 266 wheels, runs through the centre of the village. At the western end of the airstrip is a **police checkpost**.

Except during the monsoon and when there's snow between December and February, Royal Nepal Airlines have flights between Pokhara and Manang airstrip for US$50 on Tuesday, Wednesday, Saturday and Sunday mornings. They have a **booking office** here. Note that these flights operate only when the flying conditions are good and so are liable to cancellation, like the Pokhara-Jomsom flights.

Continuing along the trail to Manang, you pass the **Nepal Mountaineering Association School**, founded in 1979 by Ales Kunaver, the Yugoslav alpinist, who died in 1984. Above it is the micro hydroelectric plant serving Ongre and Manang. Power demands are outstripping supply so electricity is switched between the two villages on alternate nights, when it's working at all, that is.

Crossing the Marsyandi just before Munji, you join the high trail from Ghyaru and Ngawal.

Braga/Drakar (3450m/11,31 9ft)

The flat-roofed houses of this photogenic village are built in steep tiers against the craggy cliffs that form a natural amphitheatre around the meadow below. Above them is the region's oldest and most interesting gompa, a complex of several buildings with the three-storeyed temple at the top.

The new *Buddha Hotel*, right by the trail, is well run by a friendly lodge-owner. It's a good place to stay, particularly for the heavy-duty calories and good coffee available from the *Braga Bakery* here.

A sign on a building near the trail warns, 'Here siting, burn fire, cooking rice, dirty do is strictly prohibited'. The language may be quaint but the message is nonetheless important.

Braga Gompa Believed to be at least 500 years old, this gompa comprises three main buildings and belongs to the reformist Kagyu-pa sect of Tibetan Buddhism. Kagyu-pa was inspired by the monk Marpa who, in the 11th century, sought to make Tibetan Buddhism more spiritual.

The **main temple** is dark, mysterious and powerfully atmospheric. Bring a torch/flashlight and come up here early in the morning or late in the afternoon when the monks are worshipping and the building is filled with the fragrance of burning juniper. You enter the main sanctuary past two prayer wheels and a dingy hall, leaving your boots outside. One of the main features of this temple is the hundred or so terracotta images that line the walls and include the 39 figures of the Kagyu-pa hierarchy including Marpa and Milarepa, his disciple. The altar is an amazing jumble of butter lamps, vases of plastic flowers, masks, tinsel and photos of the Dalai Lama. Leave a donation in the big brown safe, labelled 'Donttion Box'.

The three-storeyed temple is known as the **Chorten**. The middle room is entered round the back and contains a statue of Avalokitesvara. Believed to be saviour and protector from danger he's also the ultimate in altruism, having rejected the state of nirvana when he

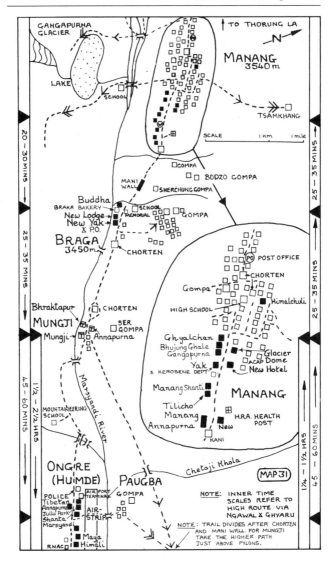

GANGAPURNA GLACIER

TO THORUNG LA

N

MANANG 3540 m

LAKE

SCHOOL

TSAMKHANG

SCALE   1 Km   1 mile

20 – 30 MINS

25 – 35 MINS

GOMPA

BODZO GOMPA

MANI WALL

SHERCHUNG GOMPA

Buddha

BRAKA BAKERY

New Lodge

New Yak & P.O.

SCHOOL

MEMORIAL

GOMPA

BRAGA 3450 m

CHORTEN

25 – 35 MINS

25 – 35 MINS

PO POST OFFICE

CHORTEN

Gompa

Himalchuli

HIGH SCHOOL

Bhraktapur

CHORTEN

MUNGJI

Mungji

SER GOMPA

Annapurna

Ghyalchan

Bhujung Ghale

Gangapurna

Glacier

ACAP Dome

Yak

& KEROSENE DEPT

New Hotel

45 – 60 MINS

1/2 – 2 1/2 HRS

Manang Shanti

MANANG

Marsyandi River

Tilicho

Manang

Annapurna

H.R.A. HEALTH POST

New

KANI

MOUNTAINEERING SCHOOL

Chetaji Khola

1/4 – 1 1/2 HRS

45 – 60 MINS

ONGRE (HUMDE)

PAUGBA

MAP 31

POLICE

Tibetan

Annapurna

Jullu Park

Shanta

Marsyandi

AIRPORT TERMINAL

GOMPA

AIR-STRIP

Maya

RNAC

Himali

NOTE: INNER TIME SCALES REFER TO HIGH ROUTE VIA NGAWAL & GHYARU

NOTE: TRAIL DIVIDES AFTER CHORTEN AND MANI WALL. FOR MUNGJI TAKE THE HIGHER PATH JUST ABOVE PYLONS.

reached it because so few other mortals had attained that stage. Above this room is another small shrine with an image of Amitabha, ('Boundless Light'); you'll need a torch as it's very dark; below is a shrine with numerous wall paintings and a large statue of Maitreya, the future Buddha whose return to earth is expected around the year 3520 AD, 4000 years after the death of the last Buddha. Between the Chorten and the main temple is another **shrine**, containing several images including Mahakala and Ma-ning.

Braga Gompa is open from 7am to 10 am and 1pm to 5pm.

Bodzo Gompa is the most interesting of the other temples between Braga and Manang but you'll need to find someone to let you in. Perched on a rocky ridge it contains fine wall-paintings and was once the centre of a large community of monks.

Manang (3540m/11,614ft)

Most trekkers make this, the largest village in the valley, a base for at least a couple of nights, while they acclimatise (see p214 for some acclimatisation trips). The views of the Annapurnas, Gangapurna and the glacial lake below it are spectacular; even more so if you climb north above Manang. From left to right the peaks are Lamjung, Annapurna II, Annapurna IV, the false peak of Annapurna III, and Gangapurna above the glacier.

The cost of a bed in and above Manang has now been pegged at Rs120 for a double room and Rs30 for a bed in a dorm, relatively high for trekking routes in Nepal. It is hoped that this doesn't encourage trekkers to hurry over the Thorung La before they are fully acclimatised. If you're travelling on a tight budget, or want to avoid the crowds, then spend a few nights in the villages of Ngawal and Ghyaru, or press on to the peaceful village of Tengi where a bed costs just a few rupees.

In Manang, the 200 or so flat-roofed houses are tightly packed together with prayer flags on long poles above them. Most of the lodges are beside fields to the south. There are several well-stocked shops (most attached to the lodges) and the wide range of goods on offer includes canned beer, cans of tuna, chocolate and cream crackers. If you anticipate a cold or snowy crossing of the Thorung La you can buy gaiters, woollen sweaters, hats and gloves. HRA sell sun block and zinc oxide to protect you from the powerful sun. You can also pick up porters here, or even a horse to help you over the pass - for around Rs3500 – or whatever you will pay!

There's an **ACAP information centre** where you can watch an interesting 30-minute video on ACAP's work, a **kerosene depot** at the Yak Hotel, a **phone office**, and a **post office** (open 10.00-16.00 Sunday to Thursday, 10.00-14.30 on Friday). Mail takes about seven days to reach Kathmandu. Testing the poste restante service here, I arrived to find my mail safely secured to the wall with nails.

Manang Gompa is in the centre of the town; the three presiding images in it are Padmasambhava ('Lotus Born'), Avalokitesvara ('Glancing Eye') and Amitabha ('Boundless Light'). Braga Gompa is, however, far more interesting and should not be missed. Nor, for your own safety, should you miss the daily lecture on AMS at the **Himalayan Rescue Association health post** (see below), if you didn't make it to one of their lectures in Kathmandu.

Accommodation Most trekkers go for the more luxurious lodge to the south of the main part of Manang. Most have large warm dining halls and varied menus including the usual trekking 'delicacies' such as chocolate cake, cinnamon rolls and apple pie. You should, however, try something of the local cuisine: buckwheat tsampa and Tibetan tea. Some lodges also make buckwheat bread; potato dishes are good, too and they all have their own specialities.

The *Yak Hotel* is very popular. The kitchen turns out good food and excellent potato dishes; try the potato cheese balls. The pizzas and Mexican queasadillas at the *Annapurna* have also been recommended. The best food in Manang, however, comes from the *Manangsangti Guest House* where Mavis Gurung, who lived in Calcutta, turns her hand to everything from Julienne salad to a curry and rice, all with excellent results.

HRA health post The Himalayan Rescue Association has done tremendous work in reducing the numbers of trekker-deaths from altitude sickness. During the trekking season this post is staffed by two foreign volunteer doctors. Their daily lectures, held each afternoon, on how to recognise the symptoms of altitude sickness and take appropriate action are both informative and entertaining. A pressure bag (see p240) is kept here for serious AMS cases. The general clinic is run for the benefit of the local people but the doctors are also happy to attend to foreigners for a small fee that goes towards running the HRA. They do stool tests, sell basic medicines (including diamox for AMS), have a book exchange and may also **change money** and travellers cheques at bank rates.

MANANG TO THORUNG LA
[MAPS 32-33, p216 & p219]
After spending a couple of nights at Manang (3540m/11,614ft) you should spend one more night between here and Thorung Phedi for acclimatisation. Two nights would be better (see below).

Leaving Manang
Tengi (3650m/11,975ft) is reached in just half an hour. There are a couple of basic lodges here, of which the *Ongme* is the best, run by a friendly woman. For the discerning trekker this is a more authentic place to stay than Manang. A hard climb follows to **Gunsang (3900m/12,795ft)** but the views back of Gangapurna and Annapurna III across the Manang Valley are a good enough excuse for frequent stops. In Gunsang take a cup of tea at the *Marsyangdi Hotel* to congratulate yourself on reaching the highest place on earth – if the sign is right you are now at '3850km' above sea level! It's a great place to stay.

Beyond Gunsang you come to **Yak Kharka** which means 'yak pastures'. True to the name grazing yaks are to be seen around this area, and across the river on the mountainside. Take care in your

---

❏ Acclimatisation advice for crossing the Thorung La
For a long time it has been known that a lot of people suffer real altitude sickness while crossing the Thorung La, although only about two die each year, unfortunately often porters. An old but only recently recognised HRA study has revealed just how many people suffer. Using an internationally recognised altitude sickness scale the study revealed that by following the usual recommended itinerary of overnight stops in Manang (two nights), Letdar, Thorung Phedi before crossing the pass led to two-thirds of trekkers suffering from moderate (not mild) AMS (for information about AMS see p240). A number also suffered severe AMS: ataxia, hallucinations and rapid fluid build up in the lungs.

Luckily the solution is simple: **spend two nights between Manang and Thorung Phed**i. This not only dramatically decreases the chance of AMS but it also gives the body a chance to get a little stronger at altitude, so making the pass crossing less arduous. The most obvious option is staying at Yak Kharka then Letdar and then Thorung Phedi but other variations include Gunsang, then Letdar, or Khangsar then Yak Kharka or Letdar.

You don't *have* to do this but it will make your trek a lot more comfortable and involve less worry. And it will save the odd life.   **Jamie McGuinness**

❏ ACCLIMATISATION TRIPS AROUND MANANG

You must spend a minimum of two nights at around this altitude (3540m/11,614ft) in order to acclimatise before moving on to sleep safely at a higher altitude. Climbing high and sleeping low is the best advice so rather than sitting in a lodge in Manang eating apple pie, you should visit some of the following:

Braga Gompa

(See p210). You could also visit Bodzo Gompa, Sherchung Gompa and, above Mungji, Ser Gompa.

Tsamkhang

Halfway up the northern cliff that rises above Manang, in a cave, is a tsamkhang (hermitage) where a characterful old lama conducts a short puja on trekkers about to cross the Thorung La. For Rs100 he'll say a prayer for you and tie a piece of red ribbon around your neck for good luck. Blessing times are 10-11am and 4-6pm. Even without the puja, the steep climb up here will help you to acclimatise and the views across the valley are stupendous. This tsamkhang is also known as Praban Gompa and Manang Vijek Gompa.

Gangapurna glacier

Across the river from Manang there are a couple of walks around the lake below this glacier.

Khangsar (3730m)

If the hustle and bustle of Manang is getting to you then escape for a night to this undeveloped village, just a 1½-2 hour walk away. There are two lodges here. The best is the *Himachuli and Laxmi Hotel* which is run by a very friendly and efficient woman. There is a small shop below the lodge where you can buy a few supplies. The *Tilicho Hotel* is more basic. From the village there are superb views up the Khangsar Khola to Tilicho Peak (7132m/23,399ft) and the Grande Barrière (so named by Herzog in 1950; see opposite p224). A trip up this beautiful valley is a great aid to acclimatisation. There's a small plain temple in the village and beyond Khangsar is Ta-hrap Gompa, built by the lama of Braga several hundred years ago.

Side trip around the Khangsar Khola valley, or on to Tilicho Tal

Maurice Herzog may have nipped up to Tilicho Tal from Manang alone with nothing more than a bar of chocolate but, having fallen in the river and spent the night in the open, he did almost die.

You'll need a sleeping bag, mat and supplies for the three-day return trip from Manang to this remote lake which lies at 4920m/16,142ft, below Tilicho Peak. A tent is not necessary as an abandoned hut now provides very basic and dirty shelter at the head of the valley. Soon the accommodation will be even better as a lodge is being constructed here. Locals in Manang should know if it has been completed. Although the paths have been improved, the difficulties of a trip up this valley should not be underestimated – there are still several precipitous sections where steady feet and a cool head are required.

● **Routes** Reach Khangsar in 1½-2 hours from Manang along either trail. The route via the ruined fort is the most direct but is dependant on the height of the river and the bridge being in place.

From Khangsar there are a couple of options for trips up the Khangsar Khola Valley. For those with only a day to spare, a long and strenuous acclimatisation trip can be made around the valley, climbing to a high point of 4800m with stunning close-up views of Tilicho Peak and the Grande Barrière. If you've got more time you could include an overnight stop in the hut at the head of the valley and then climb the long, steep trail to the small plateau overlooking Tilicho Tal, before returning. Under snow, however, the route to the lake becomes a serious mountaineering proposition with the risk of avalanche being high.

There are two main trails from Khangsar to the hut at the head of the valley. The lower route is quicker (3-4 hours), but the higher trail offers better views and acclimatisation (3¹⁄₂-5 hours). An anti-clockwise circuit combining the two offers the best of both worlds (allow 9 to 10 hours).

The higher route leaves Khangsar by the temple and climbs steadily to Tahrap gompa (40 mins to one hour). After crossing two streams you reach a hut (40 mins to one hour). The trail divides a few minutes beyond this. Take the wide upper trail which climbs steeply to a viewpoint (4800m) marked with a prayer flag (1³⁄₄ - 2¹⁄₂ hours). The trail then descends in a series of tight switchbacks down a very steep scree slope to the valley bottom (30-60 minutes). Climbing this slope would be a heart-breaking experience which is why this circuit is done this way round. Just over the bridge to the west is the two-storey hut offering shelter for those planning on climbing to Tilicho Tal.

The obvious route to Tilicho Tal (3-4 hours up; 1¹⁄₄ -2¹⁄₂ hours down) begins by climbing steeply over a ridge from behind the hut. The gradient lessens for a while before ascending in a series of steep zig-zags.

Recover your breath on the final easier haul to the small plateau at the top (5200m/17,060ft), from where there are views to the lake. Herzog refers to it as the 'Great Ice Lake' since it was covered in a thick sheet of ice when he crossed it in May 1950.

It is not possible to traverse along either shore of the lake (despite the **incorrect trails marked on many maps,** including the Schneider map) as the western side is continuously threatened by avalanche and the terrain on the eastern shore impassable. However, from late December to May, the lake is usually frozen enough to walk on (with utmost care, crampons and rope), creating a tough and dangerous alternative route to the Thorung La. Even when the lake isn't frozen it is possible to cross a pass to the north-east which will take you to the northern end of the lake. From here Herzog crossed the Tilicho Pass (5099m/16,729ft; also known as Mesokanto Pass) and descended to Thinigaun and Jomsom. Unfortunately a high-altitude army camp above Jomsom now makes this route illegal but an alternative pass to the north (marked by a few cairns) avoids this restricted area and enables a descent to Thinigaun.

Return to Khangsar along the lower route (2¹⁄₂ - 3¹⁄₂ hours). After traversing a steep landslide, avoid carrying on along a difficult middle trail and instead, descend through a small wood to a bridge over the river. Continue through the wood on the south bank of the Khangsar Khola before crossing back to the north bank over the next bridge. The route rises and falls through a forest of stunted pine crossing two main streams. At the second stream, take the lower, less obvious trail which takes you directly back to the village. The higher trail will also take you to the village, but it's a longer way round.

There is one further route up the valley which follows the south bank of the Khangsar Khola. The villagers, however, do not recommend using it as it has been destroyed by landslides in a number of places.

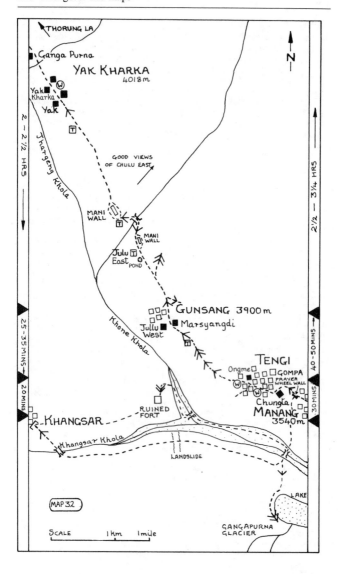

THORUNG LA

Ganga Purna

YAK KHARKA
4018m

Yak
Kharka

Yak

Jhargeng Khola

GOOD VIEWS
OF CHULU EAST

MANI
WALL

MANI
WALL

Julu
East   POND

GUNSANG 3900m

Khone Khola

Jullu
West   Marsyangdi

TENGI

Ongme   GOMPA
PRAYER
WHEEL WALL

Chungla

MANANG
3540m

RUINED
FORT

KHANGSAR

Khangsar Khola

LANDSLIDE

MAP 32

SCALE   1km   1mile

LAKE

GANGAPURNA
GLACIER

N

2 – 2½ HRS

25 – 35 MINS   20 MINS

2½ – 3¼ HRS

40 – 50 MINS   30 MINS

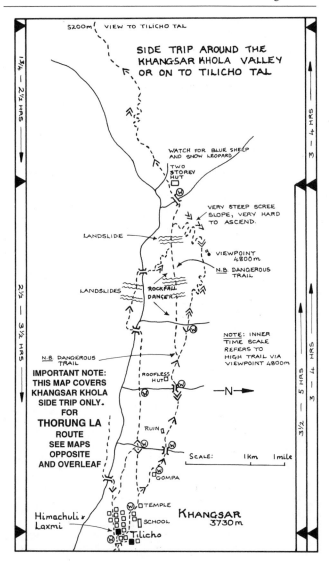

SIDE TRIP AROUND THE
KHANGSAR KHOLA VALLEY
OR ON TO TILICHO TAL

5200m VIEW TO TILICHO TAL

WATCH FOR BLUE SHEEP
AND SNOW LEOPARD

TWO STOREY HUT

VERY STEEP SCREE
SLOPE, VERY HARD
TO ASCEND.

LANDSLIDE

VIEWPOINT 4800m

N.B. DANGEROUS TRAIL

LANDSLIDES

ROCKFALL DANGER

NOTE: INNER
TIME SCALE
REFERS TO
HIGH TRAIL VIA
VIEWPOINT 4800m

N.B. DANGEROUS TRAIL

ROOFLESS HUT

IMPORTANT NOTE:
THIS MAP COVERS
KHANGSAR KHOLA
SIDE TRIP ONLY.
FOR
THORUNG LA
ROUTE
SEE MAPS
OPPOSITE
AND OVERLEAF

—N→

RUIN

SCALE: 1 Km 1 mile

GOMPA

TEMPLE

KHANGSAR 3730m

Himachuli & Laxmi

SCHOOL

Tilicho

1¾ — 2½ HRS   2½ — 3½ HRS

3 — 4 HRS   3 — 4 HRS   5 HRS   3½

efforts to photograph these shaggy creatures as they can be temperamental.

Letdar (4200m/13,780ft)

There's been considerable building activity here recently so the range of lodges should be better than the basic places that have been here for many years. ACAP has built a couple of latrines.

Check at the lodges for which side of the river you should follow between here and Thorung Phedi. ACAP recently built a new trail on the east side.

Thorung Phedi (4450m/14,600ft)

Literally 'the foot of the Thorung' this is just one very large lodge and a smaller one below it. It's a bleak spot and can seem particularly grim if you're suffering from the altitude, as many people are. The place can get very busy, particularly if

snow has closed the pass. *Thorung Base Camp Lodge*, as the original hotel is now called, has undergone considerable improvements. Some rooms even have attached bath (Rs600). All accommodation is expensive. A bed in one of the dorms is Rs90, doubles are Rs200 and triples are Rs300. Food is about 30% more expensive than in the best Manang lodges. Daal bhat is Rs180, muesli with apple Rs75 and a Coke is Rs60, more than four times the price in Kathmandu or Pokhara. Everything does, of course, have to be lugged up here just for the benefit of the trekkers. The friendly staff do an excellent job in producing good food quickly and creating a lively atmosphere, not unlike an alpine hut. The alternative is the smaller *Marsyandi Lodge* down by the river. Built around a small courtyard, it's not bad. Most people have an early

---

❑ **Safety on the Thorung La**

Although many thousands of people cross it each year, the Thorung La is a very high and potentially dangerous pass. Trek up here on a warm and sunny November day with many other trekkers for company and the route may seem innocent enough. If the weather turns or if there's snow on the ground the dangers of altitude are combined with exposure and can be lethal. Scarcely a year goes by without at least one fatality occurring here. Almost all of these could have been prevented.

For your own safety and for the safety of others:

● **Be aware of the symptoms of altitude sickness** and know what to do about them (see p240). If you feel bad at Thorung Phedi, don't press on up but go down to Letdar or below for a night.

● **Don't attempt the pass in bad weather**. The route to the top is not a simple one; it meanders round valleys and over moraines, although it's clear enough when there's no snow. If conditions don't look good, take advice from the lodge-owner at Thorung Phedi before setting out.

● **Walk in a group of at least five people** and keep together even if the weather is good and you're all feeling fine when you set off. Rik Allen, whose grave you pass near the top of the Thorung La, was travelling with only two other people. When he and the other man developed serious AMS, their companion was only able to help one of them.

● **Be properly equipped for the cold** Ensure that everyone in your group (including your porters, if you have them) has proper footwear, warm hats, gloves and jackets. Although many trekkers now cross the pass in track shoes rather than boots, their chances of getting frostbite which could lead to the amputation of toes is significantly higher than those wearing boots, if the weather turns bad.

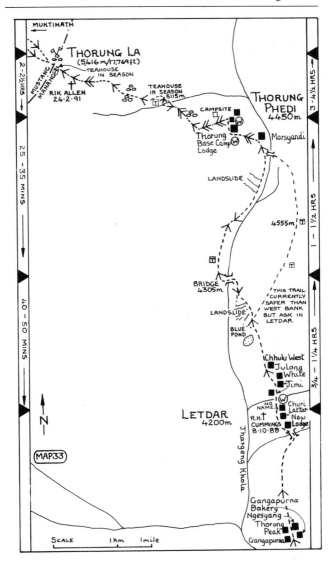

MUKTINATH

THORUNG LA
(5416 m/17,769 ft)
TEAHOUSE
IN SEASON

MUSTANG MANANG

RIK ALLEN
24·2·91

TEAHOUSE
IN SEASON
5115m

CAMPSITE

THORUNG
PHEDI
4450m

Thorung
Base Camp
Lodge

Marsyandi

LANDSLIDE

4555m

BRIDGE
4305m

LANDSLIDE

BLUE
POND

THIS TRAIL
CURRENTLY
SAFER THAN
WEST BANK
BUT ASK IN
LETDAR.

Chhuku West
Julong
White
Jimi

NO NAME

Churi
Lattar

LETDAR
4200m

R.H.
CUMMINGS
8·10·88

New
Lodge

Jhangeng Khola

N

MAP33

Gangapurna
Bakery
Ngesyang
Thorong
Peak
Grangapurna

SCALE   1km   1mile

2 - 2½ HRS

25 - 35 MINS

40 - 50 MINS

3 - 4½ HRS

1 - 1½ HRS

¾ - 1¼ HRS

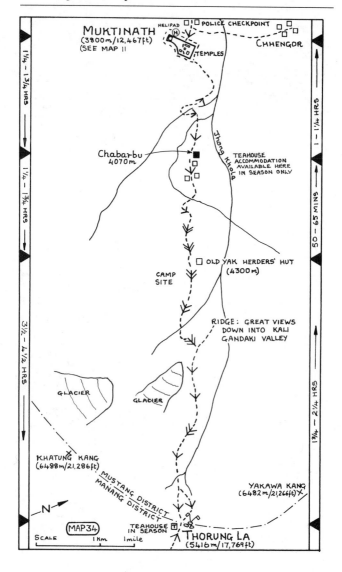

MUKTINATH
(3800m/12,467ft)
(SEE MAP 11

HELIPAD POLICE CHECKPOINT

CHHENGOR

TEMPLES

Chabarbu
4070m

Jhong Khola

TEAHOUSE
ACCOMMODATION
AVAILABLE HERE
IN SEASON ONLY

OLD YAK HERDERS' HUT
(4300m)

CAMP
SITE

RIDGE: GREAT VIEWS
DOWN INTO KALI
GANDAKI VALLEY

GLACIER

GLACIER

KHATUNG KANG
(6488m/21,286ft)

MUSTANG DISTRICT
MANANG DISTRICT

YAKAWA KANG
(6482m/21,266ft)

N

MAP 34

SCALE   1Km   1mile

TEAHOUSE
IN SEASON

THORUNG LA
(5416m/17,769ft)

1¼ – 1¾ HRS   1¼ – 1¾ HRS   3½ – 4½ HRS

1 – 1¼ HRS   50 – 65 MINS   1¾ – 2¼ HRS

supper and retire to their sleeping bags to keep warm; it can be bitterly cold here.

Leaving Phedi
You should aim to leave next morning at around 06.00, not much earlier as the steep track may be icy and dangerous in the dark. It'll probably take you around 3-4 hours to reach the top if the conditions are good and up to 4¹/₂ hours to get from there to Muktinath. Allowing for stops totalling a couple of hours along the way, you should easily reach Muktinath by 4.30pm. Make sure your water bottle is full and have as many cups of tea as you can manage before you leave. You'll acclimatise less well and feel more tired if you're dehydrated. Also, have sunscreen and a sunhat ready as it can be very hot on this exposed pass.

The route The trail begins with the ascent of the steep slope immediately behind the lodge. It's dishearteningly steep at first but becomes less so as you gain altitude. You pass many small cairns built by local travellers. About an hour above Thorung Phedi a *new hotel* is under construction. Since it's at 4800m you'd need to be well acclimatised to stay here. After about 1¹/₄ hours from Thorung Phedi you cross a small valley, descending to the stream and climbing across the far slope. At 5115m/16,781ft, there's a little *tea shop* open only during the season.

A seemingly never-ending series of false summits follow as the trail weaves through the stony moonscape. Tony and Jean Allen ask that passing trekkers check that the stones on their son's cairn are still in place. Marked with a headstone, it's in a gully just below the trail. Twenty minutes beyond is a large chorten and a short distance after this there are the prayer flags marking the top of the pass. There's a little *tea shop* here open in the season selling probably the most expensive tea in Nepal at Rs30.

Thorung La (5416m/17,769ft)
It can be fairly breezy up here so most people stay just long enough to take the commemorative photograph of themselves on this elevated spot, one of the world's highest passes. You're now standing on the equivalent of four Ben Nevises, 2¹/₂ Mt Kosciuskos, 1¹/₂ Mt Cooks and you're 938m/3077ft above the Matterhorn and 608m/1998ft higher than Mont Blanc! Unless you're a mountaineer you'll probably never reach as high an altitude in your life again.

Two peaks rise up from the saddle of the pass. To the north is Yakawa Kang (6482m/21,266ft) and to the south Khatung Kang (6488m/21,286ft). Far below you in the Kali Gandaki Valley you can just make out the fields of Kagbeni.

THORUNG LA TO MUKTINATH [MAP 34: p220]
The descent
This can be **very tough** on the knees, although it's not steep at first. You pass within about 50m of a large glacier.

The views of the mountains lining the Kali Gandaki Valley are better from about halfway down this side than from the pass itself, particularly of Dhaulagiri (8167m/26,795ft), the world's seventh highest peak.

At about 4300m/14,108ft are the ruins of a yak herder's hut. It's now roofless but the walls offer some protection to campers. The trail continues steeply down from here, crossing a stream to another collection of huts. During the trekking season one of them, *Chabarbu*, is open as a lodge with basic accommodation. There's even a curio stall though most people are more interested in resting their aching knees, attending to blisters and seeking liquid replenishment.

From here it's about an hour to the temples of **Muktinath**. The police checkpoint at **Ranipauwa** is a few minutes below where comfortable lodges await you. Turn to p165 for the continuation of this trek.

▲ Crossing the Thorung La in the opposite direction
Doing the Circuit in a clockwise direction is certainly harder but not impossible. Crossing this way

in 1950, Tilman wrote, 'This climb of nearly 5,000ft nearly broke my heart', but then he was carrying a pack full of rocks, ammonites collected in Muktinath.

You can cut about 1½ hours off the climb by spending the night at *Chabarbu* (above) but it's open only during the trekking season. A very early start is essential and if you're setting out from Ranipauwa you should aim to leave soon after 4am. It can take up to eight hours to reach the top of the pass from Muktinath. Take note of the warnings for crossing the Thorung La on p218 and if you're feeling the effects of the altitude at all in Muktinath you must not attempt the crossing.

Gorkha to Besisahar

Few trekkers take this alternative route to Besisahar because it takes longer than the direct route from Dumre and because accommodation is only very basic. The route is through low-lying villages and rice fields and can be very hot early or late in the season and sweltering during the monsoon.

Meeting few other trekkers may, however, be an attraction, and you also avoid two-thirds of the dusty Dumre-Besisahar road. The spectacularly-situated fortified palace at Gorkha is well worth seeing. Including the bus trip from Kathmandu to Gorkha, this route will take three days, giving you time on the first afternoon to look round Gorkha.

Gorkha (1200m/3937ft)

Famous as the town from which the whole country was conquered in the 18th century, and also for giving its name to one of the world's most famous fighting forces (see p60), modern Gorkha looks just like any other bazaar in Nepal. But 250m/820ft above is an architectural gem, Gorkha Durbar, the fortified palace and temple of the kings of Gorkha. Originally built by Ram Shah in the early

17th century, it was expanded by Nepal's best-known king, Prithvi Narayan Shah, to commemorate his conquest and unification of the country in 1769.

You won't regret the half-hour slog up the hill to **Gorkha Durbar**. The views from the crenellated walls are superb and include Dhaulagiri and Manaslu to the north. In the western half of the palace is the Kali temple (so holy that only the King and the priests are allowed inside). The courtyard outside flows with the blood of sacrificed goats at Dasain (October) and Chaitra Dasain (late March). The palace living-quarters were in the eastern half of the complex. Guards forbid photography inside the main palace complex but you can take photos of the views and fine Newar carvings that decorate the eaves and windows.

Trails lead to the look-out posts of Upallokot and Tallokot. In the town is **Tallo Durbar**, an 18th century Newar-style building which is thought to have been used as the administrative headquarters. It's currently being restored and turned into a museum. The new statue of Prithvi Narayan Shah should now be on display in the park above the bus stand.

Accommodation The smart new *Hotel Gorkha Prince* (☎ 20131) has large clean double rooms for Rs150 with shared bathroom and Rs300 with attached. There is a good rooftop restaurant here. A more intimate place to stay is the *Gorkha Lodging Centre*, in fact, just a few rooms that the pharmacy lets out. They charge Rs150 for a double or triple. The *Hotel Pamper* has good value double rooms with communal bathroom for Rs60, or Rs100 with attached bath.

The *Hotel Gorkha Bisauni* is rather overpriced with attached doubles for Rs 300, Rs 200 without. There's also a dormitory for Rs 50 per bed. The hotel has a good restaurant, and you can make international calls from here.

The *Gorkha Hill Resort* (☎ 227929) is an up-market hotel just off the road, 5km before you reach Gorkha. Rooms are US$30/40.

Other services The town is the head-quarters of Gorkha district, and public services include a post office, bank and health post. International calls can be made from many of the hotels.

Buses Most buses leave early in the morning so you should check departure times the night before. There are several buses a day to Kathmandu (Rs65-85, six to seven hours) including a Sajha bus at 06.45 and 13.00 (tickets from the office beside Swagat Hotel). Buses to Pokhara (Rs65, five hours) leave at 06.00 and 09.15. You can also get buses from here to Bhairawa/Sunauli (the border with Uttar Pradesh, India), Birgunj (the border with Bihar, India) and Bharatpur (on the Terai).

Get a direct bus if you want a seat. If you can't get a direct one you could take any bus from Gorkha to Anbu Khaireni (the junction with the Kathmandu-Pokhara road, 20km from Gorkha) and pick up another from there.

GORKHA TO CHEPE GHAT
[MAPS 35-36, p224-5]

Allow ample time for the first section from Gorkha to Chorkate as the route down to the Daroundi Khola can be difficult to follow. Ask directions frequently. Do so, in fact, until you reach the Besisahar road, since you come to numerous tricky junctions along this route. A porter-guide as far as Chepe Ghat might be useful.

Leaving Gorkha

There are several trails down to the Daroundi Khola from Gorkha. For the most direct route, turn left before the temple and pass the barracks. The trail is fairly level to start with, then it loses height out of the town, eventually dropping steeply through the forest down paved

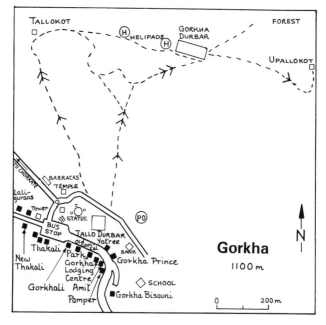

Gorkha
1100 m

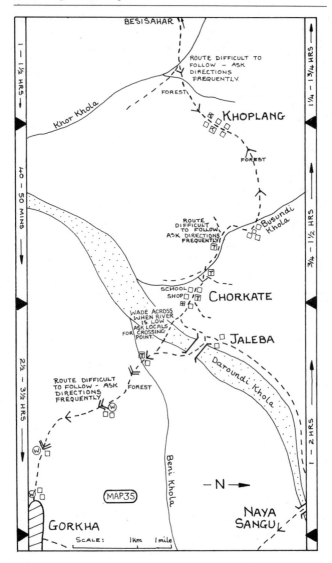

(Opposite) Top: The Grande Barrière(see p215). **Bottom:** Tengi and the Manang Valley (photos: Charlie Loram).

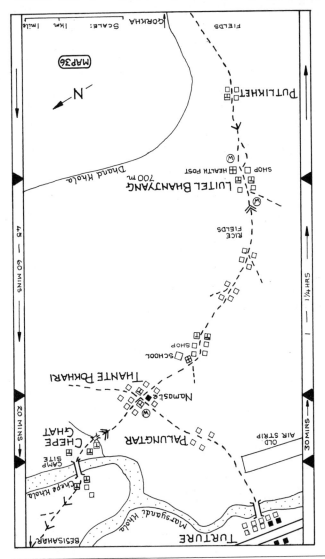

(Opposite) Top: Prayer flags and a cairn mark the Thorung La (5416m/17,769ft).
Bottom: Crossing the Thorung La after an October snowfall (photo: Charlie Loram).

steps. Wade across the Daroundi Khola if the level is low enough or cross on the big blue bridge upstream at Jaleba. The alternative route to this will take you on a much longer jaunt to the north, crossing the river at Naya Sangu.

Chorkate is the first village you come to; nothing more than a couple of tea shops and a school. Cross the Busundi Khola a few minutes later and follow it upstream. After 20-30 minutes follow the left-hand valley and climb for a further 20-30 minutes to **Khoplang**, another small village. Descend through a forest and 30-40 minutes later you come to a major trail. Turn right over a small stream and follow this better trail between fields to the few houses that are **Putlikhet**.

Luitel Bhanjyang is on the crest of a low pass, though at 700m/2297ft it hardly deserves to be known as such. There are tea houses and a health post here. If you're feeling drained by the heat buy a packet of powdered glucose from the shop. Washed down with water it's a good source of instant energy.

Continue through rice fields. Beside the trail, you'll see the pink powder-puff flowers of the sensitive plant. Touch these small fern-like plants and the leaves instantly fold up.

Thante Pokhari This is quite a large place with **post office** and bank but no exchange facilities. There's basic tea house accommodation, although Chepe Ghat by the river is more pleasantly located. From here a path, passing the Palungtar airstrip that served Gorkha before the road reached it, leads you to Turture in about an hour. Turture is on the way to Besishahar but if you want to steer clear of the dusty road for as long as possible continue north through Chepe Ghat.

Chepe Ghat This small village is on the Chepe Khola, a tributary of the Marsyandi that forms the border between Gorkha and Lamjung districts. There are basic tea houses here where you can unroll your sleeping bag for the night and you can swim in the river by the bridge.

CHEPE GHAT TO TARKUGHAT [MAPS 21-22: p193-4]

Ascend from Chepe Ghat and after 20 minutes you reach a small settlement amongst the mango groves. Continue along the level trail, high above the Chepe Khola, through the strung out village of **Damilikua**. After the village there are views down to the Marsyandi, the river you'll be following all the way to Manang. The trail drops steeply to the large village of **Tarku Ghat** where you cross the river to join the road to Besishahar. See p192 for the continuation of this route to Besishahar.

Pokhara to Khudi
(via Begnas Tal)

BEGNAS TAL TO KHUDI [MAPS 37-41]

This route is beginning to develop as an alternative to the not particularly pleasant Besishahar to Dumre road. The views are superb, excellent from the ridge between Nalma and Begling Pani, but the climb up here is very tough – particularly if you're just starting your trek. The trail is not, however, always easy to find so you'll need to ask directions frequently or take a guide. Lodges are basic in comparison to those in the Kali Gandaki, and, since the first part of the trek is at low altitude, it can be very hot. The trek to Khudi will take 2-3 days. The best lodges on this trek are probably those at Karputar and Nalma.

Begnas Tal (700m/2296ft)

There are frequent buses from Pokhara to **Begnas Tal** where you'll find several lodges by the lake. You won't need to stay here, however, if you get an early morning bus from Pokhara. The **New Begnas Lodge** has clean double rooms with communal bath for Rs100 and with attached

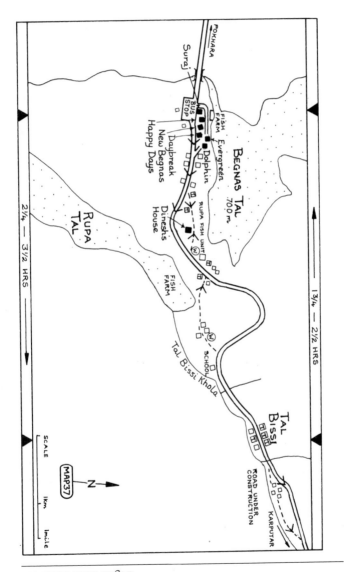

MAP 37

N

SCALE

1 km.

1 mile

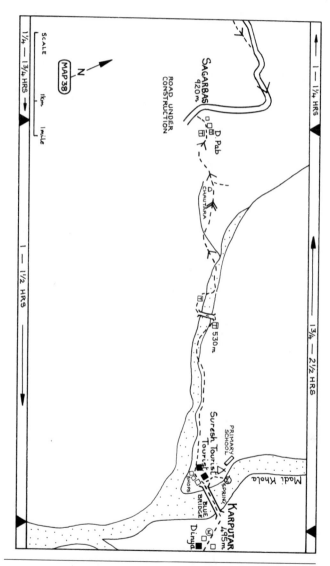

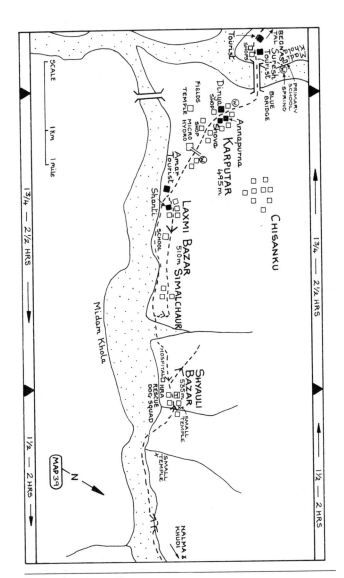

bath for Rs250. Situated at the top of a long flight of steps, the friendly *Dolphin Lodge* has double rooms with communal bath for Rs100. The mountain views are fantastic.

It is sometimes possible to get a lift in a jeep along the rough road between Begnas Tal and Sagarbas, so enquire in Begnas Tal to see if one is available. Those on foot can follow the road all the way to Sagarbas, taking shortcuts where possible to make the walking more interesting; ask the locals to point them out. There are some basic tea houses at **Tal Bissi** and a couple of well-stocked ones at **Sagarbas.**

The trail from here can be hard to follow. Descend steeply through rice fields and then a forest. As you come out of the forest the trail follows a small stream which soon joins a larger one. Continue downstream, crossing it a few times before walking through rice fields.

Karputar has several simple lodges. Just before the big blue bridge, the *Suresh Tourist Lodge* is reasonable and close enough to the river for a swim. The main part of the village is across the bridge; the *Dinya Hotel* here looks good.

Continue through fields, passing the pipework of the micro hydro plant. **Laxmi Bazar,** which you reach in about 45 minutes, has two very simple lodges. There is a choice of trails from here: either past the school and through the forest, or along the large irrigation channel to the Midam Khola, which you may have to wade across. Ask locally for the best route. The trail follows the river bed before climbing above the blue roofed hospital buildings at **Shyauli Bazar.** Descend back to the river which you must follow as best you can, occasionally detouring up the bank to avoid obstacles, until you reach a few buildings on the north bank. Climb over the shoulder behind them to the bridge over the Midam Khola. Cross to the hamlet of **Nalma Phedi** where there are two basic lodges and a shop.

Steps begin the long 600m grind up to the ridge-top village of Nalma. Thankfully the first part of the climb is through the shade of the forest and several conveniently spaced chautara provide much needed resting places along the trail. The gradient eases as you emerge from the trees, climbing easily through fields to the first cluster of houses. The main part of the village is still a short climb above.

Nalma is just over half way up the climb to the highest point on the long ridge which curves gracefully to Baglung Pani in the north. The views to the mountains are magnificent. There are two reasonable lodges here: **Bhim Guest House** is a friendly place and the owner also runs a small shop; the *Annapurna Guest House* has been relocated to a new building which promises to be good.

The steeper sections of trail ahead are made easier by ancient stone steps that lead you ever upward, through the hamlet of **Purana Gaon** and past a small temple dedicated to Shiva. Continue along the crest to the highest section of the ridge, where you can enjoy some short sections of level walking before descending the west side to avoid a large cliff. Climb the short distance to Baglung Pani.

Baglung Pani has mountain views to rival some of Nepal's better known beauty spots – without the crowds. They are best appreciated from the hill by the secondary school, either early in the morning or around sunset. This necessitates a stay at one of the three lodges in the village; don't expect any luxuries.

From the far right corner of the village playing field take the left path which descends through the forest and then steeply across fields. Cross the bridge over the Bhoran Khola and turn immediately right (east) along the north bank. It is possible to follow the river all the way to **Sera**, but the higher level trail along an irrigation ditch is easier. From here it is only a short distance to **Khudi** where you join the main trail up the Marsyandi.

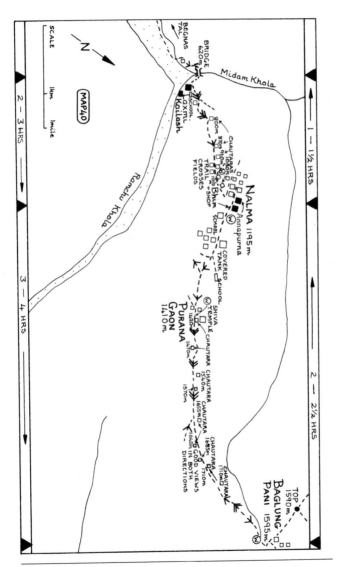

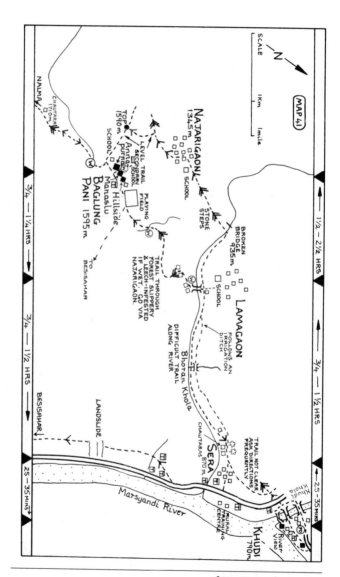

SCALE
N
1Km.
1mile

MAP 41

NATARIGAON
1345m.

SCHOOL

SCHOOL

STONE
STEPS

BROKEN
BRIDGE
935m.

TOP
1590m.
Annapurna
SECONDARY
SCHOOL
LEVEL TRAIL

Hillside

Manaslu

BAGLUNG
PANI 1595m.

PLAYING
FIELD

TRAIL THROUGH
FOREST SLIPPERY
& LEECH-INFESTED
IF WET: GO VIA
NATARIGAON.

LAMAGAON

SCHOOL

FOLLOWS AN
IRRIGATION
DITCH

Bhotan Khola

DIFFICULT TRAIL
ALONG RIVER

CHAUTARA
1710m.

NALMA

To
BESISAHAR

LANDSLIDE

BESISAHAR

CHAUTARAS

SERA
870m.

TRAIL NOT CLEAR
ASK DIRECTIONS
FREQUENTLY

Marsyandi River

Khudi khola

RURAL
TRAINING
CENTRE

River-
View

KHUDI
790m.

½ — 2½ HRS

¾ — 1½ HRS

¾ — 1½ HRS

25 — 35 MINS

¾ — 1¼ HRS

¾ — 1½ HRS

25 — 35 MINS

The preceding trail guide was deliberately not written on a 'Day 1, Day 2' basis to encourage trekkers to travel at their own pace and not stop all in the same places. Some guidelines are, however, necessary for overall planning. These itineraries are based on a leisurely pace and to allow overnight stops in the more interesting villages. Walking more quickly you could easily reduce them by several days. See p243 for maximum recommended daily altitude gains.

Jomsom Trek

Day 1	Pokhara to Hille/Tirkhedunga (1540m)
02	Ghorepani (2750m)
03	Tatopani (1190m)
04	Ghasa/Kalopani (2010m/2530m)
05	Marpha (2670m)
06	Kagbeni (2800m)
07	Jharkot (3550m)
08	Muktinath (3800m)
09	Jomsom (2710m)
10	Tukuche/Khobang (2590m/2560m)
11	Kalopani/Ghasa (2530m/2010m)
12	Tatopani (1190m)
13	Ghorepani/Beni (2750m/830m)
14	Birethanti/Baglung (1050m/970m)
15	Pokhara (850m)

Annapurna Sanctuary

Day 1	Pokhara to Birethanti (1050m)
02	Ghandruk (1939m)
03	Chomrong (2050-2170m)
04	Bamboo (2400m)
05	Deurali (3200m)
06	Machhapuchhre Base Camp/Annapurna BC (3700m/4130m)
07	Dovan (2600m)
08	Chomrong (2050-2170m)
09	Landruk (1550m)
10	Dhampus/Pokhara (1650m/850m)

Annapurna Circuit

Day 1	Kathmandu - Dumre - Besisahar* (820m)
02	Bhulebhule/N/gadi (840m/930m)
03	Syanje(1100m)
04	Tal (1700m)
05	Dharapani (2160m)
06	Chame (2670m)
07	Pisang (3200-3300m)
08	Manang (3540m)
09	Manang (3540m)
10	Letdar (4200m)
11	Thorung Phedi (4450m)
12/13	Muktinath (3800m)
14-20	to Pokhara (see above)

*Add 2 days if walking from Dumre or Gorkha, add 3 days from Pokhara.

APPENDIX B: NEPALESE EMBASSIES

Australia: Melbourne
Suite 1, Level 5
277 Flinders Lanet
Vic 8009
(☎ 03-9650 6683; a 30 day
visa currently costs A$80)

Australia: Perth
Suite 2, 16 Robinson St
Perth, WA 6009
(☎ 386 2102)

Australia: Sydney
3rd Lvl, 441 Kent St
Sydney, NSW 2060
(☎ 02-9264 5909)

Belgium
21 Ave Champel B-1640
Rhode St Genese
(☎ 02-358 5808)

Canada
Royal Bank Plaza
South Tower,
Toronto
(☎ 416-968 7252)

China
No 1 Sanleitaniliujie
Beijing (☎ 532 1795)
Norbulinka Rd 13
Lhasa, Tibet
(☎ 36890)

Denmark
2 Teglgaardstraede
1452 Copenhagen
(☎ 312 4166)

Finland
Kaisaniemenkarul B a
00100 Helsinki
(☎ 13 11 62 30)

France
45 bis rue des Acacais
75017 Paris
(☎ 46 22 48 67)

Germany
Im Hag 15,
D-53179 Bonn
(☎ 0228-343097)
Ehrenbreitsteiner Strasse 44
80993, München
(☎ 089-1436 5260)

India
1 Barakhamba Rd
New Delhi 110001
(☎ 332 9969)

Italy
Piazzale Medaglia
d'Orro 20,
Roma (☎ 06-348176)

Japan
14-9 Tokoroki
7-chome Setagaya-ku
Tokyo 158
(☎ 3705 5558)

New Zealand
Lady Hillary
Hon Consul General
Auckland
(☎ 09-520 3169)

Norway
Haakon VIIs gt-5B
0116 Oslo
(☎ 283 5510)

Sweden
Eriksbergsgatan 1A
S-11430 Stockholm
(☎ 679 8039)

Switzerland
Asyistrasse 81
CH-8030 Zurich
(☎ 475 993)

Thailand
189 Soi 71, Sukhumvit
Bangkok 10110
(☎ 391 7240)

United Kingdom
12a Kensington Palace
Gardens London W8 4QU
(☎ 0171-229 1594; open
10.00-12.00, Mon to Fri;
a 30 day visa currently
costs £20)

USA: Atlanta
212 15th St NE
Atlanta GA 30309
(☎ 404-892 8152)

USA: Chicago
1500 Lake Shore Dve
Chicago IL 60610
(☎ 312-787 9199)

USA: Dallas
16250 Dallas Parkway
Suite 110, TX 75248
(☎ 214-931 1212)

USA: Los Angeles
11661 San Vicente Blvd
Suite 510, CA 90049
(☎ 310-420 4099)

USA: New York
247 W 87th St Apt 12G
NY 10024
(☎ 212-874 2306)

USA: San Francisco
909 Montgomery St
CA 94133
(☎ 415-434 1111)

USA: Tiffin
Heidelburg College
Tiffin
OH 44883
(☎ 419-448 2202)

USA: Washington
2131 Leroy Place
NW Washington
DC 20008
(☎ 202-667 4550)

INTRODUCTION

The Nepal Mountaineering Association (NMA) has classified 18 peaks in Nepal as 'trekking peaks', a misleading name because all involve climbing. Ranging from 5650-6500m (18,537-21,325ft) some are, however, appropriate heights to combine within a trekking programme. 'Limited bureaucracy peaks' would be a better name.

Permits and costs

The procedure for obtaining a permit is streamlined in comparison to the months of planning required for expedition peaks. It's therefore possible to arrive in Kathmandu, organise a trekking peak trip from scratch and be on the trail in just under a week. At present the rules are biased towards larger groups because the fee is a flat rate – the same for one person as for ten. The noticeboards at the HRA, KEEP's Trekkers Information Centre and the Kathmandu Guest House are the best places to advertise for partners. Since the permits must be obtained in Kathmandu, it is difficult to meet potential partners and arrange things in Pokhara.

The 18 peaks are divided into two categories: 12 'A' group peaks above 6000m 19,685ft and 6 'B' group peaks below 6000m/19,685ft. 'A' group permits cost US$300 £200 and 'B' group, US$150/£90. An NMA-registered sirdar must accompany the group for the entire trek and if you wish he can act as guide, rather than overseer. This is to ensure that every climbing trip is organised as a fully guided group trek, involving porters (who must all be insured) and tents, and costing at least US$20/£13.50 per person per day. Some trekking companies are willing to waive this rule.

Equipment and safety

If climbing in a trekking company group headed by a climbing guide, then harnesses and ropes will be used on every one of the peaks below, whether for crevasse danger or steep slopes. Nepali guides are accomplished at fixing ropes but generally don't have any idea of how to rope up properly for glacier travel or to set up a belay, or belay using a climbing rope. Unbelievable, but true. The only way to find out if they do know is to ask the guide to demonstrate. If climbing without a guide, recognising your personal limits is important, this is the Himalaya after all. Some of these peaks are 'straightforward' but what this really means is that to be safe you don't need a shop-ful of karabiners, ice-screws, snow-stakes and rock racks – just a partner, rope, a few bits of protection, experience, this gear, good weather and an overriding urge to die of senility.

The routes mentioned below cover the least difficult way up some of the main trekking peaks in the region. For proficient technical alpinists none of the routes is particularly challenging **under good conditions**. For safety-conscious amateurs, they have the potential to provide satisfaction and experience without excessive danger.

Acclimatisation and itinerary planning

Heading straight up to high altitude for the first time, even if following the recommended guidelines, is usually a shock to everyone's system. The effort required for walking, let alone climbing, uphill at 5000m is much greater than you might think. So a sensible acclimatisation programme is essential: use the 300m a day rule, not only to avoid altitude sickness, but to give your body time to gain strength. Also plan in extra days for less than perfect weather. These are two significant factors that the majority of trekking companies ignore, and common causes of failure. Almost invariably a trekking itinerary with a couple of days thrown in for a climb doesn't result in a successful ascent. Plan the trip as a peak expedition, with the trek in and out.

Further information

Bill O'Connor's *The Trekking Peaks of Nepal* is the standard reference but it's better on some peaks than on others. There are notable gaps and errors in the descriptions of climbs for the peaks below. You should also check out other sources of information. Try www.trailblazer-guides.com/trek-nepal.

ANNAPURNA SANCTUARY REGION PEAKS

● **Mardi Himal (5587m/18,333ft)** Overshadowed by Machhapuchre to the north, Mardi Himal receives only a few ascents a year. The most common climbing route takes the south ridge for a straightforward ascent using a snow gully. It is also possible to climb using the SSW ridge (Mardi Himal trek) but this involves a bit of rock climbing too. One of the attractions of this peak is the remoteness. Just to get to the base camp takes 3-5 days wilderness trekking.

● **Hiun Chuli (6441m/21,132ft)** The formidable front wall of the Sanctuary has a fearsome reputation and there is no 'standard' route up. Any route is a challenging technical climb with devilish route finding, and is best tackled in true expedition style.

● **Tharpu Chuli/Tent Peak (5663m/18379ft)** Lying right in the middle Sanctuary surrounded by 7000m peaks, this is the most popular of the Sanctuary peaks. The route packs a few surprises and some intricate route finding but its lower altitude makes it suitable for shorter itineraries.

● **Singu Chuli/Fluted Peak (6501m/21,329ft)** Also lying entirely within the Sanctuary, north of Tharpu Chuli, most attempts are combined with an attempt on Tharpu Chuli as a warm-up. The access is more challenging, and the mountain is, too, so few commercial groups tackle it.

MANANG REGION PEAKS

● **Pisang Peak (6091m/19,987ft)** This is often touted as the easiest of the peaks near Manang, but this is considerably under-estimating the difficulty of the rock sections, especially if the least bit wet or snow-covered. Chulu Far East is more straightforward yet receives surprisingly little attention. Trekking companies seem fond of attempting this as a three-day side trip from Pisang village, forgetting that virtually nobody can acclimatise in this time.

● **Chulu East (approx 6200m/20,336ft)** and **Chulu Far East (6060m/19,877ft)** Very few maps accurately mark the four Chulu peaks but the altitudes give away their locations. The east peaks are accessed from the same base camp but are quite different mountains. Far East should be the 'Island Peak' (in the Everest region and the most popular limited bureaucracy peak) of the Annapurnas. There are two routes to base camp, both interesting. Then from a high camp clambering over rough, steep scree leads to a broad glaciated ridge with slopes of varying angles. On some sections fixed rope would be useful for a larger group but for smaller teams climbing alpine style with several ropes will do. Note that the majority of climbing sherpas don't know how to set up belays, and rely on fixed ropes.

Chulu East is quite a different proposition requiring much more commitment and alpine experience. From the col on the glaciated ridge you have to descend and cross a broken glacier then climb steep scree slopes to gain a relatively straightforward but high ridge. Setting up a second high camp (Camp 1) is a necessity.

● **Chulu West (6419m121,055ft)** and **Chulu Central (6558m/21,515ft)** The West peak is the Mera (Everest region and second most popular of the limited bureaucracy) of the Annapurnas, little more than a long tough snow slog for a high summit. The difference is that between base camp and high camp the steep loose rock requires fixing ropes. The experienced and sure-footed can get away with a couple of 20m sections while larger groups require something like 300m. Acclimatisation is the key to success, and a little luck. Not everyone, even if well acclimatised, can cope with sleeping at 5600m. Also, if there is a single cloud in the area, it will be on Chulu West. The Central peak is not attempted by commercial groups, being an even longer slog, with a sometimes tricky rock section to the actual summit.

OTHER PEAKS

These peaks are likely to be designated as trekking peaks in 1999, provided the Ministry of Tourism approves the applications.

● **Thorungtse (6032m/19,790ft)** and **Khatung Kang (6484m/21,273ft)** lying immediately south of Thorung La, many a mountaineer has admired these peaks while crossing the pass, and some have admired them closer than others. Moderate mostly unbroken glacier slopes and short rock scramble lead to a false summit, which has often been solo-ed. I have called this peak Thorungtse here. The real summit, Khatung Kang, requires far more commitment and climbing steeper, more exposed slopes.

● **Dhampus Peak (6013m/6035m)** Best approached from Dhampus Pass or from Hidden Valley, this peak is little more than a rock scramble in good conditions, although there is also a short stretch of ice to be crossed too. From the summit the Annapurnas and Nilgiris smack you in the face with their size and sheerness, Tukuche and Dhaulagiri make you gulp, they are so close, and Manaslu, shimmering 100 kms away, still looks too huge to be true. And the view stretches into Mustang to the Tibetan border.

APPENDIX D: THE SIKLES TREK

A model eco-trek – Ghalekhark-Sikles Circuit

The following information was kindly supplied by Juddha Bahadur Gurung, Project Manager/Conservation Officer, Ghalekharka-Sikles Trekking Circuit Development Projects (ACAP).

Introduction

Annapurna Conservation Area Project (ACAP) has realised that the Annapurna trek which accounts for 61% of trekking tourism of the country has to be managed in such a way that the region will not be adversely affected by tourism. To minimise the tourists' impact on the fragile environment eco-tourism is considered essential. A model was developed and launched in the Annapurna Region.

This week-long trek begins and ends in Pokhara. Basic camp facilities: camping grounds with toilets, bathroom, safe drinking water, kitchen, porters' shelter, rubbish bin/pits and signposts along the trail have been established. Trekking permits are required. Contact ACAP for more information.

The route

The trek starts from west of Pokhara, either from Milanchowk or from Bhunpare, both half an hour from Pokhara by taxi or bus.

● **From Milanchowk** Cross the new bridge at Mardikhola, and then climb approximately 50m to level ground. Within 45 minutes from Milanchowk a cultivated field and the scattered settlement of Bhallabot is reached. From here, another two and half hours' walk leads to the first camp-site.

This site is called **Kharpani** (Tatopani) where there are hot springs by the Seti River. Group trekkers usually camp here but individual trekkers use the community-owned lodge at Diprang, which is reached 30 minutes before Kharpani camp-site. Next day you pass through Gurung settlements of Chaura and Chyangling before crossing the Sardikhola. Another 30 minutes' climb through a Tamang village, lies the second camp-site, Ghalekharka.

● **From Bhunpare** Cross a patch of riverine forest beside the canal. After 30 minutes Chitepani is reached on a level trail. An hour beyond is Tallakot, with pleasant views of settlements along the bank of Seti River and peaks including Machhapuchhre. After crossing the Bhujungkhola bridge, Bhujungkhola village is reached within an hour. Then a climb of 1½ hours leads to Ghalekharka.

Both trails meet at **Ghalekharka** where a **Tourist Information Centre** is located. Shortly after Ghalekharka, you enter the natural zone and then climb up a steep trail which passes through a huge forest. Reach the top of the hill, Jhakarphulan (2600m) within three hours.

Nyaulikharka, the next camp-site, is reached in an hour. Group trekkers halt here for a night but individual trekkers have to walk further a three to four hours to reach human settlements.

From Nyaulikharka you cross a rhododendron and broad-leaf mixed forest to reach **Parche/Sikles**, one of the largest Gurung settlements. There are camp-sites located in Parche and in Sikles. Individual trekkers have to stay at a community-owned lodge situated close to the Parche camp-site. Normally, visitors take one day off and participate in various recreational activities. You can climb a nearby viewing point to watch the avalanches on Annapurna II. In Sikles village, at ACAP Regional Headquarters, a brief talk can be given and video/slide organised. There's also a new Natural and Cultural History Museum, Ama Toli (the mother group) from the respective local settlement will perform folk dances. The collected donation is used for local infrastructure development and conservation. Other activities that can be organised include weaving demonstrations of wool and nettle fibres. It's also possible to see the spiritual traditional dance called Ghantoo but this needs special request and prior notice. With a week's notice you can go on a three-day honey hunting expedition, staying with families in the area.

Leaving Sikles you descend for 90 minutes into the Madikhola valley at Sonda. Follow the right bank of the river for at least an hour to Chansu. At this point you can go either to **Yangjakot** (two hours) or to Lamakhet (one hour). Yangjakot village is a large Gurung settlement. There is a camp-site for group trekkers and a hotel for individual trekkers. In Yangjakot you can see another Gurung spiritual dance, Kusunda Ghantoo, quite different to that of Sikles. It takes place around the last week of April or first week of May.

After leaving Yangjakot, two hours' descent brings you to Bhaise (1½ hours from Lamakhet). Then it's a two-hour climb to **Kalikasthan** camp-site. Four lakes (Rupa, Begnas, Khaste, Maide) and panoramic views are the main attractions of the camp-site. From Kalikasthan it takes one hour to reach **Begnas** where you can catch a taxi or bus back to Pokhara.

An illness may be caused by the planets. In such a case, it is useful to make a boat from the leaf of a sal tree and float it down the river. The boat should contain some barley, mas (black pulse), linseed and a lighted wick. If the boat is carried away by the current, rejoice, for the patient will soon recover. If it sinks or describes circles in the water, alas! there is little hope of recovery. **Kesar Lall** *Nepalese Customs and Manners*

REDUCING THE RISKS OF GETTING ILL

Trekkers, like other travellers in the developing world, seem to relish horror stories about the life-threatening diseases they might contract on the trail. Whilst Nepal does indeed have all the serious health problems of a very poor country, if you follow the guidelines below for reducing the risks the worst that you're likely to pick up is a mild bout of diarrhoea.

Before you arrive in Nepal
● Have all the required inoculations in good time (see p53)
● Check that your footwear is comfortable and will support your ankles. This is particularly important if you're doing a long trek such as the Annapurna Circuit
● Ensure you're in good health at the start of your holiday. If you're tired and run-down at the beginning of your trek your trek resistance will be lowered
● To reduce the effects of jet-lag, set your watch to Nepal time as soon as you board the plane, avoid alcohol but drink as much other liquid as possible, don't over-eat and try to get some sleep.

In Nepal
● Drink only purified water, bottled (Coke, Fanta etc) and hot drinks (tea, coffee, boiled milk, hot lemon)
● Eat only food that has just been cooked and is still hot or fruit you can peel yourself. And eat enough – as much carbohydrate and protein as you can manage. You'll burn it all off on the trail.
● Avoid ice-cream, salads and raw vegetables, and food from roadside stalls.
● If you're going to be trekking at altitude it is vital to follow the advice on acute mountain sickness (AMS or altitude sickness) given below.
● Take care of your feet, keeping them clean and dry. Stop and deal with a blister as soon as you feel it forming (see p245).
● Don't get knocked off the trail by a mule train or a yak. Stop on the mountain side of the path and let them pass.
● Slow down! Don't forget that this is a holiday not a competition to cover the routes faster than everyone else. Trekking before dawn (except where absolutely necessary) or after dark increases the risk of turning an ankle.
● In areas of increased natural danger (high passes, rarely-used routes) travel in a group of at least five people (see p218).

FIRST AID KIT
Some trekkers carry far too many pills and potions with them, including several potentially dangerous drugs they wouldn't know how to use if they got ill. Self-diagnosis can be very difficult and cases where trekkers have made themselves even more ill by taking the wrong drugs are not unknown. If you're trekking in a remote area a comprehensive medical kit could save a life. In the Annapurna region, however, there are

health posts in many villages and they stock some medicines. For a basic first aid kit the following items should suffice:

- **Plasters/bandaids**
- **Moleskin** or **Second Skin** for treating blisters. In Britain Second Skin can usually be found at hiking/camping shops.
- **Bandage** for a sprained ankle or weak knee. An elasticated support (*Tubigrip*) may be useful if you are prone to knee or ankle problems.
- **Scissors/penknife**
- **Antiseptic cream** (eg *Savlon*)
- **Aspirin/paracetamol** for pain-relieving. Aspirin is also effective for reducing swelling.
- **Cough/throat lozenges** Sore throats are not uncommon. Lozenges containing anaesthetic (eg *Merocaine*) offer most relief.
- **Emergency Medical Kit** Also known as an 'Anti-Aids Kit', this contains sterilised syringes, needles and suture materials needed by a doctor in an emergency. They're widely marketed in the West.
- **Oral rehydration solution** (*Dioralyte*) to replace salts and minerals lost through diarrhoea. *Jeevan Jal* is the Nepali equivalent.
- **Drugs** The two most useful drugs to take with you are easily available in Nepal without a prescription. Buy six to eight tablets of **Tinba** (also known as Tinidazole) for the treatment of giardia and either **Ciprofloxacin** (20 x 500mg) or **Norfloxacin** (12 x 400mg) as a general antibiotic.

HEALTH FACILITIES IN THE ANNAPURNA REGION

Along the main trails described in this book there are hospitals at Pokhara, Gorkha, Besisahar, Jomsom and Baglung as well as numerous small health posts in villages, as marked on the route maps.

During the main trekking season the Himalayan Rescue Association operates a health post in Manang, staffed by Western volunteer doctors.

MOUNTAIN RESCUE

There are actually fewer emergency situations where a helicopter rescue is the best option than one might suppose. It can take many hours to reach a radio to get a message to the Royal Nepal Army who operate the rescue missions. The flight may be delayed if the weather is bad and will not even take off without an assurance of payment, since operational costs are more than US$600 per hour. Your embassy will usually be contacted and in turn will need to get in touch with your relatives. It is, therefore, vital to fill in a form giving trek details and the names of next of kin for your embassy in Kathmandu before you go trekking. The Himalayan Rescue Association (see p112) hold stocks of these forms.

If the patient could possibly be suffering from altitude sickness the most important thing is descent as fast as possible. Death could occur long before the arrival of the helicopter so carry the patient to a lower altitude without delay.

WATER PURIFICATION

The rule is simple: don't drink any liquid anywhere in Nepal that hasn't been purified. Beware also of innocent-looking streams high in the mountains since these may be polluted either by even higher human habitation or by animal faeces. Also be wary of restaurant signs that inform you that 'All Water is Filtered and Boiled'. If you haven't watched what you're about to drink being purified, don't drink it or even wash your teeth in it.

Staying healthy in Nepal is all about reducing the risks of getting ill. Using one of the methods below, it's not difficult to minimise the chances that you'll become ill from something you drink.

Boiling
Current research shows that water need be brought only to the boil (even at altitude) to kill the bugs in it. Given the shortage of firewood in the country and the large quantities of water that would need to be boiled up along the main routes to satisfy the needs of thirsty trekkers it's neither feasible nor ecologically sound to recommend this as a purification method. Tea, coffee, hot lemon and other drinks made from boiling water are, however, generally safe.

Filtering
You'll see large water filters in some of the lodges along the trails. These do nothing more than filter out some of the sediment in the water. They don't make it safe to drink. In some parts of the Annapurna region, however, the water has a high mica content so it's a good idea to fill your bottle from one of these filters before purifying it using one of the chemical methods described below.

A number of portable filters have come on the market over the last decade which also include a chemical purification stage in their filtration process. They may be effective but are expensive and heavy to carry.

Chemical purification
The most useful chemical for water purification is iodine. Chlorine based tablets (eg Puritabs), widely available in the West, are not recommended for use in Nepal unless combined with a fine filter since they're not effective against giardia and amoebic cysts.

Some people find the chemical taste of treated water reassuringly safe but if you don't like it, neutralise it by adding vitamin C or disguise it by adding fruit juice powders. These seem to be the most refreshing when only small quantities are added.

● **Tincture of iodine** This is the method most widely used by trekkers for water purification. Since it's available in a range of concentrations you must know the strength in order to determine the quantity to use. Although it's available in Nepal, it's best to buy tincture of iodine in the West where you can be sure of the concentration. For a 2% solution, the dose is 5 drops per litre of clean water which must then stand for 20-30 minutes. If the water is cloudy double the dose. For a 10% solution use a fifth of the dose but wait for the same amount of time before drinking the water. You need a dropper to dispense the correct dose.

Wrap the bottle and dropper in more than one plastic bag. An iodine leak in the centre of a pack can be a very messy business.

● **Iodine tablets** There are a number of brands on the market in the West (eg Potable Aqua and MicroPur). They are sold at ACAP offices around the trek. One tablet purifies a litre of water in about ten minutes.

● **Iodine solution** Marketed as Polar Pure, iodine crystals are dissolved into a solution that is then added to your drinking water. Accidentally swallowing these crystals could kill you but a filter on the bottle prevents this happening.

DIARRHOEA
Diarrhoea seems to be one of the biggest fears amongst Westerners visiting a developing world country for the first time but it's important not to get things out of proportion. Few cases result in total loss of bowel control. If you get diarrhoea it will probably be several loose movements a day for just a few days. Diarrhoea is caused

by drinking or eating something contaminated by human faeces. The potential for contamination of this kind in a poor country is great but you can significantly reduce the risk by ensuring that everything you drink is either boiled or purified and that all food is freshly cooked. Stick to fruit that can be peeled. Wash your hands frequently.

In their desire to regain control over their bowels Westerners are all too keen to take something. There are, however, several different causes for the intestinal infections that cause diarrhoea, making diagnosis difficult. Very often, the diarrhoea will clear up on its own in a few days. Avoid preparations like Imodium or Lomotil (except for long bus journeys) since these merely paralyse the bowel and are not a cure for the infection. If the diarrhoea does not clear up by itself the most reliable method of diagnosis is a stool test. Since you may be several days' walk from a clinic you may need to do some self-diagnosis. Dr David Schlim, the medical director of CIWEC clinic in Kathmandu, produces an excellent pamphlet (*Understanding Diarrhea in Travelers*) which is available at the clinic.

Bacterial diarrhoea

Also known as travellers' diarrhoea' (since it's the most common form of diarrhoea in travellers) this is caused by a change in diet. Even in the West your diet includes some bacteria but these are recognised by your body and so do not cause a reaction. Foreign bacteria may result in a bout of diarrhoea.

● **Symptoms** Loose stools that may be frequent and watery, sometimes accompanied by vomiting, abdominal pain and fever. There may be some blood, pus or mucus in the stools.

● **Treatment** Since it often goes away by itself, you should leave well alone for the first few days but drink plenty of fluids. It's most important not to become dehydrated. Oral Rehydration Solution (*Dioralyte/Jevan Jal* etc) can be useful; Coke or Pepsi (sugar-rich) are also good but get the fizz out first. If you feel you want to eat, stick to a plain diet (boiled rice or dry biscuits). If there is no improvement after five days, take 400mg Norfloxacin every 12 hours for three days.

Giardia

A single-celled parasite (*Giardia lamblia*), three times the size of the red blood cell, causes this unpleasant diarrhoeal disease. It's unpleasant not only for the sufferer but also for his or her companions since symptoms include 'rotten egg' burps and wind. Although other travellers may lead you to believe otherwise, it's not nearly as common as bacterial diarrhoea.

● **Symptoms** As well as foul smelling burps and frequent wind, other uncomfortable symptoms include a gut that rumbles like an underloaded washing-machine producing only a few loose motions each day.

● **Treatment** Take four 500mg Tiniba (a total of 2g) all at once. This single dose treatment is effective in 90% of cases. Don't mix this with alcohol.

Amoebic dysentery

There are several different species of amoeba that cause infection and symptoms but amoebic dysentery occurs rarely in trekkers.

● **Symptoms** These vary from occasional loose stools and abdominal pain that occur in cycles (clearing up after a few days – then returning) to frequent and sometimes bloody diarrhoea. The result is weight loss and extreme fatigue.

● **Treatment** Since the treatment involves a large dose of a powerful drug, it would be best to seek medical opinion and, if possible, a stool test rather than relying on self diagnosis. If it is established that you have amoebic dysentery, the treatment is 2g (4 x 500mg tablets) of Tiniba daily for three days.

ACUTE MOUNTAIN SICKNESS (AMS)

In the late 1960s and early 1970s, when trekkers in Nepal could be numbered in hundreds rather than in tens of thousands, about ten trekkers a year died from AMS in the country. Now that so much more is known about this sickness there are only one or two AMS-related deaths each year here. Given, however, that AMS is entirely preventable if certain precautions are taken, this is one or two lives lost unnecessarily.

The important thing to remember is that it is the speed of ascent not the altitude itself that causes AMS. The body takes several days to adapt to an increase in altitude. The higher you go above sea-level, the lower the barometric pressure, resulting in less oxygen reaching your lungs with each breath you take. At 2500m/8202ft it's about 25% lower but up to this altitude the effects of the altitude are rarely felt; at 5416m/17,769ft (the Thorung La, high point on the Annapurna Circuit trek) the pressure is almost 50% lower.

Prevention

● **Don't exceed the recommended rate of ascent** To prevent AMS you must not ascend too quickly since your body needs time to become accustomed to the thinner air. You should take two to three nights to reach 3000m or 10,000ft and spend the subsequent nights at about 300m or 1000ft above the previous night's altitude. After each 1000m or 3000ft gain in altitude above 3000m or 10,000ft you should have a rest day and spend two nights (rather than one) at the same altitude.

It should be stressed that this is the absolute maximum rate of ascent and that even if you do not exceed it you may still get some symptoms of mild AMS since people adapt at different rates. Some doctors recommend taking three nights to reach 3000m or 10,000ft and then ascending 300m or 1000ft for only the first two days above 3000m or 10,000ft (ie to 3600m or 12,000ft) and there-after only 150m or 500ft a day.

You should also be aware that being young and fit is no advantage against AMS. In fact, these people are probably more likely than older trekkers to get AMS symptoms since they are able to walk further and higher each day. Men and women are almost equally likely to get AMS.

● **Drink plenty of liquids** Try to drink at least four litres of liquid (water, tea, soup etc) per day at altitude. Passing large amounts of clear-coloured urine is a good sign that your body is adapting to the altitude. If your urine is dark yellow or orange coloured you are becoming dehydrated. Avoid alcohol at altitude.

● **Eat well** You should eat a diet that is rich in carbohydrates (potatoes, chapattis, pancakes, sugar etc). You may lose your appetite at altitude but it's important to try to eat even so; your body's energy consumption is probably far higher than usual.

● **Avoid over-exertion** Take the steep hills slowly at altitude, giving yourself adequate rest-breaks at frequent intervals.

● **Look out for symptoms of AMS** as listed below and take the required action. In Manang (on the Annapurna Circuit trek) there are afternoon lectures at the Himalayan Rescue Association Health Post which are worth attending.

If you feel ill, unless you know that whatever is causing your symptoms is definitely not AMS, the best advice is to assume that it is. The symptoms may be divided into two groups: mild/benign AMS and serious/malignant AMS. In both cases descent brings immediate relief of symptoms.

● **Using Diamox** There seems to be much debate in the medical profession over whether drugs like acetazolamide (Diamox) should be taken to prevent AMS. They are not effective in all cases but may be worth considering if you have had problems acclimatising in the past. Diamox is widely available in Nepal.

☐ **SERIOUS AMS SYMPTOMS – IMMEDIATE DESCENT!**

● Persistent, severe headache
● Persistent vomiting
● Ataxia – loss of co-ordination, an inability to walk in a straight line, making the sufferer drunk.
● Losing consciousness – inability to stay awake or understand instructions.
● Liquid sounds in the lungs
● Very persistent, sometimes watery, cough
● Difficulty breathing
● Rapid breathing or feeling breathless at rest
● Coughing blood, pink phlegm or lots of clear fluid
● Severe lethargy
● Marked blueness of face and lips
● High resting heartbeat – over 130 beats per minute
● Mild symptoms rapidly getting worse

Symptoms and treatment

• **Mild/benign AMS – Don't go higher!** The symptoms of this primary stage of AMS are not dangerous in themselves but provide vital early warnings that must not be ignored. They include: headache (which may get worse during the night), nausea and loss of appetite, difficulty in sleeping (note that it could be dangerous to take sleep-ing-pills) and light-headedness.

If you experience any of these symptoms and they do not go away you should not go higher but spend a rest day at the altitude you've reached. If they get worse you should descend. This may not need to be all the way down to the previous lodge: only a few hundred metres lower may make all the difference.

• **Serious/malignant AMS – Descend immediately!** There are two types of serious AMS: high altitude cerebral oedema (swelling of the brain) and high altitude pul-monary oedema (where fluid builds up in the lungs). Both can be fatal.

Symptoms include extreme tiredness, loss of co-ordination, delirium and even-tual coma, painful headache, frequent vomiting, cyanosis (blueness of the lips), shortness of breath, coughing attacks producing pink, brown or white sputum, bub-bling breath or rapid heartbeat at rest (110 or more beats per minute).

Recognising the signs of serious AMS may be very difficult since your judgment can be affected. It's very important to let other people know how you feel and watch for symptoms of AMS in them. If you're travelling with porters this goes just as much for them as for your foreign companions.

Immediate descent to a lower altitude is of paramount importance. The patient may need to be carried by porters or on a horse or yak. If you're trekking with a group it's important that the interests of the patient are put above the group's schedule. There have been cases where AMS sufferers died being carried over high passes so as not to disrupt a group's schedule.

If you are trekking above Manang try to make for the Himalayan Rescue Association's Health Post in the town. As well as several drugs used in the treatment of AMS, they also have a pressure bag (Gamow Bag). Patients are zipped into this large air-proof bag and it is then inflated using a foot-pump. This increases the pres-sure inside the bag to simulate a lower altitude.

Visit the Himalayan Rescue Association in Kathmandu for further information about AMS.

CARE OF FEET, ANKLES & KNEES

A twisted ankle, swollen knee or a septic blister on your foot could ruin your trek so it's important to take care to avoid these. Choose comfortable boots with good ankle support. This is particularly important if you're doing one of the longer treks. Avoid trekking in the dark and don't carry too heavy a load. Wash your feet and change your socks regularly. During lunch stops take off your boots and socks and let them dry in the sun. Attend to any blister as soon as you feel it developing.

Blisters

There are a number of different ways to treat blisters but prevention is far better than cure. Stop immediately you feel a 'hot spot' forming and cover it with a piece of mole-skin or Second Skin. One trekker suggests using the membrane inside an egg-shell as an alternative form of Second Skin.

If a blister does form you can either burst it with a needle (sterilised in a flame) then apply a dressing or alternatively build a moleskin dressing around the unburst blister to protect it.

Sprains

You can lessen the risk of a sprained ankle by wearing boots which offer good ankle support and by watching where you walk. If you do sprain an ankle, cool it in a stream and keep it bandaged. If it's very painful you may need to stop for a few days and rest with your leg up and bandaged. Aspirin is helpful for reducing pain and swelling.

Knee problems

These are most common after long stretches of walking down-hill. It's important not to take long strides as you descend; small steps will lessen the jarring on the knee. It may be helpful to wear knee supports for long descents (eg Thorung La to Muktinath), especially if you have had problems with your knees before.

OTHER HEALTH PROBLEMS

Bedbugs and scabies

You'll probably only have problems with these night-time companions if you borrow quilts or blankets in the lodges. If you don't use a sheet-sleeping bag with a rented sleeping-bag there's a slight chance of scabies.

Bed-bugs may disturb your sleep and leave rows of itchy bites but they tend not to hitch a ride in your sleeping-bag when you leave since there's nowhere to hide. The tiny mites that cause scabies, however, are difficult to shake out of a sleeping-bag. They cause trails of little itchy red bites all over the body and you'll need to visit a health post for some scabies powder, wash all your clothes and air your sleeping-bag in the sun.

Boils

Staphylococcal skin infections cause painful pus-filled boils that may erupt on any part of the body. They're most common during the monsoon period and require antibi-otic treatment. Visit a clinic in Kathmandu after your trek.

Constipation

Surprising as it may seem, constipation does affect some trekkers, although it's not nearly as common as diarrhoea.

The trekking diet can contain fairly large quantities of the roughage necessary to prevent constipation so more likely causes are dehydration (you can't drink too much) and psychological problems associated with the lack of Western plumbing!

The problem usually resolves itself without recourse to laxatives. If constipation occasionally troubles you, however, it might be helpful to bring laxatives with you.

Coughs and colds

These are common in Nepal and many trekkers succumb to them. Aspirin can be taken for a cold; lozenges containing anaesthetic are useful for a sore throat, as is gargling with warm salty water. Drink plenty.

A cough that produces mucus has one of a number of causes; most likely are the common cold or irritation of the bronchi by cold air which produces symptoms that are similar to flu. It could, however, point to AMS. A cough that produces thick green and yellow mucus could indicate bronchitis. If there is also chest pain (most severe when the patient breathes out), a high fever and blood-stained mucus, any of these could indicate pneumonia, requiring a course of antibiotics. Consult a doctor.

Exposure

Also known as hypothermia, this is caused by a combination of not wearing enough warm clothes against the cold, exhaustion, high altitude, dehydration and lack of food. Note that it does not need to be very cold for exposure to occur. Make sure everyone (porters included) is properly equipped.

Symptoms of exposure include a low body temperature (below 34.5°C or 94°F), poor co-ordination, exhaustion and shivering. As the condition deteriorates the shivering ceases, co-ordination gets worse making walking difficult and the patient may start hallucinating. The pulse then slows and unconsciousness and death follow shortly. Treatment involves thoroughly warming the patient quickly. Find shelter as soon as possible. Put the patient into a sleeping-bag with hot water bottles (use your drinking water bottles). Another person should get into the sleeping-bag with the patient to warm him or her up.

Frostbite

The severe form of frostbite that affected Maurice Herzog on the 1950 Annapurna expedition (he lost all his fingers and toes) rarely happens to trekkers. You could, however, be affected if you get stuck or lost in the snow on a high pass such as the Thorung La. Ensure that all members of your party are properly kitted out with thick socks, boots, gloves and woolly hats.

The first stage of frostbite is known as 'frostnip'. The fingers or toes first become cold and painful, then numb and white. Heat them up on a warm part of the body (eg an armpit) until the colour comes back. In cases of severe frostbite the affected part of the body becomes frozen. Don't try to warm it up until you reach a lodge/camp. Immersion in warm water (40°C or 100°F) is the treatment. Medical help should then be sought.

Gynaecological problems

Periods may become irregular or even stop altogether but this should not cause concern. The menstrual cycle may be upset by travel and the strenuous exercise required on some treks.

If you have had a vaginal infection in the past it would be a good idea to bring a course of treatment in case it recurs.

Haemorrhoids

If you've suffered from these in the past bring the required ointments or suppositories with you since haemorrhoids can flare up on a trek, particularly if you get constipated.

Leeches

The fear of leeches amongst first-time trekkers seems to be out of all proportion to reality. They are not several inches long, they can't give you anaemia, Aids or any other disease. In the main trekking seasons you rarely see leeches. They come out in force during the monsoon and are particularly numerous in the rhododendron forests around Ghorepani in the Annapurna region. They crawl up your boots and on to your feet and legs where they take their fill of blood before dropping off. To remove a leech apply salt, iodine or a lighted cigarette.

Snowblindness

It's important to wear sunglasses when walking through snow to prevent this uncomfortable, though temporary, condition. Ensure everyone in your group, including porters, has eye protection. The cure for snow-blindness is to keep the eyes closed, lying down in a dark room. Eye-drops and aspirin can be helpful.

If you lose your sunglasses a piece of cardboard with two narrow slits (just wide enough to see through) will protect your eyes.

Sunburn

Protect against sunburn by wearing a hat, sunglasses and a shirt with a collar that can be turned up. At altitude you'll also need sunscreen for your face.

AFTER YOUR TREK

Any leftover medicines and bandages that you may have will be welcomed at the Himalayan Rescue Association in Kathmandu. If they don't need them they can redistribute them to other charities in Nepal that do.

If you get ill after you've returned home it's vital to let your doctor know that you've been abroad. There have been cases where a serious illness picked up abroad has been misdiagnosed and wrongly treated leading to the death of the patient. Note that if you've been taking anti-malarials it's most important to continue the course for four to six weeks after you leave a malarial region

---

APPENDIX F: FLORA AND FAUNA

The flora and fauna of the Annapurna region are particularly diverse, largely the result of wide variations in altitude and climate. An outline is given below; for more information consult the identification guides mentioned on p50.

FLORA

Sub-tropical plants are found at altitudes of around 1000m (eg Pokhara), where trees include the chestnut, schima, alder, chir pine and cotton tree.

In the temperate zone (2000-3000m) there are forests of broad-leafed trees such as rhododendron, conifers (spruce, silver fir, deodar, Himalayan cypress, hemlock) and a variety of oaks. In high damp areas bamboo is found.

Some conifers (silver fir, blue pine) grow also in the lower regions of the sub-alpine zone (3000-4200m). Birch and juniper are found in the upper regions. In the alpine zone (4200m and above) there is juniper and alpine grassland, with a wide diversity of flowers including primula, saxifrage, buttercups, gentian and edelweiss.

MAMMALS

Domestic animals you will see include water buffalo, mules and horses and, at higher elevations, yaks. Although wild mammals are varied in this region, they are not frequently encountered by trekkers. You may, however, see the long-tailed grey langur (Hanuman monkey) and, on the route to the Sanctuary, the vole-like mouse hare (Royle's pika). You might catch a flash of the yellow-throated marten but you're unlikely to see the (nocturnal) red panda, the rare snow leopard and Himalayan musk deer. The barking call of the Indian muntjac (barking deer) is occasionally heard and the tahr (wild goat), goat-antelopes such as the goral and serow, and the bharal (blue sheep, main prey of the snow leopard) may sometimes be seen.

BIRDS

The avifauna of Nepal is extremely rich with more than 800 species having been recorded within the borders of this small country. In the Annapurna Conservation Area alone, 441 species have been identified. (See p13 for agencies that operate bird-watching treks here).

The following information was supplied by Simon Cohen (UK).

Trekkers can't fail to notice the wealth of birdlife in the Annapurna region. This account concentrates on the species that are easy to see and to identify. Although examined by habitat along the route to the Annapurna Sanctuary the information is transferable to corresponding areas within the region.

For a bird-watching trek, the size and weight of binoculars are important considerations; I'd recommend taking a good quality pair of 8x30 binoculars. Larger objective lenses make the binoculars too bulky, while higher magnifications with objective lenses 40mm make them too dark. You'll also need a notebook and identification guide (see p50).

Pokhara and Phewa Tal

The numerous lodges and restaurants here have been built amongst pre-existing farms and many of the birds you see are typical of rural Nepal. Tree sparrow, jungle myna, pied bush-chat, magpie robin, red-vented bulbul and common swallow are all easy to spot around the town. The flowering trees and shrubs in the gardens of the lodges attract grey-headed myna, blue-throated barbet, warblers like the diminutive tailor bird and the golden oriole. In the surrounding farmland you may see black-headed shrike, black drogo and stone-chat.

The lake and its banks provide important habitat for a number of species. Most obvious are the white egrets that can be seen flying back and forth across the water, feeding in the shallows or roosting in the large trees along Lakeside. Three species are found: the cattle egret, the little egrets and the smaller, browner paddybird. Pied kingfisher are common but the shyer common kingfisher is generally seen only beside smaller streams. On the open water of the lake there are dabchick and coot.

Hillside villages

In Ghandruk, Chomrong and other hillside villages, the clusters of slate-roofed houses set amongst the terraced rice and corn fields offer a home to a similar range of birds as are found in the rural areas of Lakeside. Common myna, red-vented bulbul, dark grey bush-chat are numerous around the edges of the fields. Himalayan tree-pie, black-headed sibia and Himalayan greenfinch may be seen amongst the scrub around the paddies, while the streams attract grey wagtails and black redstarts. Overhead, Nepal house martins glide, catching insects to take back to their nests under the eaves of village houses.

Bamboo forest

Not generally good bird-watching country, bamboo forest is dense, dark and can be extremely wet. You tend to spend more time watching your feet than the birds and you'll certainly hear more than you see. The most likely birds that you'll come across

are the noisy laughing thrushes; their cackling and squealing calls are most entertaining. The white-throated laughing thrush is the most common of the eleven species that
occur in the Annapurna Conservation Area.

Mixed forest

The mixed forest in the region (between Chomrong and Ghorepani, for example) comprises a great variety of trees, with different areas dominated by rhododendron, oak,
chestnut and sometimes deodar. The forest may appear devoid of birdlife but this can
change within minutes as large mixed feeding flocks sweep though the trees in 'bird
waves', consisting mainly of warblers and tits. The more easily identified species are
the black-faced warbler, grey-headed flycatcher, yellow-bellied fantail, as well as
green-backed, coal and grey tits. You may also see the treecreeper, and the Darjeeling
pied or golden-backed woodpeckers. With luck you may cross paths with two or three
'bird waves' in a day.

In winter the Himalayan monal (Danphe), the colourful pheasant that is Nepal's
national bird, descends to the forests from its summer habitat above the treeline. Not
often seen, the crimson horned pheasant (the satyr tragopan but confusingly called
'monal' in Nepali) is found as high as 3800m in summer but comes down to the rhododendron forests in winter.

Above the treeline

At altitude the forests begin to thin, giving way first to sparse birch woodland, then to
dwarf willow and juniper scrub, and eventually to rough grassland. The birch and
scrub (eg above Hinko Cave) attracts flocks of black tits as well as mixed flocks of
red-headed bullfinch, Himalayan greenfinch and rosefinch. Their place is taken by
blue-fronted redstart, Northern wren and Tickell's leaf warbler as the birch disappears,
leaving thick growths of willow and juniper.

By around 3500m or 11,500ft, the higher altitude species like the plain mountain
finch join the rosefinches and wrens amongst the dense scrub (below the
Machhapuchhre weather station, for example). Above 4000m or 13,000ft (eg around
Annapurna Base Camp) only the hardiest species remain: the plain mountain finch,
pipit, blue-fronted redstart and hill pigeon. In autumn trekkers may find the very tame
Alpine accentor around Base Camp. Another winter visitor, although much more elusive, is the wallcreeper which may be seen on the steep rock faces above the glaciers.

Rivers

Wider, slower rivers The slower stretches of these rivers (eg near Birethanti) provide pools that are attractive to the common kingfisher; the brown dipper and little
forktail are also seen. By the rivers, the alluvial grasslands often grazed by mules and
buffalo are good for pied and grey wagtails, and whistling thrush.

Wooded gorges Where the streams pass through the jungle they often cut deep,
narrow gorges (eg between Banthanti and Deurali). The brown dipper and little forktail are still present, the latter being particularly fond of these heavily wooded areas.
Another bird characteristic of these shady ravines is the plumbeous redstart. Except in
areas of densest cover riverchats abound along the streams and in many dry areas
higher up. The riverchat is probably the one bird that every trekker will spot: its bril-
liant plumage of white cap, red belly, black face and wings, and its constantly wagged
tail make it easy to recognise.

Mountain streams above the treeline In summer the brown dipper and grey
wagtail move up here to feed and breed, descending to lower, less exposed areas by
October. The plumbeous redstart and whistling thrush may venture up here but this is
really the domain of the riverchat, which can also be found in the dry ravines running
up from the streams.

Vultures and eagles

Seeing a large bird of prey cruising high over a village or circling a distant peak, most trekkers assume it to be an eagle; in fact, most will be vultures. At lower levels around the villages you may see white-backed, long-billed and Egyptian vultures. As you go higher you enter the realm of the larger king (black) and Himalayan griffon vultures and the bone-eating lammergeyer (bearded vulture).

Eagles do occur in the Sanctuary. The largest of them is the golden eagle, which hunts across huge territories amongst the highest peaks. The black eagle is easier to spot, above the forest canopy in the valleys. The crested serpent eagle can be observed hunting snakes, lizards and small mammals around the villages.

APPENDIX G: NEPALI WORDS AND PHRASES

Many Nepalis, especially those used to dealing with foreigners, can speak some English. It is, however, really worth making the effort to learn even a few Nepali phrases since this will positively affect the attitude of the local people towards you and you'll be made all the more welcome.

Derived from Sanskrit, Nepali shares many words with Hindi and is also written in the Devanagari script. For many of the people you speak to Nepali will, in fact, be their second language.

Nepali includes several sounds not used in English. The transliterations given below are therefore only approximate. However since pronunciation varies across the country your less-than-perfect attempts will probably be understood as just another regional variation.

Namasté

Probably the first word learnt by the newly-arrived foreigner in Nepal is this greeting, which is spoken with the hands together as if praying. Its meaning encompasses 'hello,' and 'goodbye,' as well as 'good morning,', 'good afternoon,' or 'good evening'. *Namaskar* is the more polite form.

General words

How are you?	*Bhaat khanu-boyo?* (Have you eaten your dal bhaat?)
Fine thanks	*Khai-é* (I have eaten)
Please give me	..... *di-nus*
Do you speak English?	*Angrayzi bolnoo-hoon-cha?*
Yes/no	(see below)
Thank you	*Dhan-yabad* (not often used)
Excuse me (sorry)	*Maf-garnus*
good/bad	*ramro/naramro*
cheap/expensive	*susto/mahongo*
Just a minute!	*Ek-chin!*
brother/sister	*eai/didi* (used to address anyone of your own age)
Good night	*Sooba-ratry*
Sweet dreams	*Meeto supona*

Questions and answers

To ask a question, end the phrase with a rising tone. An affirmative answer is given by restating the question without the rising tone. 'No' is translated as *chaina* (there isn't/aren't any) or *hoi-na* (it isn't/they aren't).

What's your name?	*Topaiko* (to adult)/*timro* (child) *nam ke ho?*		
My name is	*Mero nam ..... ho.*		
Where are you from?	*Topaiko/timro dess kay ho?*		
Britain/USA	*Belaiyot/Amerika*		
Australia/New Zealand	*Australia/New Zealand*		
Where are you going?	*Kaha janné?*	I'm going to	*..... janné*
Are you married?	*Bebah bo sokyo?*		
Have you any children?	*Chora chori chon?*	boy/girl	*chora/chori*
How old are you?	*Koti borsa ko boyo?*		
What is this?	*Yo kay ho?*		

Directions

Ask directions frequently and avoid questions that require only 'yes' or 'no' as a reply.

Which path goes to ....?	*........janay bahto kun ho?*
Where is ...?	*.....kaha cho*
lodge/hotel	*bhatti*
shop	*possol*
latrine	*charpi*
What is this village called?	*Yo gaon ko nam kay ho?*
left/right	*baiya/daiya*
straight ahead	*seeda jannus*
steep uphill/downhill	*bhiralo matti/talla*
far away	*tadah*
near	*nadjik*

Numerals/time

1 *ek*; 2 *du-i*; 3 *tin*; 4 *charr*; 5 *panch*; 6 *chho*; 7 *saat*; 8 *aatt*; 9 *nau*; 10 *dos*; 11 *eghaara*; 12 *baahra*; 13 *tehra*; 14 *chaudha*; 15 *pondhra*; 16 *sora*; 17 *sotra*; 18 *ottahra*; 19 *unnice*; 20 *beece*; 25 *pochis*; 30 *teece*; 40 *chaalis*; 50 *pachaas*; 60 *saati*; 70 *sottorri*; 80 *ossi*; 90 *nobbi*; 100 *say*; 200 *du-i say*; 300 *tin-say*; 400 *charr say*; 500 *panch say* ; 600 *chho say*; 700 *saat say*; 800 *aatt say*; 900 *nau say*; 1000 *hozhar*

How much/many?	*Kati?*
What time is it?	*Kati byjhay?*
It's three o'clock	*Tin byjhay*
hours/minutes	*ghanta/minoot*
today	*ajaa*
yesterday	*hidjo*
tomorrow	*bholi*
day after tomorrow	*parsi*

Food and drink

restaurant/inn	*bhatti*	cheese	*cheese*
Please give me...	*......di-nus*	boiled egg	*phul*
mineral water	*khanni-paani*	omelette	*unda*
tea	*chiya*	salt	*noon*
coffee	*coffee*	spicy hot	*piro*
milk	*dood no*	chillis	*korsani china*
boiled milk	*oomaleko-dood*	sugar	*chinni*

Food and drink (cont)

honey	*maha*
beer	*beer*
rice spirit	*ruxi*
Cheers!	*Khannus!*
chicken	*kookhura-ko massu*
buffalo	*rango-ko massu*
pork	*sungur-ko massu*
rice	*bhaat*
lentils	*dal*
vegetables (cooked)	*takaari*
potatoes	*aloo*
bread	*roti*
It tastes good	*Ekdum meeto*

APPENDIX H: GLOSSARY

ama	mother
beni	rivers' confluence
bhatti	simple hotel
Brahmin/Bahun	Hindu high priest caste
cairn	pile of stones marking a route ('stone men')
chang	home-brew made from barley or rice; also 'north'
chhu	river
chhusa	crop-growing area above main village
chorten	Tibetan stupa (see below)
chotar	prayer flag pole beside house
crampons	spikes that strap on boots to aid walking on ice
crevasse	dangerous cracks in a glacier
cwm	valley shaped like an amphitheatre (Welsh)
dal bhaat	staple meal of lentils and boiled rice
deorali	pass
dhai	curds
dingma	clearing
doko	woven, load-carrying basket
drangka	stream
ghat	river bank or bridge
goan/gau	village
gompa	Buddhist temple (literally: 'meditation')
goth 'goat-h'	shelter or temporary house
gunsa	'winter place', where early crops are grown
himal	snowy mountains
kang	mountain
kani	entrance arch
kharka	grazing ground (Nepali)
khola	stream

kosi	river
kund	lake
la	pass
lha	fenced herding area
lho	south
mani wall	wall of stones carved with Buddhist mantras
mantra	prayer formula
névé	smooth high snow-field, accumulation area of a glacier
nup	west
phu	high altitude grazing area at the end of a valley
piton	spike hammered into a rock crack for climbing security
pokhri	lake
prussiks	loops of cord used to climb a vertical rope
rakshi	local distilled spirit
ri	ridge or soft peak
saddhu	Hindu ascetic
satu	flour
serac	large block of ice typically found in an icefall
shar	east
Sherpa	of the Sherpa people
sherpa	trekking group assistant
solja/suchia	salt-butter tea
stupa	hemispherical Buddhist religious monument
suntala	mandarin orange
tal	lake
tika	holy mark placed on forehead
trisul	trident carried by worshippers of Shiva
tsampa	roasted barley flour
tse	peak
tsho/cho	lake
yersa	crop-growing area above main village

INDEX